How the
FORKS OVER KNIVES
Documentary and Book Are Changing Lives

"I watched *Forks Over Knives* in November of 2011, then I took the book to my doctor and discussed quitting my statin drug for cholesterol. He was intrigued but not convinced it was a good choice. In December I took the plunge and went completely plant-based. Yesterday I had my six-month checkup: I was taken off all medication—blood pressure and cholesterol—plus I had lost weight. I feel great, and now my doctor is reading the book."

—Mary Yeaple, North Pole, Alaska

"I received the book and the movie as a gift, and they have given my family more than I could have dreamed. I love to cook and I love to impress my guests, so at first I thought this was going to be very difficult. But after looking up recipes and trying it for just one week, we all had more energy and felt much better . . . in one week! I thought my children would have a problem but they love fruits and veggies! This is not just another diet—this is a new way of living, an eye-opener to health. So many people are dependent on medications, and sometimes they don't even make you feel better—you are just told you need them in order to live. There are other solutions—and there is science that proves it!"   —Katisha Conner, Centralia, Washington

"I have eaten a plant-based diet since I first watched this wonderful film 23 weeks ago. I have lost 25 pounds of body fat. I have lowered my triglycerides by over 125 points. My waist has dropped three inches. Most importantly, I feel happy and healthy every day now. I sleep well and wake up rested. My brain seems better able to focus on my tasks, and I can complete a to-do list without pause. I know that this plant-based lifestyle works. I am careful not to call this a diet. A diet ends. This is how I live now."   —Christopher H., Spring Park, Minnesota

"After kidney cancer, being diagnosed with atrial fibrillation, pacemaker surgery, and diabetic artery disease, my husband finally decided to take our daughter's recommendation of your book seriously. I purchased the book as well as the video and Dr. Esselstyn's book. In less than two weeks, my husband's blood pressure is down, he has lost five pounds, and his glucose readings have dropped a whopping 60 points and he is decreasing the units of insulin he takes! We can't wait to share the books and video with his cardiologist."   —Joanne Clark, Lakeside, Texas

"My wife and I both read Dr. T. Colin Campbell's *The China Study*, and that book set us on the path toward veganism and a plant-based diet. Together, Dr. Campbell's book and your film changed our lives forever. My wife and I have been on a plant-based, vegan diet for the past six months, and we have never felt better."   —Jacob Song, Torrance, California

THE EXPERIMENT

BECAUSE EVERY BOOK IS A TEST OF NEW IDEAS

"I owe the authors of *Forks Over Knives* a big thank-you! I'm a 74-year-old woman, descended from Wisconsin dairy farmers and midwestern beef, hog, and chicken farmers, so I was raised on a meat- and dairy-based 'standard American diet.' I adopted a whole-foods, plant-based diet about eight months ago. Wow! I dropped 25 pounds without even trying, totally lost the painful arthritis symptoms that have bothered me for decades, and can now breathe normally without allergies for the first time ever!"   —Phyllis Kaufman, Lacey, Washington

"A heart attack turned my life upside down two years ago. Then my husband and I discovered Dr. Campbell, Dr. Esselstyn, and *Forks Over Knives*. Within six months of beginning plant-based eating, I lost 40 pounds without effort and am off a lifetime of medications. Now I teach classes about the extraordinary health benefits of plant-based eating and never miss an opportunity to show the life-changing film *Forks Over Knives*."   —Dorothy Greet, Lewes, Delaware

"I'm a stage IV breast cancer thriver, diagnosed in September 2008. I decided to take matters into my own hands instead of letting cancer take me over. I made a quick adjustment to my diet, removing white flour, white sugar, and dairy. Today I eat a vegan diet. I watched *Forks Over Knives* and I think it was so well done. I've also really enjoyed the *Forks Over Knives* book; my kids especially like the muffins. The best news for me is that I've been cancer-free for about two years! Thank you for spreading the word!"

—Robin Page, founder of Live Squared nutritional consulting, Libertyville, Illinois

"My wife and I started a plant-based diet in January 2012 on the day I turned 44. As of June 2012, I have lost around 40 pounds and she has lost around 37. I really didn't have to try, the weight just came off—I weigh less now than when I graduated high school. I have taken up kayaking and have much more energy than before. I love my new lifestyle—thanks for the movie and the information."   —John Witt, Max Meadows, Virginia

"I have been a type 1 diabetic for almost 40 years, and a lifelong emphasis on plant-based nutrition has been very significant to my health. Most people I know cannot believe I spent two thirds of my life as a diabetic. *Forks Over Knives* is inspiring me to make even greater progress toward a vegan lifestyle. My vigor in regular exercise and running is unabating, and I am enjoying new foods and flavors. My blood-sugar levels are as good as ever, and I never have that heavy feeling in my stomach that comes from eating calorie-dense and high-fat foods. I hope there will be a part two to *Forks Over Knives*."   —Dave Bishton, Longmont, Colorado

"The documentary was a huge wake-up call, so we purchased the book and 'jumped in.' My husband and I have already lost weight and feel younger and more vibrant. Our three kids ask for fruit and veggies! Our six-year-old no longer wants the processed school lunches that now 'taste funny' to her. I feel like we are tasting food for the first time. This is amazing and we are encouraging others to make the change!"   —Denise DeLallo, Webster, New York

OVER 300 RECIPES FOR PLANT-BASED EATING ALL THROUGH THE YEAR

FORKS OVER KNIVES®

THE COOKBOOK

DEL SROUFE

WITH DESSERTS BY
ISA CHANDRA MOSKOWITZ

AND WITH RECIPE CONTRIBUTIONS BY JULIEANNA HEVER,
JUDY MICKLEWRIGHT, AND DARSHANA THACKER

THE EXPERIMENT
NEW YORK

The Experiment, LLC
220 East 23rd Street, Suite 600
New York, NY 10010–4658
theexperimentpublishing.com

Forks Over Knives® is a registered trademark of Monica Beach Media.

The Experiment's books are available at special discounts when purchased in bulk for premiums and sales promotions as well as for fundraising or educational use. For details, contact us at info@theexperimentpublishing.com.

Many of the designations used by manufacturers and sellers to distinguish their products are claimed as trademarks. Where those designations appear in this book and The Experiment was aware of a trademark claim, the designations have been capitalized.

The statements expressed in this book are not meant to be a substitute for professional medical advice. Readers should seek their own professional counsel for any medical condition or before starting or altering any exercise or dietary plan.

Sroufe, Del.
  Forks over knives--the cookbook : over 300 recipes for plant-based eating all through the year / Del Sroufe;
with desserts by Isa Chandra Moskowitz ; and with recipe contributions by Julieanna Hever, Judy Micklewright, and Darshana Thacker.
      pages cm
  Includes index.
  ISBN 978-1-61519-061-4 -- ISBN 978-1-61519-159-8 (ebook)
1. Vegetarian cooking. I. Title.
  TX837.S717 2012
  641.5'636--dc23
                                2012021683

ISBN 978-1-61519-061-4
Ebook ISBN 978-1-61519-159-8

Cover design by Sarah Smith
Photography by Cara Howe
Food styling by María del Mar Sacasa | ENNIS, Inc.
Photo assistance from Jeri Lampert
Photo production and prop styling by Lukas Volger
Text design by Pauline Neuwirth, Neuwirth & Associates, Inc.

Manufactured in China

First printing August 2012
30 29 28 27 26 25 24 23

Contents

STEWS AND CHILIES

WRAPS AND SPREADS

Lettuce Wraps

Tortilla Wraps

Spreads

PASTA AND NOODLES

Pasta and Noodle Salads

Warm Pasta Dishes

THE AMAZING BEAN

GREAT GRAINS

Rice Dishes

Corn, Polenta and Millet Dishes

Quinoa and Other Grain Dishes

CASSEROLES

DESSERTS

THE COOKBOOK

INTRODUCTION

Forks Over Knives has become synonymous with a healthy, whole-foods, plant-based way of eating. First, the feature documentary made a clear and persuasive case for why this diet can save your life, and the companion book *Forks Over Knives: The Plant-Based Way to Health* followed with personal stories from those living on the plant-based frontier and with specific guidance for all those seeking to embrace a truly healthy way of eating.

That book contained recipes simple and delectable enough to ease anyone into the plant-based lifestyle. But those hoping to take on a fully whole-foods, plant-based diet for *life* are hungry for a complete guide to cooking with the whole-plant foods that are most recommended: the fruits, vegetables, whole grains, tubers, and legumes that are the foundation of this way of eating. Newcomers to the lifestyle especially want more recipes, enough to provide themselves and their loved ones with varied, satisfying, healthful dishes every meal of the day, every day of the year, every year of their lives. This book is intended to provide just that: an eclectic collection of healthy recipes drawing inspiration from cuisines all over the world. The recipes range from the simple to the celebratory and cover every meal (yes, even dessert!). Whether you are a complete home-cooking novice, an old hand in the kitchen but new to exclusively whole-plant cooking, or even an experienced plant-based kitchen pro, this cookbook will have something for you.

First, though, allow me to introduce myself: I'm Chef Del. I'm proud to have contributed seven recipes to the original companion work *Forks Over Knives: The Plant-Based Way to Health*, and I'm now incredibly excited to bring you this new addition to the *Forks Over Knives* lineup. For six years I've worked as chef and co-owner of Wellness Forum Foods, a plant-based meal delivery and catering service that emphasizes healthy, minimally processed foods and offers cooking classes to the public. I've worked in vegan and vegetarian kitchens for twenty-two years, and I've also been a vegan personal chef.

I'm also delighted to be joined here by four other plant-based champions: Isa Chandra Moskowitz (who has provided an entire chapter of delicious plant-based desserts), Julieanna Hever, Judy Micklewright, and Darshana Thacker. (See page 319, About the Author and Contributors, for more about each of us.) We know how good whole-foods, plant-based eating can be, and in *Forks Over Knives—The Cookbook*, we show you, too.

We've formulated this cookbook to make it easy for you to find whatever type of food you are looking for. We begin with the **BASICS.** The nearly two dozen recipes in this chapter are staples that you'll use in a wide variety of other recipes throughout the cookbook. You can also use them as building blocks for your own plant-based creations. In this section you'll find numerous sauce recipes, some familiar and some unusual, and a whole array of condiments, from oil-free Mayonnaise (page 28) to Pineapple Sweet-and-Sour Sauce (page 33).

The subsequent chapters include:

▶ **BREAKFASTS,** including quick and easy recipes like smoothies and muesli, and hearty meals like Breakfast Rancheros (page 55)

▶ **SALADS,** made from fresh vegetables and fruits as well as filling beans and grains

▶ **SOUPS,** including more than thirty delicious options, from Cream of Broccoli Soup (page 89) to Julieanna Hever's Fall Harvest Vegetable Chowder (page 95)

▶ More than twenty hearty and nourishing **STEWS AND CHILIES,** including Darshana Thacker's Indian Zuppa with Tomatoes and Fava Beans (page 114)

▶ Lettuce and tortilla **WRAPS,** filled with everything from simple beans and rice to roasted red pepper spread to fajita fixings

▶ A wide range of **PASTA** and **NOODLE** dishes for every season and occasion, whether it's a quick weeknight meal or a dinner party for twelve

▶ Special **STIR-FRIED, GRILLED AND HASHED VEGETABLE** dishes, including Cauliflower "Steaks" (page 174) and Vegetable White Bean Hash (page 182)

▶ Everything from tomatoes and mushrooms to cabbage and potatoes **STUFFED AND BAKED** with tasty vegetable- and grain-based fillings

▶ **BEANS**, showing their amazing versatility in dishes like Judy Micklewright's Cuban-Style Black Beans with Cilantro Rice (page 204)

▶ **GRAINS,** with enticing recipes featuring rice, corn, polenta, millet, quinoa, bulgur, barley, and more

▶ **CASSEROLES,** providing recipes for everything from Mac and "Cheese" (page 252) to Moroccan-Style Shepherd's Pie (page 263)

▶ And last but not least, Isa Chandra Moskowitz's **DESSERTS** chapter, proving that low-fat, whole-grain, plant-based desserts can taste great without eggs, butter, or any other dairy.

At this point, you might be wondering, *What about vitamins, potassium, or calcium? What about calorie counts and carbohydrates, fat, and protein?* If you've seen the film or read the first *Forks Over Knives* book, you may remember that good health can be achieved only by focusing on adopting an overall healthful dietary pattern: a low-fat, plant-based diet composed of whole foods. Don't worry about eating particular foods in order to get enough of certain nutrients. Focus instead on eating (and enjoying!) the wide variety of fruits, vegetables, beans and legumes, whole grains, and other ingredients used in our recipes, over the course of each day, each week, each month, and each year. These foods combined will naturally steer you on your way toward optimal health.

We have included desserts in this book, which we are sure you will find delicious! Keep in mind that most of the desserts contain some amount of added sugar (although the recipes in this book are lower in sugar than many you will find). The added sugar is a source of concentrated calories without the fiber that helps regulate blood sugar and makes you feel full. So it is important to remember that desserts are treats—something you eat on a special occasion, but not every day.

We have elected not to include nutrient data for recipes to avoid encouraging the tendency to get hung up on nutrient tallying or calorie counting. Forget about the numbers! Just pay attention to your body's natural hunger signals and eat the low-fat, nutrient-rich, plant-based recipes presented here, and you will reap the myriad benefits that come with doing so.

Just what are those benefits, exactly? If you're already eating the whole-foods, plant-based way, then you've likely already discovered a wide variety of advantages, not only for your personal health but also for animal welfare and for the environment. If not, you might want to check out the "Good for Animals" and "Good for the Environment" sections in Part One of *Forks Over Knives: The Plant-Based Way to Health*. Even if you have read those sections, the social and economic advantages of this eating style are worth highlighting again here:

Your Health and the Cost of Health Care

If you consume a typical Western diet, most likely you live in a country like the United States, a country with the most expensive health care in the world and some of the *least* healthy people. Sadly, as the costs of health care continue to rise and the health of the population continues to decline, we face a growing economic and social crisis. This, however, is a crisis that need not grow any more. Once we wake up to the problem, we can regain control of our own health care, starting at our family's breakfast table.

We can make a significant dent in both our own and our society's health care expenses by paying attention to the foods we eat. Any number of diseases—cardiovascular disease, diabetes, obesity, and more—can be not only prevented, but in many cases *reversed* with the right diet: a whole-foods, plant-based diet. By eating this way, you can cut down on increasingly expensive medical bills and insurance costs. As a bonus, you'll even likely slash your weekly grocery bills, because the healthiest foods, like beans, grains, fruits, and vegetables, also tend to be less expensive than the highly processed foods that are currently making us sick. The whole-plant foods that feature in these recipes are readily available in most places and—while they haven't been spared the price increases that have affected all kinds of food in the last several years—they remain far more affordable than most red meat, poultry, dairy items, and processed foods, products on which consumers pay a premium for not only manufacturing and production, but for research and development, packaging, and shipping.

Being sick not only comes with the out-of-pocket expenses for increasingly expensive medical bills and insurance (and the hidden, behind-the-scenes expenses that insurance companies handle), but also negatively impacts the things that matter most in your life, whether it's spending time with family and friends; achieving your physical, mental, and personal goals; making a difference in your community; or just *living*. The costs of disease are not just high for you—they're high for everyone around you, too.

KEY TIPS AND TECHNIQUES FOR SHOPPING, PREPPING AND COOKING

Do More, Save More

Preparing foods from scratch is far less expensive than buying foods already prepared—and for those who are in the habit of doing so, it's often a pleasure to see raw ingredients transformed into nourishing foods for themselves, their family, and their friends. Consider, for example, that canned beans cost 3 to 4 times as much as dried beans that you cook yourself. Not only will you be saving money by cooking your own, you can feel confident that the meals you prepare with those beans won't contain all the extra preservatives and sodium that standard canned beans can bring to a meal.

Sometimes, though, buying butternut squash or other vegetables already prepped is a time-saving option for when you want to cook with such ingredients but just can't find the time to do the prep work. Buying such vegetables already prepped will cost you more than if you buy a whole squash and peel it, seed it, clean it, and cut it up yourself—but even though it will be more expensive, it's better to take a shortcut than to not cook with healthy, whole-food ingredients. The key point is this: The more cooking (and prepping) you are willing and able to do, the cheaper your food bill will be. Sure, it's fine to buy canned vegetables and pre-prepped foods for when you need to get a healthy meal ready in a hurry, but the more you do on your own, the more money you will save. (Also check out the Time-Saving Tips on page 9.)

Buy in Bulk

Buying dried beans is less expensive than buying canned ones, but buying dried beans in bulk can be even less expensive. Many supermarket chains—and nearly all food co-ops and health food stores—sell dry goods in bulk, so you can buy as much or as little as you need of any number of foods, particularly beans, grains, pastas, seeds, dried fruits, and the like. Depending on where you live, you can also start a buying club, which is similar to a food co-op but without the overhead of a permanent location. In buying clubs (often predecessors to food co-ops), members order directly from a distributor and have food delivered in bulk quantities to a designated drop-off location.

Buy Produce in Season

In most locales, not only are fresh strawberries less tasty in the middle of winter, but paying for out-of-season produce to be shipped thousands of miles is costly to you and to the environment. Seek out the freshest seasonal produce you can find. There are now over 7,000 farmers' markets, large and small, across the United States, and their popularity continues to grow. By buying produce at farmers' markets, you're not only going home with seasonal, fresh produce, you're also helping to sustain small-scale farmers, whom we all owe a big thank-you for doing the incredibly hard work of growing our food without commercial pesticides. Buying from farmers' markets also promotes crop diversity, since small farmers are able to (and must) grow a wider variety of foods than large-scale growers, whose livelihood depends on mass-producing just one or two crops, such as corn or soybeans.

Composting

The more home cooking you do with whole-plant foods, the less garbage your kitchen will generate from plastic and paper packaging. Plus, more of the refuse you do generate will be green waste, which can go right into the compost bin. The majority of any waste generated from making the recipes in this cookbook will be safe for your compost bin—fresh fruit and vegetable skins, the sodden mush of vegetables leftover after you make homemade Vegetable Stock (page 23), tough outer lettuce leaves, and so much more. Some municipalities give away bins at no or very low cost, and once it's set up, a working compost bin can turn fruit and vegetable waste into nutrient-rich compost in a matter of weeks. If you're not able to set up a compost bin, but you'd like to compost your green waste, it's worth investigating to see if a local neighborhood or community garden will accept such waste—many will.

Cooking Beans

Beans and legumes vary in their cooking times and their yields, and a variety of factors, including the age of the beans (which may not be knowable), can affect the cooking time. Generally, though, quick-cooking legumes like red and green lentils are done in about 25 minutes, while longer-cooking beans, like black beans, can take up to 2 hours to cook.

Before cooking, pick through and discard any shriveled beans or stones, which are sometimes found among dried beans. Then rinse the dried beans thoroughly in a colander under cool water.

To reduce their cooking times, most beans should be soaked overnight in cold water; since dried beans can soak up more water than you might think, be sure the water covers the beans by several inches. In the morning, drain off the soaking water and transfer the beans to a pot. Add enough fresh water to cover the beans by at least 3 inches, bring them to a boil, and then lower the heat and cook at a simmer until they are tender.

If you realize you won't have time to cook beans after all and have already soaked them overnight, don't throw them out! Just change the water and leave them to soak in the fridge for up to another 2 days, changing the water every 12 hours or so.

If you forget to soak the beans the night before, you can use what is known as the quick-soaking method. Place the dried beans and enough water to cover them in a pot. Bring the beans and water to a boil, turn off the heat, and let them sit for an hour (or even less, if you're time-constrained—but do try to let them sit for at least 15 minutes). Drain off the water, add enough fresh water to cover them by 3 inches, and bring the pot to a boil again. Cook the beans until they are tender.

Again, it can be difficult to pinpoint cooking times for beans and legumes (versus grains, where cooking times are usually more consistent), but here are some general cooking times and yields for the dried beans used in this cookbook:

BEAN (1 CUP DRIED)	COOKING TIME	YIELD (COOKED)
Adzuki	50–60 minutes	3 cups
Anasazi	55–60 minutes	2–2½ cups
Black	1½ hours	2–2½ cups
Black-eyed peas	50–60 minutes	2 cups
Cannellini	50–60 minutes	2½ cups
Chickpeas (Garbanzo)	1½–2 hours	2 cups
Fava, skinned	50–60 minutes	1½ cups
Great northern	1½–1¾ hours	2½ cups
Kidney, red	55–65 minutes	2–2¼ cups
Lentils, brown	40–50 minutes	2–2½ cups
Lentils, green	40–50 minutes	2 cups
Lentils, red	20–25 minutes	2 cups
Lima	50–60 minutes	2 cups
Mung	50–60 minutes	2 cups
Navy	55–65 minutes	2½ cups
Pinto	1½ hours	2½ cups
Split peas, green	45 minutes	2 cups

Cooking Grains

The technique for cooking most grains is generally the same as it is for cooking dried beans: Place the water (or an equal amount of vegetable stock) and the grains in a pot just large enough to hold both (avoid using too large of a pot). Bring it to a boil, covered, and cook, still covered, over medium heat until the water is absorbed. The cooking time and amount of water needed for each grain vary, but here is a general guide for cooking times and yields for the grains used in this cookbook:

GRAIN (1 CUP DRIED)	WATER	COOKING TIME	YIELD (COOKED)
Barley, pearled	3 cups	45–55 minutes	3½ cups
Brown rice, including brown basmati and wild rice blends	2 cups	45–50 minutes	2½ cups
Bulgur	2 cups	15 minutes	2½ cups
Millet	3 cups	20 minutes	3–3½ cups
Quinoa	2 cups	15 minutes	2½ cups
Spelt berries, whole	2–3 cups	40–50 minutes	2½ cups
Wheat berries, whole	3 cups	1¾–2 hours	3–3½ cups
Wild rice	3 cups	50–60 minutes	4 cups

Special Chopping Techniques: Matchsticks and Chiffonade

To cut vegetables like carrots or zucchini into matchsticks, slice the vegetable carefully into long, thin strips using a sharp knife or, if you have one, a mandoline. Then cut the strips into 2½-inch lengths. Stack the shorter lengths neatly on top of each other and then cut the stack lengthwise into ¼-inch sticks.

To cut basil or other large leafy herbs or greens into a chiffonade, stack the leaves neatly on top of each other and then, starting with the short side, roll them up tightly. Cut across the roll thinly to achieve ribbons.

Dry or Water Sautéing

Because the recipes in this book do not use processed oils, when a recipe calls for sautéing ingredients—such as onions, garlic, and vegetables—it makes use of a dry- or water-sauté method, where only enough water is added to keep the ingredients being cooked from sticking to the pan as you stir them. Nonstick skillets are more conducive to dry or water sautéing than other skillets, but they are not required.

Peeling Tomatoes

Peeling fresh tomatoes is easy once you get the hang of it. In a small saucepan, bring to a boil enough water to cover your tomatoes. Meanwhile, wash the tomatoes, and then with a sharp knife score (make shallow cuts in) each tomato at the stem end with an "X."

When the water boils, carefully drop the tomatoes into the boiling water, reduce the heat to a simmer, and cook for no more than one minute. You may begin to see the flaps of skin peel back from the scoring. But even if you don't, remove the tomatoes with a slotted spoon after no more than one minute, plunge them in ice-cold water, and then when they are sufficiently cooled, peel each tomato with a sharp knife.

Some skins may slip right off, but if you find it difficult to remove the skin from a tomato, return that tomato to the simmering water, and boil it for another 30 seconds or so.

Preparing Winter Squash

To prepare winter squash, lay the squash on its side and cut a thin piece off the bottom of the squash. This allows you to stand the squash up on its end and keep it stable while you peel the sides. Remove the skin using either a very sharp knife or a vegetable peeler. Once you have peeled the squash, halve it vertically (through the blossom and stem ends), scoop out the seeds with a spoon, lay the halves flat on a cutting surface, and cut them lengthwise into long strips. Finally, cut those strips into cubes.

Roasting Peppers

To roast peppers on a gas stovetop, hold the whole pepper over an open flame and roast, turning frequently, until the pepper is black all over. You can either hold it by the stem, if it is strong and sturdy enough, or use heatproof tongs; either way, use caution. To roast peppers in an oven, put washed peppers in a cast-iron skillet or roasting pan, and roast them for 45 minutes to 1 hour at 400°F. Remove the pan from the oven, put the peppers into a plastic bag or heat-proof container with a lid, and let them sweat until cooled. When the peppers are cool, peel off the charred or blackened skin; the degree to which it is charred will depend on the roasting method and the extent to which the peppers have been roasted. Perfectly roasted peppers will retain their body but will be softened throughout, and the skin will slip right off.

Salt and Pepper

Recipes that call for salt and/or pepper nearly all specify "to taste" rather than give precise quantities. Many people prefer to cook with little to no salt, while others prefer not to grind on copious amounts of pepper. We are all encouraged to limit our salt consumption—the recommended daily sodium intake is 1,500 milligrams, equal to less than a teaspoon—so go light on the salt. When you do use salt, I recommend sea salt or kosher salt, which, unlike table salt, contain no chemicals such as silicon dioxide, dextrose, and aluminum silicate and retain the salt's natural minerals. As for pepper, if you're a fan of it, invest in a good grinder if you don't already have one and buy whole peppercorns (try to see if you can find them in bulk bins, where they are typically much less expensive than where they are sold in jars in the spice aisle).

About Sulfites and Sulfur Dioxide

Some recipes call for unsulfured molasses and dried fruit, which means foods that have not been treated with sulfur dioxide. Sulfur dioxide functions as a preservative and bleaching agent and can cause allergic reactions in many people, especially people with asthma.

Time-Saving Tips

Read the entire recipe before embarking on it to make sure that you have all the necessary ingredients and that you're prepared to make any additional recipes that may be called for (such as a recipe of No-Cheese Sauce, page 29, that needs to be prepared before you can make Curried Potato Soup with Corn and Red Pepper, page 91). It's always a good idea to prep vegetables while water is coming to a boil, a sauce is simmering, or the oven is preheating. Depending on the recipe, you may want to do *all* of your prep before embarking on the cooking; stir-fries especially benefit from being fully prepped, with all ingredients in easy reach of the stove, before the actual cooking begins.

If you find yourself frequently returning to recipes that use beans (or even cooked brown rice, for example), you may also find it a time-saver to make a large batch of beans and keep recipe-size portions in the freezer. They'll keep for up to several months in the freezer, and that way, you get all the health and savings benefits of making your own beans (see page 6) without spending hours ahead of time soaking and cooking them.

Using Fresh and Dried Herbs

All the herbs used in the recipes in the book are presumed to be fresh, unless they are specified otherwise. While it's certainly preferable to use fresh herbs whenever possible, sometimes the herbs called for are not in season, or you just can't find them easily in your local store. If you need to substitute dried herbs, that's fine, but remember that dried herbs are more potent than fresh herbs, so you'll need less for the recipe. Dried herbs will begin to lose their potency about six months after their packaging has been opened, and while they're still usable, they won't have the same amount of flavor as those from a freshly opened package. When substituting dried herbs for fresh, the general conversion is 1 part dried to 3 parts fresh. Here are some approximate conversions for the common measurements used in this book:

FRESH	DRIED
¼ cup	1½ tablespoons
1 tablespoon	1 teaspoon
1½ teaspoons	½ teaspoon
1 teaspoon	¼ teaspoon
½ teaspoon	1 pinch

Toasting Nuts

The most fail-safe way to toast raw nuts is to place them on a rimmed baking sheet in a 350°F oven for 5 to 8 minutes. Pine nuts will take just 5 minutes to toast, whereas almonds will take about 10 minutes. Other larger nuts can take anywhere from 10 to 15 minutes. Do not leave the nuts unattended; they can go from perfectly toasted to irretrievably burnt in a matter of a minute or two. A good rule of thumb is, the moment you can smell them, they're done (or were done two minutes earlier). If toasted nuts stayed in the oven a few minutes too long, rather than letting them cool on the baking sheet, you can help forestall any further cooking by transferring them to a heat-proof dish the moment you remove them from the oven and letting them sit at room temperature.

Toasting Seeds and Spices

To toast whole seeds and spices, place them in a dry skillet over medium heat, stirring constantly to keep them from burning. The seeds are done when they become fragrant and start to turn darker, or in the case of some seeds, including sesame, start to pop. Most seeds will take no more than a few minutes to toast, so be sure not to leave them unattended.

Zesting and Juicing Citrus

Fresh lemon or lime juice and zest appear often in the recipes in this book—a touch of citrus juice and/or zest brings a bright, fresh zing to foods in a way no other ingredient quite can. Citrus juicers and reamers come in a wide variety of shapes and types, starting at the bottom of the spectrum with very simple wooden reamers. Mexican squeezers, a small step up, are more widely available than others and come in three basic sizes, each painted a bright color: yellow for lemons, green for limes, and orange for oranges. At the high end of the spectrum are electric juicers with varying features. For the amounts called for in the recipes in this book, one Mexican squeezer or a simple wooden citrus reamer is all you really need.

As for making citrus zest, Microplane zesters are widely available with different size blades and can do a spectacular job creating fine shreds of zest. Alternatively, you can buy a zester that, pulled along the surface of a piece of citrus, generates strips of zest that you can then chop as finely as you'd like. (See the photo below for an example.)

Cooking Basics

- ► Almond milk, unsweetened (I prefer almond milk, but there are many other types of plant-based milk, such as rice, soy, oat, and hemp)
- ► Barley
- ► Beans and legumes, assorted, dried (see page 5 for cooking instructions) and canned (low-sodium or no-salt-added varieties if possible)
- ► Brown basmati rice
- ► Brown rice
- ► Brown rice noodles
- ► Buckwheat groats
- ► Bulgur
- ► Dijon mustard
- ► Dried fruits (such as apples, apricots, cranberries, currants, dates, and raisins)
- ► Millet
- ► Nuts and seeds (use them sparingly because of their high fat content)
- ► Oats, rolled or steel-cut
- ► Quinoa
- ► Soy sauce, low-sodium
- ► Tomatoes, canned (diced, crushed, paste, and pureed)
- ► Tortillas, corn or whole wheat
- ► Vinegar, assorted (such as balsamic, brown rice, red wine, and apple cider)
- ► Wheat berries and spelt berries
- ► Whole-grain pasta, such as macaroni, penne, and spaghetti

Herbs and Spices

- ► Allspice, whole and ground
- ► Ancho chile powder
- ► Basil, dried
- ► Bay leaf, dried
- ► Cardamom, pods and ground
- ► Cayenne pepper
- ► Cinnamon, sticks and ground
- ► Cloves, whole and ground
- ► Coriander, whole and ground
- ► Crushed red pepper flakes
- ► Cumin, whole and ground
- ► Curry powder
- ► Dill, dried
- ► Fennel, whole and ground
- ► Fenugreek
- ► Garam masala
- ► Garlic powder
- ► Ginger, ground
- ► Mustard powder
- ► Nutmeg, ground
- ► Onion powder
- ► Oregano, dried
- ► Paprika, smoked and sweet
- ► Peppercorns, black, whole and ground
- ► Rosemary, dried
- ► Saffron
- ► Sage, dried
- ► Salt
- ► Tarragon, dried
- ► Thyme, dried

- ► **ALMOND BUTTER**

- ► **APPLESAUCE (UNSWEETENED)**

- ► **COCONUT FLOUR** is a gluten-free flour made from dried coconut meat. Coconut flour can dry out baked goods if overbaked, so monitor baking times carefully. Increasingly available in large supermarkets, coconut flour is also available in health food stores and online.

- ► **DRY SWEETENER** is a general term for non-liquid sweeteners. There are many kinds available, some more natural than others. Some sugars, like white table sugar, are bleached, sometimes chemically and sometimes using charred cow bones. The dessert recipes in this book were designed to be made using evaporated cane juice or cane sugar. Sucanat, date sugar, and maple sugar are other options, all with slight variations in flavor. *All* sugar has had the fiber and most if not all of the vitamins and minerals removed, so it should be enjoyed only on occasion.

- ► **FLAXSEEDS AND GOLDEN FLAXSEEDS (GROUND)**

- ► **GRAIN-SWEETENED CHOCOLATE CHIPS** use malted grains as a source of whole-food sweetness. Many manufacturers have discontinued them because of their gluten content, so if you are gluten intolerant or can't find them, opt for plant-based dark or semisweet chocolate chips or carob chips.

- ► Pure **MAPLE SYRUP** is divided into two main categories, Grade A and Grade B. Grade B maple syrup tends to be more affordable than Grade A and to have a more pronounced maple flavor. Pancake syrup, table syrup, or maple-flavored syrup should not be substituted, as they often consist primarily of high-fructose syrup.

- ► **OAT FLOUR** is made from whole oats. You can find it among the alternative flours at many grocery stores, or you can make your own by pulsing rolled oats in a blender or food processor. One cup of oats yields about ⅔ cup oat flour. If you follow a gluten-free diet, choose certified gluten-free oats or oat flour.

- ► **ROLLED OATS** are also known as old-fashioned oats. Choose a certified gluten-free variety if you follow a gluten-free diet.

- ► **PUMPKIN PUREE** should be 100 percent pure, not the pie filling variety.

- ► **SORGHUM FLOUR** is milled from sorghum, one of the oldest cultivated grains. It is high in fiber and gluten-free, with a mild taste and dense texture.

- ► **SPELT FLOUR** is made from spelt, an ancient grain with a mellow nutty flavor. Spelt is not gluten-free but is considered more easily digestible than wheat. It can be found in health food stores and large grocery stores with gluten-free aisles.

- ► **WHOLE WHEAT PASTRY FLOUR** is essential for many of the desserts in this book. Finely milled from white wheat, it gives baked goods a light, fluffy texture. Whole wheat pastry flour is available in grocery stores, sometimes in the bulk section. If you cannot find it, you can substitute spelt flour or white whole wheat flour.

- ► Pure **VANILLA EXTRACT** is made from vanilla beans and lends a delicious hint of vanilla to many desserts. It is worth the money to buy pure vanilla extract rather than the cheaper imitation version, which leaves baked goods with a bitter taste.

The following ingredients are all called for in recipes in this book, although they don't appear as often as the items in the Pantry Basics (page 12).

- ▶ **ARROWROOT POWDER** is used as a thickener in sauces in much the same way that cornstarch is. It is the dehydrated root of the plant of the same name, and unlike cornstarch, it is a minimally processed food.

- ▶ **BRAGG LIQUID AMINOS** is a gluten-free, non–genetically modified soy-based product used in the same way you would use soy sauce.

- ▶ **BROWN RICE FLOUR**, milled from unhulled rice kernels, is a whole-grain, gluten-free alternative to whole wheat flour.

- ▶ **BROWN RICE SYRUP** is made by cooking brown rice with enzymes to break down the starches and then straining off the resulting liquid and boiling it down in the same way you would to make maple syrup.

- ▶ **CHIPOTLE PEPPERS** are dried, smoked jalapeño peppers.

- ▶ **COCONUT MILK (LITE)** is a rich milk made from the liquids in coconut meat. Lite coconut milk generally has less than half the fat of regular coconut milk. Though coconut milk is high in saturated fat, it is cholesterol free. Lite coconut milk is available in most supermarkets, either with other plant-based milks or in the Asian specialty section. It comes canned, in aseptic packages, and in powdered form.

- ▶ **COCONUT WATER**, not to be confused with coconut *milk*, is a clear, nutty, and mildly sweet liquid tapped from the center of young, green coconuts. Coconut water is naturally free of fat and cholesterol and is rich in electrolytes, particularly potassium. It is available in health food stores and many grocery stores.

- ▶ **DATE MOLASSES** is a cooked version of date syrup (see below) and usually has most of the fibers removed.

- ▶ **DATE SYRUP** is a popular sweetener in Middle Eastern cooking and can be made by soaking dates in water and pureeing the dates with the soaking water to make a syrup.

- ▶ **KAFFIR LIME LEAVES** are a fragrant seasoning popular in Asian cooking, and they have a flavor so distinct that most recipes do not give a substitute for it. The leaves can be found fresh or dried in Asian grocery stores.

- ▶ **KIMCHI** is a popular condiment in Korea, made with cabbage and hot peppers, although vegan kimchi is not as common as kimchi that has been made with some kind of fish. The flavor is very pungent and usually very hot.

- ▶ **KOMBU,** a seaweed that can be found in natural food stores and Asian grocery markets, is used to make beans more tender during cooking and is the base for many broths in Asian soup recipes.

- ▶ **MEDJOOL DATES** are one of the many varieties of fruits from date palm trees. Medjool dates are larger and sweeter than many of their cousins.

14

► **MELLOW WHITE MISO** (look for low-sodium varieties) is made by fermenting soybeans, often with other grains. It is used to flavor sauces and soups, and it makes a great salad dressing.

► **NUTRITIONAL YEAST** is a deactivated yeast that comes in flaked or powdered form. It is popular in plant-based cooking for its umami, "cheesy" flavor and strong nutritional profile. Some find that it is an acquired taste, so when it is called for in the recipes in this book, it is generally optional—but I encourage you to try it!

► **PORCINI MUSHROOMS** are earthy-flavored mushroom from Italy. Outside of Italy, they may be purchased in dried form.

► **SAMBAL OELEK** (Indonesian chili sauce) is another distinct condiment used in Asian cooking. It has quite a kick and should be used sparingly if you are not sure how much heat you can take.

► **TAHINI** is a paste made of ground, most often preroasted, sesame seeds. It can be found in many grocery stores alongside other Middle Eastern products.

► **THAI RED CURRY PASTE** is a popular condiment in Thai cooking and has a distinct pungent flavor. It is made from shallots, garlic, ginger, chiles, and spices.

► **TOFU, EXTRA FIRM SILKEN,** is a particular type of tofu that, despite its "extra firm" name, is soft and creamy. Like other forms of tofu, it takes on the flavor of whatever food it is cooked with. In this book, it is used for sauces, salad dressings, and puddings.

► **VEGAN WORCESTERSHIRE SAUCE** is made without anchovies, which is a common ingredient in traditional Worcestershire sauce. It adds a salty, tangy pungent flavor to many dishes.

The following is a list of some basic tools that will help you to prepare easy, delicious, healthy, plant-based meals.

▶ **BLENDER.** Handy for making smoothies or combining mostly liquid ingredients. Because of the toughness of kale and some other green vegetables that are often added to smoothies, consider buying a blender with a strong motor, such as a Blendtec or Vitamix.

▶ **CITRUS REAMER OR SQUEEZER.** Very useful if you like using juice from fresh citrus fruits. See Zesting and Juicing Citrus (page 10).

▶ **COLANDER.** Perfect for draining steamed vegetables and pastas and for rinsing berries or beans.

▶ **COOKIE SHEETS.** For baking healthy whole-grain cookies.

▶ **COOLING RACKS.** For cooling baked goods.

▶ **CROCK-POT OR SLOW COOKER.** A great appliance for making soups, stews, and casseroles. Just add all the ingredients, turn it on, and forget about it!

▶ **CUTTING BOARD.** You will get a lot of use out of this kitchen staple. Choose wood or plastic, depending on your preference. On a plant-based diet there is no need for concern about cross-contamination among raw foods.

▶ **FOOD PROCESSOR.** Absolutely essential for making dips, dressings, spreads, sauces, and other thicker-consistency condiments.

▶ **GLASS BOWLS.** For mixing ingredients for baking, marinades, salsas, and so on. Those with lids are also convenient for storage.

▶ **GLASS COUNTERTOP CANISTERS WITH LIDS.** For storing everything from flour to dried beans.

▶ **IMMERSION BLENDER.** This is a handy tool for making creamy soups or blending hot liquids right in the pot. You can blend ingredients without the extra mess or danger of transferring hot soup in batches between the pot and a conventional blender.

▶ **KNIVES.** You really need only one good long knife—find one that you really like, and keep it sharp. You'll also want a small paring knife and a short, serrated knife—these are key for cutting avocados, mangoes, and other whole foods that require some dexterity.

▶ **MANDOLINE.** Not essential, but very useful for thinly slicing vegetables. Many mandolines have multiple settings for different thicknesses and cuts. But be careful—mandoline blades are extremely sharp and unforgiving, so follow the manufacturer's instructions and be sure to use safety guards and other mechanisms designed to ensure that food gets sliced, not fingers.

▶ **MEASURING CUPS AND SPOONS.** You will want the following sizes for measuring dry goods: ¼ cup, ⅓ cup, and ½ cup. You will also want a 1-cup, as well as a

2- or 4-cup glass measuring cup with a spout, for liquids. Convenient sizes for measuring spoons are: ¼ teaspoon, ½ teaspoon, 1 teaspoon, and 1 tablespoon.

▶ **MUFFIN PANS OR CUPS, NONSTICK OR SILICONE.** To make the oil-free muffins and cupcakes in this book, we recommend a high-quality nonstick muffin pan such as the Wilton brand pans. If you prefer, you can use silicone pans or cups, but be sure to choose 100% silicone products, like those made by Betty Crocker; other products not only are less effective but also tend to leach and smell.

▶ **PARCHMENT PAPER.** For occasional oil-free brownies and cookies.

▶ **PIZZA STONE, WOODEN PIZZA PEEL, AND PIZZA CUTTER.** To make great plant-based, cheese-free pizzas!

▶ **POTS AND PANS.** In various sizes for everything from bread and brown rice to soups and stir-fries. The most convenient sizes you need are: 1-, 2-, 4-, and 8-quart saucepans with covers; a 12-inch nonstick skillet with a cover; a 9-inch square cake pan; a 9 x 13-inch baking pan; and a 9 x 5-inch loaf pan. Nonstick pans are a good choice, especially for dishes that require baking or sautéing, as are clay pots.

▶ **RICE COOKER.** Cooks any grain perfectly, including brown rice, quinoa, barley, and more. Just throw your grain in with the right amount of water (see page 6) and go for a jog or drive a carpool—when you get home, dinner will be done!

▶ **ROLLING PIN.** For making your own whole wheat pizza dough or healthy cookie dough.

▶ **SCISSORS.** Useful for more things than you can imagine, including opening tofu containers, snipping cilantro, preparing whole peeled tomatoes, and more. Wash them in the dishwasher just as you would a knife.

▶ **SPATULAS.** At least one straight spatula, one spatula with an angled handle, and one rubber scraper spatula.

▶ **SPICE RACK.** Should include a variety of spices and herbs, including sweet and savory flavors (see the Herbs and Spices Pantry Basics, page 12).

▶ **SPOONS, FOR MIXING AND STIRRING.** Be sure to include a slotted spoon, a wooden spoon, a sturdy metal spoon, and a soup ladle.

▶ **STEAMING BASKET OR BAMBOO STEAMER.** Steaming is the best way to cook vegetables, since it cooks the vegetable while letting it retain the most nutrients possible.

▶ **VEGETABLE PEELER.** Makes short work of peeling everything from potatoes to butternut squash. Some vegetable peelers come with various blade attachments, such as julienne, crinkle cut, and slicing.

▶ **WHISK.** For combining baking ingredients and whipping up your own dressings and vinaigrettes. It's most convenient to have a variety of different sizes.

Cooking Equipment and Your Budget

Although there are many items in the equipment list on the previous pages, many recipes in this book can be prepared with one pot or pan. Aside from that, you could get by with just a blender, for making smoothies, and a slow cooker, which allows you to start your meals in the morning and then come home from work or class to have dinner ready (or to prepare breakfast overnight—see Slow-Cooked Steel-Cut Oats, page 48). Many salad and wrap recipes require little or no equipment. (See also "If You're a Student and Living in a Dorm," below, for more about cooking equipment for college students.)

IF YOU'RE A STUDENT AND LIVING IN A DORM

Every August and September, students move into dorm rooms on their college or university campuses. If you live in a dorm, you are usually required to purchase a meal plan as part of your housing contract, tying up any monetary freedom you may have to pursue healthier options. A few food service providers allow students to use their meal plans to purchase ingredients to use in community kitchens for meal preparation, but if not, cafeteria food may be all that is available to you, and you will have to make do with it, whatever its limitations.

If your goal is to eat a whole-foods, plant-based diet based on recipes like those in this book, even the most progressive campus dining services may prove challenging. While campus dining services are more aware than they've been in many years that many students don't want to eat just pepperoni pizza and hamburgers, a whole-foods, plant-based diet may still not be on the radar of most food service directors. Your ability to educate and influence these directors will vary from campus to campus, as will your ability to navigate the available food choices.

At the very least, seek out and speak with the food service director about making some of the foods already available more healthy. Ask that steamed vegetables not be tossed with oil, or that veggie burgers be made with whole grains and without added fat. However, some colleges and universities do make an effort to work with students to improve their campus food. Penn State (University Park), for example, has a vegetarian advisory board where vegetarians, the executive chef, the campus dining director, and others meet to discuss student issues and new recipe ideas. The board even has a Facebook page to facilitate easy communication.

Larger universities usually have many options for dining—cafeterias with salad bars, fast-food chains, and even smoothie stands. Nearly all colleges have salad bars, which are usually a good bet. Fresh tofu and vegetables, brown rice, beans, mixed salad greens, fresh fruit, and whole-grain breads are staples of the best-stocked salad bars. You may even be able to use salad bar ingredients to prepare your own healthy meals in a community kitchen (see "Cook in a Community Kitchen," on the following page). Raw vegetables, beans, and grains can be found in salad bars and used in many of the recipes in this book. (One problem with that approach, however, is that many meal plans do not allow you to take more than a piece of fruit from the dining hall.)

Depending on the facilities provided by your college or university, you may be able to cook for yourself, but the ability to prepare healthy meals in a dorm setting can vary greatly and depends on a number of factors—the housing contract governing your dorm, the type of food service offered on campus, the availability of community kitchens, the willingness of campus food service to work with your diet, and your budget. Some campus dorms have community kitchens, stoves, ovens, microwaves, and maybe even cooking utensils. Others may have only a microwave and a 2-by-2-foot refrigerator.

If you are cooking the recipes in this book in your dorm room, and a microwave is all you are allowed to have, you can still prepare most of them. The one big drawback to a microwave is that it does not brown foods well, so if you can afford one, and are permitted to, buy a microwave that doubles as a toaster oven—this will allow you to prepare foods that are browned the way you would expect them to be if they were prepared in a conventional oven.

Other options include:

▶ **BECOME A MEMBER OF YOUR LOCAL FOOD CO-OP OR START A BUYING CLUB IN YOUR DORM.** Buying in large quantities is a great way to reduce the cost of foods. It's also a great way to create community wherever you live. Focus on whole-food staples, such as rice, beans, and local fruits and vegetables.

▶ **START A COOKING CO-OP.** Being a part of a cooking co-op can save money, and it can also reduce the amount of already limited time most of us have to cook. By sharing food preparation with another person, or group of people, you may have to cook only every third or fourth day, depending on how many people are members of your co-op. Keep in mind that you will want to find people who want to cook the way you do, with a whole-foods, plant-based approach.

If you want to start a cooking co-op, approach the food service operation on campus and see if can use your meal plan to purchase ingredients for your community kitchen. Campus food service providers have amazing buying power and access to a huge resource of raw materials, and many of the recipes in this book are made with ingredients that can be found in most grocery stores, or easily through wholesale distributors.

▶ **COOK IN A COMMUNITY KITCHEN.** If you have access to a community kitchen, you can stock it inexpensively by purchasing equipment at thrift stores or garage sales. I buy stainless steel pots and pans when I can find them used, but I usually avoid purchasing used nonstick pans—they are often chipped, and I don't want Teflon flakes in my food. I also purchase food processors, blenders, slow cookers, and most of my utensils used. Most of the time these appliances are in good to excellent condition and cost only a fraction of what I would pay for new ones. If you can afford one, buy a vacuum sealer. It allows you to make large batches of food, individually package them, and then freeze them. You can then reheat the packages by dropping them into a pan of boiling water for 5 minutes or so. It's not only a cheap option—it's a great time-saver, too.

Reading Ingredient Labels—A Recap

IN AN IDEAL WORLD, everyone would be eating whole foods that arrive without any kind of plastic packaging and, therefore, without that long list of ingredients telling you what's inside—some of it good, much of it bad, and some of it simply mysterious, such as strange compounds that sound less like food and more like something concocted in a chemistry lab.

In the real world, however, even people who have considered themselves healthy, whole-plant eaters for years consume some multi-ingredient foods, which are therefore processed to some degree. Some of these even contain those mystery ingredients. Given this reality, here is some advice on choosing processed products when you must purchase them.

The ingredient list is the most important piece of text on a product's packaging because it shows, in descending order by weight, everything you are about to put into your body. Be wary of label manipulation. For example, manufacturers often alter their ingredients lists to make it seem as if certain foods are included in lesser quantities than they actually are. This happens most often with sugars. In a practice commonly known as "ingredient splitting," manufacturers use more than one kind of sweetener, such as cane sugar, corn syrup, beet sugar, fructose, and so on, to push what might have been the top-listed ingredient (i.e., heaps of sugar) farther down the list so that healthier ingredients can be listed first.

Likewise, expect the unexpected. Foods that you may imagine to be whole and healthy may not be. For example, you may think that you know which foods are high in sodium and which are low, but look again: A seemingly innocent can of vegetable juice may contain up to half of your daily allowance of salt.

Unwanted foods pop up in unexpected places. Dairy appears more often than you would think in products that may not seem to be dairy foods at all: potato chips, breakfast cereals, tomato sauces, and many other nondairy foods. Even some so-called dairy-free "cheeses" actually contain cow's milk derivatives. These dairy products are often listed using terms that you might not recognize, such casein, whey, whey protein, albumen, caseinate, sodium caseinate, lactose, lactic acid, rennet, and rennin, to name a few.

Serving size and the number of servings per container are two other key pieces of package information. One of the ways that manufacturers fool consumers into buying their products is to make them seem lighter on calories and fat by reducing the serving size listed on the container. For instance, there's one product in most kitchens whose label indicates that it contains no fat, and yet it is 100 percent fat—cooking spray. The reason cooking spray can be all fat and yet call itself "nonfat" is that, according to the Food and Drug Administration, any food that contains less than a half-gram of fat per serving can be called "fat free." A single serving of cooking spray is one incredibly quick spritz—small enough to be less than a half-gram of fat—but most cooks use much more than that. Remember: Cooking spray is just fat under a "fat free" label. And, if you aren't careful to check the number of servings included in that bottle of juice or can of soup (often 2.5 servings or more), you may think you're consuming a lot less sugar or sodium than you in fact are.

Of course, one way to avoid confusion over food labels is to purchase only whole-plant foods. Broccoli, cabbage, bananas, oats, lentils, and other whole-plant foods need no ingredient lists. However, if they had labels, they would look great! Because the recipes in this book rely on ingredients like these—no mystery ingredients there—you can feel confident when cooking them that you're giving your body just what it needs and nothing else.

In short, choose wisely when you must choose packaged foods—and the rest of the time, focus on whole-foods, plant-based recipes made in your own kitchen, like the ones you'll find in the following pages.

By now, we hope you're starting to get excited about the many benefits that cooking and eating the whole-food, plant-based way can bring to you, your loved ones, your community, and the world. By cooking the *Forks Over Knives* way, you can save money on medical bills and groceries, discover new and intriguing ingredients and techniques, and even bring your community together in the pursuit of health. It's all as simple as getting into the kitchen and getting started. So flip through the pages, check out your kitchen cupboards, write up a shopping list, and let's get cooking!

NOTE ▶ Throughout the following chapters, the 📷 indicates that a recipe is pictured in the book's four-color photo insert, which is situated following page 144.

Vegetable Stock

MAKING YOUR OWN vegetable stock is as easy as chopping the vegetables. Double, triple, or quadruple the recipe and freeze some for later use. This is my go-to stock recipe, but you can use whatever vegetables you have available. A good rule of thumb is to use vegetables that you may be using in the recipe in which you plan to use the stock. For example, if you are making a soup with corn, add the corn cob to the stock. If you are making a potato and leek soup, use some of the leek greens and potato peelings in the stock. However, be careful to avoid adding strongly flavored vegetables like Brussels sprouts or beets, as they can overpower the finished product. And do not use vegetables that are past their prime—if you would not add them to the soup, you should not add them to the stock. I like browning the vegetables first, as it helps concentrate their flavors.

MAKES ABOUT 6 CUPS

> **1 large onion, peeled**
> **2 large carrots, peeled**
> **2 celery stalks**
> **8 cloves garlic, peeled and smashed**
> **8 sprigs parsley**
> **½ cup green lentils, rinsed**

Scrub the vegetables and chop them roughly into 1-inch chunks. In a large pot, add the onion, carrots, celery, garlic, parsley, and lentils and cook them over high heat for 5 to 10 minutes, stirring frequently. Add water 1 to 2 tablespoons at a time to keep the vegetables from sticking to the pan. Add 2 quarts of water and bring to a boil. Lower the heat and simmer, uncovered, for 30 minutes. Strain the stock carefully and discard the solids.

NOTE ▶ Vegetable stock keeps for up to a week in the refrigerator and several months in the freezer. Freeze stock in ice cube trays, and then keep frozen stock cubes on hand to add to dishes that call for small quantities of stock or water.

Basil Pesto

TRADITIONAL PESTO IS made with Genovese basil, pine nuts, olive oil, and Parmesan cheese. The flavor is rich, and a little goes a long way. This healthy version has all the flavor of the traditional version without the oil or cheese, and just a touch of fat in the nuts. For a really low-fat version, make the sauce without the nuts and use low-fat silken tofu. And for an unusual twist, try it with arugula instead of the basil.

MAKES ABOUT 1 CUP

2 cups packed basil or arugula

¼ cup pine nuts, toasted (see page 10)

4 cloves garlic, peeled and chopped

2 teaspoons fresh lemon juice

Salt to taste

½ package extra firm silken tofu (about 6 ounces), drained

¼ cup nutritional yeast, optional

Combine the basil, pine nuts, garlic, lemon juice, salt, tofu, and nutritional yeast (if using) in the bowl of a food processor and puree until smooth and creamy.

Spicy Cilantro Pesto 📷

AN APPEALING ALTERNATIVE to traditional basil pesto, this goes well with a variety of foods, including Pinto Bean Stew with Hominy (page 115) and Quinoa-Stuffed Tomatoes (page 188).

MAKES ABOUT 1 CUP

2 cups packed cilantro

¼ cup hulled sunflower seeds, toasted (see page 10), optional

1 jalapeño pepper, coarsely chopped (for less heat, remove the seeds)

4 cloves garlic, peeled and chopped

Zest and juice of 1 lime

Salt to taste

½ package extra firm silken tofu (about 6 ounces), drained

¼ cup nutritional yeast, optional

Combine the cilantro, sunflower seeds (if using), jalapeño pepper, garlic, lime zest and juice, salt, tofu, and nutritional yeast (if using) in the bowl of a food processor and puree until smooth and creamy.

Tomato Sauce

THIS IS MY go-to sauce for anything from Eggplant Rollatini (page 196) to Millet Loaf (page 236). You can also toss it with cooked whole-grain pasta and sautéed vegetables for an easy meal.

MAKES 4 CUPS

> **1 medium yellow onion, peeled and diced small**
> **6 cloves garlic, peeled and minced**
> **6 tablespoons minced basil**
> **2 tablespoons minced oregano**
> **One 28-ounce can diced tomatoes, pureed**
> **Salt to taste**

Place the onion in a large saucepan and sauté over medium heat for 10 minutes. Add water 1 to 2 tablespoons at a time to keep the onion from sticking to the pan. Add the garlic, basil, and oregano and cook for another 3 minutes. Add the pureed tomatoes and salt and cook, covered, over medium-low heat for 25 minutes.

Roasted Red Pepper Sauce 📷

THIS SAUCE IS as versatile as any tomato sauce. Toss it with pasta for a quick meal, serve it over steamed vegetables and brown rice, or use it as a dip for vegetables.

MAKES 2 CUPS

> **One 12-ounce package extra firm silken tofu, drained**
> **2 large red bell peppers, roasted (see page 8) and seeded**
> **3 cloves garlic, peeled and chopped**
> **2 tablespoons chopped dill**
> **1 teaspoon salt**
> **½ teaspoon freshly ground black pepper**
> **Zest of 1 lemon**

Combine all ingredients in the bowl of a food processor and puree until smooth and creamy. Refrigerate in an airtight container until ready to use.

Fresh Tomato Salsa

HERE'S ANOTHER MUST-HAVE recipe for using ripe, garden-fresh vegetables. I am not a fan of salsa made with out-of-season tomatoes, so in the off-season, I use my favorite store-bought salsa instead.

MAKES ABOUT 4 CUPS

> **3 large ripe tomatoes, diced small**
> **1 small red onion, peeled and diced small**
> **½ cup finely chopped cilantro**
> **1 to 2 jalapeño peppers, minced (for less heat, remove the seeds)**
> **2 cloves garlic, peeled and minced**
> **3 tablespoons fresh lime juice**
> **Salt to taste**

Combine all ingredients in a large bowl and mix well. Store refrigerated until ready to serve.

Salsa Verde 📷

SALSA VERDE IS a popular Mexican salsa made tart by tomatillos, which, by the way, are not green tomatoes. Many recipes add lime juice to the dish, but I find that it needs no more tang so I use the lime zest instead. Use this salsa on enchiladas, or anywhere you would use salsa.

MAKES 3 CUPS

> **1 pound tomatillos (about 16 medium), husks removed, coarsely chopped**
> **2 poblano peppers, roasted (see page 8), peeled, and seeded**
> **6 green onions (white and green parts), chopped**
> **2 cups chopped cilantro leaves and tender stems**
> **4 cloves garlic, peeled and chopped**
> **1 serrano chile, chopped (for less heat, remove the seeds)**
> **Zest of 2 limes**
> **Salt to taste**

Combine all ingredients in the bowl of a food processor and puree until smooth and creamy.

Not-So-Fat Guacamole

FAT-FREE GUACAMOLE HAS been around in one form or another for a while. Most recipes taste good, but you can often tell they're not made with avocados, the traditional primary ingredient. While I can't promise that my recipe tastes just like the original version, this healthy alternative uses both broccoli and edamame to fool the taste buds just a little more. Serve this low-fat version of the very popular Mexican condiment wherever you would serve traditional guacamole, such as with enchiladas, burritos, or as a dip for vegetables.

MAKES 2 CUPS

> 1 cup shelled edamame
> 1 cup broccoli florets
> Zest of 1 lime and juice of 2 limes
> 2 Roma tomatoes, diced
> ½ small red onion, peeled and diced small
> ¼ cup finely chopped cilantro
> 1 clove garlic, peeled and minced
> Salt to taste
> 1 pinch cayenne pepper, or to taste

1. Place the edamame in a medium saucepan and add water to cover. Bring to a boil and cook for 5 minutes. Drain and rinse the edamame until cooled.
2. Steam the broccoli in a double boiler or steamer basket for about 8 minutes, or until very tender. Drain and rinse the broccoli until cooled.
3. Add the edamame and broccoli to a food processor and puree until smooth and creamy. Add water if needed to achieve a creamy texture. Put the pureed mixture into a bowl and add the lime zest and juice, tomatoes, onion, cilantro, garlic, salt, and cayenne. Mix well and chill until ready to serve.

Tofu Sour Cream

USE THIS HEALTHY dairy alternative in any dish that calls for sour cream. Serve it with baked potatoes and fresh chives, with tacos or enchiladas, or with Mushroom Stroganoff (page 152).

MAKES 1½ CUPS

One 12-ounce package extra firm silken tofu, drained
1 tablespoon fresh lemon juice
1 tablespoon red wine vinegar
Salt to taste

Combine all ingredients in a blender and puree until smooth and creamy. Chill until ready to serve.

VARIATION

▶ For a spicy version, omit the salt and add 1½ teaspoons of ancho chile powder and ½ teaspoon of cayenne pepper.

Mayonnaise

FOR A LOWER-FAT version, use lite silken tofu instead and you'll add only 2 grams of total fat to the recipe.

MAKES 1½ CUPS

One 12-ounce package extra firm silken tofu, drained
1 teaspoon dry mustard
½ teaspoon onion powder
½ teaspoon garlic powder
½ teaspoon salt, or to taste
3 tablespoons red wine vinegar

Combine all ingredients in the bowl of a food processor. Puree until smooth and creamy.

No-Cheese Sauce

THIS LOW-FAT SAUCE makes great Mac and "Cheese" (page 252) or Baked Ziti (page 251). Best of all, it takes only about 5 minutes to put together. It may seem as though this recipe will not work in a blender, but with a little patience it does. If your onions are strong, blanch them in boiling water for a few minutes, or sauté them over medium heat for about 5 minutes before adding them to the blender.

MAKES ABOUT 2½ CUPS

> 1 large yellow onion, peeled and coarsely chopped
>
> 1 large red bell pepper, seeded and coarsely chopped
>
> 3 tablespoons cashews, toasted (see page 10), optional
>
> 1 tablespoon tahini, optional
>
> 1 cup nutritional yeast
>
> Salt to taste

Combine all ingredients in a blender in the order given and puree until smooth and creamy, adding up to ½ cup of water if necessary to achieve a smooth consistency.

VARIATIONS

▶ Use an equal amount of roasted red bell peppers in place of the raw pepper.

▶ Combine the prepared sauce with a jar of store-bought salsa or a recipe of Fresh Tomato Salsa (page 26), and use it as a dip for vegetables.

▶ Add ½ teaspoon of nutmeg with the salt.

Cauliflower Béchamel

CREAM SAUCES ARE used in many recipes from pastas to soups and stews, but most plant-based "cream" sauces, usually made from soy, leave something to be desired. This sauce, made from pureed cauliflower, is a great substitute for traditional cream versions, but it is also a delicious sauce—period. Use it wherever you want a creamy texture in a dish—for instance, in Spinach and Sweet Potato Lasagna (page 267) or Penne with Spinach Béchamel (page 151).

MAKES ABOUT 3½ CUPS

> **1 large head cauliflower, cut into florets (about 3 cups)**
> **Unsweetened plain almond milk, as needed**
> **1 medium yellow onion, peeled and diced small**
> **2 cloves garlic, peeled and minced**
> **2 teaspoons minced thyme**
> **¼ cup finely chopped basil**
> **¼ cup nutritional yeast, optional**
> **¼ teaspoon ground nutmeg**
> **Salt and freshly ground black pepper to taste**

1. Add the cauliflower to a large pot and add water to cover. Bring to a boil over high heat and cook until the cauliflower is very tender, about 10 minutes. Drain the excess water and puree the cauliflower using an immersion blender or in a blender with a tight-fitting lid, covered with a towel, in batches if necessary. Add almond milk, if needed, to achieve a creamy consistency. Set the puree aside while you prepare the rest of the ingredients.

2. Place the onion in a large skillet or saucepan and sauté over medium heat for 10 minutes. Add water 1 to 2 tablespoons at a time to keep the onion from sticking to the pan. Add the garlic, thyme, and basil and cook for another minute. Add the nutritional yeast (if using), nutmeg, and salt and pepper and cook for 5 minutes, or until heated through.

3. Add the onion mixture to the cauliflower puree and blend until smooth, adding up to ½ cup of water if necessary to achieve a smooth consistency.

VARIATION

▶ Using only the cauliflower and almond milk (if needed), follow step 1. Use 1½ cups of the plain puree as a substitute for one 12-ounce package of extra-firm silken tofu in any savory recipe in this book, if you wish to avoid soy.

Nitter Kibbeh

ETHIOPIAN CLARIFIED BUTTER is usually made from spices cooked in fat. This version suspends the flavor in caramelized onions to make a relish can be used in traditional recipes like Ethiopian Lentil Stew (page 125) or as a topping for baked potatoes or steamed sweet potatoes, or mixed into cooked rice or quinoa for a flavorful change.

MAKES 1½ CUPS

> **2 pounds yellow onions, peeled and diced small**
> **9 cloves garlic, peeled and minced**
> **1 tablespoon grated ginger**
> **½ tablespoon turmeric**
> **¼ teaspoon ground cardamom**
> **½ teaspoon ground cinnamon**
> **⅛ teaspoon ground cloves**
> **⅛ teaspoon ground nutmeg**

Place the onions in a large skillet over medium heat. Stir frequently, adding water only as needed to keep the onions from sticking to the pan, and cook for about 20 minutes, or until the onions are browned. Add the garlic, ginger, turmeric, cardamom, cinnamon, cloves, and nutmeg and cook for 5 minutes. Add ¼ cup of water and scrape the bottom of the pan with a spatula to pick up and incorporate the bits on the bottom of the pan. Transfer the mixture to a blender and puree, adding water as needed to make a smooth and creamy consistency. This will keep, refrigerated, for up to 7 days.

Coriander Chutney 📷

A STAPLE IN Indian dishes, chutney is as common in the East as ketchup and salsa are in the West, and just as versatile. Serve this condiment with any curry dish or as a flavorful addition to a sandwich or wrap.

MAKES ABOUT 1 CUP

½ teaspoon cumin seeds, toasted (see page 10) and ground
½ teaspoon yellow mustard seeds, toasted and ground
1 large bunch cilantro
1 small yellow onion, peeled and chopped
¼ cup unsweetened coconut
3 tablespoons grated ginger
2 serrano chiles, stemmed (for less heat, remove the seeds)
Zest and juice of 2 lemons
Salt to taste

Combine all ingredients in a blender and blend on high until smooth. Add water as needed to achieve a thick paste.

Mango Chutney

SERVE THIS SWEET and spicy chutney with any curry dish, in a wrap with rice and stir-fried vegetables, or to liven up simple beans and rice.

MAKES ABOUT 2 CUPS

2 to 3 mangoes, peeled and diced (about 2 cups)
1 small yellow onion, peeled and minced
½ cup golden raisins
1 jalapeño pepper, seeded and minced
2 tablespoons brown rice syrup
Zest of 1 lime and juice of 2 limes
2 teaspoons grated ginger

Combine all ingredients in a large saucepan with ½ cup of water and bring to a boil over high heat. Reduce the heat to medium-low and simmer, uncovered, until thickened, about 15 minutes.

Pineapple Chutney

PINEAPPLE CHUTNEY IS a great condiment to have on hand when you want to add a kick to beans and rice dishes, wraps, or even stir-fries. If you prefer less heat, you can cut back on the jalapeño peppers. And if you are not a cilantro fan, try mint instead.

MAKES 1½ CUPS

½ **medium yellow onion, peeled and diced small**
1 **tablespoon grated ginger**
2 **jalapeño peppers, seeded and minced**
½ **tablespoon cumin seeds, toasted (see page 10) and ground**
½ **fresh pineapple, peeled, cored, and diced**
½ **cup finely chopped cilantro**
Salt to taste

Place the onion in a large skillet or saucepan and sauté over medium heat for 7 to 8 minutes. Add water 1 to 2 tablespoons at a time to keep the onion from sticking to the pan. Add the ginger, jalapeño peppers, and cumin seeds and cook for another 4 minutes. Add the pineapple and remove the pan from the heat. Stir in the cilantro and salt.

Pineapple Sweet-and-Sour Sauce

THIS UNUSUAL SAUCE goes well with a variety of dishes, such as Spicy Sweet-and-Sour Eggplant (page 177) and the Sweet-and-Sour "Meatball" Stir-Fry (page 221). There are many variations on sweet-and-sour sauce, but this is one of my favorite recipes. The brightness of the pineapple juice pairs well with all kinds of vegetables and grains, and this sauce is a great one to have on hand for a last-minute stir-fry.

MAKES 2 CUPS

1½ **cups unsweetened pineapple juice**
¼ **cup apple cider vinegar**
¼ **cup low-sodium soy sauce**
1 **clove garlic, peeled and minced**
¼ **cup plus 2 tablespoons brown rice syrup, more to taste**
2 **tablespoons arrowroot powder, dissolved in ¼ cup cold water**

Combine the pineapple juice, vinegar, low-sodium soy sauce, garlic, and brown rice syrup in a saucepan. Bring the pot to a boil and whisk in the arrowroot mixture. Cook until thickened, about 1 minute.

Kombu Broth 📷

THIS IS A versatile broth used to make miso soup and any number of Asian noodle soups. Kombu is a seaweed that can be found in natural food stores and Asian grocery markets.

MAKES 6 CUPS

One 6-inch piece kombu

Bring 8 cups of water to a boil in a large saucepan. Add the kombu and simmer, uncovered, over medium heat for 20 minutes. Let cool, then store in an airtight container for up to 2 weeks.

Easy Miso Sauce

SERVE THIS FLAVORFUL sauce with steamed vegetables and brown rice for a quick and tasty meal. There are many flavors of miso on the market, but I recommend a mellow white miso because it will not overpower other flavors in dishes. Mirin is a sweet Japanese cooking wine, widely available in the international sections of supermarkets and at specialty grocers.

MAKES ¾ CUP

⅓ cup Kombu Broth (above)
¼ cup plus 2 tablespoons mellow white miso
3 tablespoons mirin
3 tablespoons sake

In a medium saucepan, bring the kombu broth to a boil and add the miso, mirin, and sake. Remove the pan from the heat and whisk the mixture until smooth and creamy.

Ponzu Sauce 📷

THIS CITRUS-BASED SAUCE, used as a dip in Japanese cooking, is a versatile condiment. Use it alongside vegetables or as a sauce for stir-fry or noodle dishes.

MAKES ABOUT 1¾ CUPS

Zest and juice of 2 lemons
Zest and juice of 2 limes
¼ cup brown rice vinegar
¾ cup low-sodium soy sauce
¼ cup sake
¼ cup date molasses or brown rice syrup

Combine all ingredients in a bowl and whisk until smooth. Store refrigerated in an airtight container for up to 1 week.

Chinese Brown Sauce

DOUBLE OR TRIPLE this sauce and keep some on hand for last-minute stir-fried vegetables.

MAKES ¾ CUP

⅓ cup low-sodium soy sauce
⅓ cup Vegetable Stock (page 23), or low-sodium vegetable broth
¼ cup date molasses or brown rice syrup
2 teaspoons grated ginger
2 cloves garlic, peeled and minced
2 teaspoons arrowroot powder

Combine all ingredients in a medium saucepan and cook over medium heat until thickened, about 5 minutes. Store refrigerated in an airtight container for up to 1 week.

Barbecue Sauce

RECIPE BY JULIEANNA HEVER

BAKE THIS INTO tofu, tempeh, or seitan for a spicy and pungent kick. Or simply serve as a dipping sauce or poured over whole grains or legumes.

MAKES 2 CUPS

One 6-ounce can tomato paste
½ cup pineapple juice
¼ cup 100% pure maple syrup
3 tablespoons low-sodium soy sauce, or Bragg Liquid Aminos
2 tablespoons apple cider vinegar
2 tablespoons stone-ground mustard
1 tablespoon minced ginger
1 to 2 cloves garlic, peeled and minced
½ teaspoon chipotle powder
½ teaspoon paprika or smoked paprika
½ teaspoon freshly ground black pepper
¼ teaspoon onion powder
¼ teaspoon cayenne pepper

1. Combine all ingredients in a blender and blend on high until smooth.
2. Serve immediately or keep in an airtight container in the refrigerator for up to 4 or 5 days.

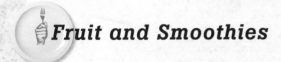

Fruit and Smoothies

Fruit Salad

FRUIT SALADS CAN be as simple as a few fresh fruits chopped and served in a bowl. While I've specified fruits here, feel free to vary the recipe based on whatever is in season. Start with fresh, great-tasting fruits and you won't need to do much besides eat them.

SERVES 4

1 pint fresh strawberries, stems removed, sliced
1 pint fresh blueberries
2 cups seedless grapes
1 ripe pear, cored and diced
2 tablespoons fresh lemon juice
2 tablespoons date syrup, optional
Pinch ground cinnamon

Combine all ingredients in a bowl and mix well. Chill until ready to serve.

VARIATION
▶ Make this into a fruit gazpacho by adding pineapple juice to cover the fruit, plus 2 to 3 tablespoons of finely chopped mint.

Mean Green Smoothie 📷

EVEN IF YOU don't like kale, you won't notice it in this drink. This delicious, plant-based smoothie is an excellent way to add more greens to your diet. The smoothie gets most of its sweetness from the dates, so decrease the amount if you don't have much of a sweet tooth.

SERVES 1

1 cup unsweetened almond milk, or water
1 cup frozen berries
1 banana, peeled
2 cups kale, ribs removed, coarsely chopped
½ cup pitted and coarsely chopped Medjool dates, or to taste

Combine all ingredients in a blender and process until smooth and creamy.

Spicy Tropical Green Smoothie

RECIPE BY JULIEANNA HEVER

THIS BRIGHT AND refreshing beverage will wake up your taste buds with ice-cold flavors of the tropics.

SERVES 1

> **2 cups tightly packed spinach leaves**
>
> **1 cup frozen pineapple chunks**
>
> **1 cup frozen mango chunks**
>
> **1 small tangerine, peeled and pitted, or juice of 1 lime**
>
> **1 cup coconut water**
>
> **¼ teaspoon cayenne pepper (optional)**

Combine all ingredients in a blender and blend on high until smooth. Enjoy cold.

Very Berry Smoothie 📷

WHEN BERRIES ARE in season, their flavor is perfect. You can also make this easy breakfast any time of year with frozen berries.

SERVES 1

> **1½ cups unsweetened almond milk, plus more as needed, or water**
>
> **1 cup berries, such as strawberries, blueberries, or raspberries**
>
> **½ cup pitted and chopped Medjool dates, or to taste**

Add all ingredients to a blender and process until smooth and creamy. Add more almond milk if necessary to achieve a smooth consistency.

Banana Cranberry Smoothie

BANANAS, CRANBERRIES, AND dates come together to make this sweet and tangy breakfast drink. I like it with almond milk, but you can use whichever plant-based milk you prefer.

SERVES 1

> 1½ cups unsweetened plant-based milk, or water
>
> 1 cup frozen cranberries
>
> 1 large banana, peeled
>
> ½ cup pitted and chopped Medjool dates, or to taste

Combine all ingredients in a blender and process until smooth and creamy.

Strawberry Peach Smoothie

BUY FRESH FRUIT at the farmers' market when it is in season and freeze some to have on hand for smoothies. It's an excellent way to get the wholesome benefits of seasonal fruits throughout the year.

SERVES 1

> ½ cup chopped frozen strawberries
>
> ½ cup frozen peach slices
>
> 1½ cups unsweetened plant-based milk, plus more as needed
>
> ½ cup pitted and chopped Medjool dates, or to taste

Combine all ingredients in a blender and process until smooth and creamy. Add more plant-based milk, if needed, to achieve a smooth consistency.

Chunky Monkey Smoothie 📷

THIS IS A quick, filling, and tasty breakfast that's ready in less than 5 minutes. If you prefer, use any other nut butter in place of the peanut butter and substitute carob powder if you prefer it to cocoa. If you don't have bananas in your freezer, use fresh instead and add a few ice cubes to the blender.

SERVES 1

> **1 cup unsweetened almond milk, plus more as needed, or water**
> **2 medium frozen bananas, peeled and cut into chunks**
> **1 tablespoon peanut butter**
> **½ cup pitted and chopped Medjool dates, or to taste**
> **1 tablespoon unsweetened cocoa powder**

Combine all ingredients in a blender and process until smooth and creamy. Add more almond milk as needed to achieve a smooth consistency.

Pumpkin Pie Smoothie

THIS SMOOTHIE COULD easily be dessert on Thanksgiving. It's like having pie without any of the extra fat or sugar.

SERVES 1

> **1 cup unsweetened almond milk, or water**
> **½ cup pumpkin puree**
> **½ cup ice cubes**
> **4 Medjool dates, pitted and chopped, or to taste**
> **¼ teaspoon pure vanilla extract**
> **¼ teaspoon ground cinnamon**
> **Pinch ground nutmeg**

Combine all ingredients in a blender and puree until smooth and creamy.

Gingerbread Smoothie

THIS SMOOTHIE IS almost a dessert in a glass. It makes a great holiday breakfast treat. I prefer unsweetened almond milk in this recipe, but you can use whichever plant-based milk is your favorite.

SERVES 1

1½ cups unsweetened plant-based milk, or water

1 teaspoon unsulfured molasses, or to taste (see page 9 for more about sulfites and sulfur dioxide)

6 Medjool dates, pitted and chopped, or to taste

½-inch piece ginger, peeled and grated, or to taste

Pinch ground cinnamon

Pinch ground nutmeg

2 to 3 ice cubes

Combine all ingredients in a blender and process until smooth and creamy.

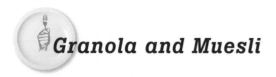
Granola and Muesli

Stove Top Granola

THIS EASY GRANOLA comes together quickly and is a perfect breakfast food when you don't want to heat up the oven. Be careful toasting the oats on the stove top—they go from toasted to burnt in a flash.

MAKES TWELVE ½-CUP SERVINGS

> **5 cups rolled oats**
> **¾ cup date molasses or brown rice syrup**
> **1 tablespoon ground cinnamon**
> **½ teaspoon salt, or to taste**
> **1 cup chopped dried fruit (such as apples, apricots, dates, raisins, cranberries, or blueberries)**

1. Toast the oats in a saucepan over medium-low heat, stirring constantly, for 4 to 5 minutes, or until lightly toasted. Transfer them to a large bowl.
2. In the same saucepan, add the date molasses and bring it to a boil over medium-low heat. Cook for 1 minute. Remove from the heat. Add the toasted oats, cinnamon, and salt to the molasses and mix well. Pour the cereal onto a nonstick baking sheet and let it cool to room temperature.
3. When the cereal is cool, transfer it to a large bowl and stir in the dried fruit. Store in an airtight container for up to 2 weeks.

Basic Baked Granola

LEAVE OUT THE sugar and the oil found in most commercial granolas, and what do you have? A great-tasting granola that's really healthy.

MAKES SIXTEEN ½-CUP SERVINGS

> 8 cups rolled oats
> 1½ cups pitted and chopped dates
> Zest of 2 oranges
> 1 teaspoon ground cinnamon
> 1 teaspoon pure vanilla extract
> 1 teaspoon salt, or to taste

1. Preheat the oven to 275°F.
2. Add the oats to a large mixing bowl and set aside. Line two 13 x 18-inch baking pans with parchment paper.
3. Place the dates in a medium saucepan with 2 cups of water, bring to a boil, and cook over medium heat for about 10 minutes. Add more water if needed to keep the dates from sticking to the pan. Remove from the heat, add the mixture to a blender with the orange zest, cinnamon, vanilla, and salt, and process until smooth and creamy.
4. Add the date mixture to the oats and mix well. Divide the granola between the two prepared pans and spread it evenly in the pans. Bake for 40 to 50 minutes, stirring every 10 minutes, until the granola is crispy. Remove from the oven and let cool before storing in airtight containers (the cereal will get even crispier as it cools).

Banana Almond Granola

THIS RECIPE WAS inspired by my favorite banana almond muffins. Whether in muffins or in cereal, bananas and almonds pair perfectly.

MAKES SIXTEEN ½-CUP SERVINGS

> **8 cups rolled oats**
> **2 cups pitted and chopped dates**
> **2 ripe bananas, peeled and chopped**
> **1 teaspoon almond extract**
> **1 teaspoon salt, or to taste**
> **1 cup slivered almonds, toasted (see page 10), optional**

1. Preheat the oven to 275°F.
2. Add the oats to a large mixing bowl and set aside. Line two 13 x 18-inch inch baking pans with parchment paper.
3. Place the dates in a medium saucepan with 1 cup of water, bring to a boil, and cook over medium heat for 10 minutes. Add more water if needed to keep the dates from sticking to the pan. Remove from the heat and add the mixture to a blender with the bananas, almond extract, and salt. Process until smooth and creamy.
4. Add the date mixture to the oats and mix well. Divide the granola between the two prepared pans and spread evenly in the pans. Bake for 40 to 50 minutes, stirring every 10 minutes, until the granola is crispy. Remove from the oven and let cool before adding the slivered almonds, if desired (the cereal will get even crispier as it cools). Store the granola in an airtight container.

Banana, Date and Coconut Muesli

THIS IS MY favorite way to eat muesli. It's sweet without added sugar, and I love the flavor of the toasted coconut.

SERVES 2

> **1 cup rolled oats**
> **¾ cup unsweetened almond milk**
> **½ cup pitted and chopped dates**
> **¼ cup unsweetened coconut, toasted (see page 10)**
> **1 banana, peeled and sliced**

Combine all ingredients in a bowl and let soak 15 minutes.

Apple Cinnamon Muesli

GRANNY SMITH APPLES give this cereal a mild tartness, but feel free to use your favorite apples, or even pears.

SERVES 2

1 cup rolled oats

¾ cup unsweetened almond milk

½ cup raisins

¼ teaspoon ground cinnamon

2 tablespoons date molasses or brown rice syrup, optional

1 Granny Smith apple

1. Combine the oats, almond milk, raisins, cinnamon, and date molasses (if using) in a bowl and let soak 15 minutes. When you are ready to serve the cereal, grate the apple into the cereal (or core and chop the apple separately before adding it to the cereal) and combine well.

Banana Granola Parfait 📷

PARFAITS—LAYERED DISHES OFTEN served in glasses, and often for dessert—can also be served for breakfast. This elaborate presentation is perfect for Sunday brunch with friends or family, or for other occasions when you're entertaining guests. If you don't have fancy parfait glasses, you can use wineglasses, or just serve it family-style in a large bowl (preferably glass, so that the attractive layers of the dish are visible).

SERVES 4

FOR THE BANANA CREAM:

> One 12-ounce package extra firm silken tofu, drained
>
> 2 ripe bananas, peeled and coarsely chopped
>
> 2 tablespoons fresh lemon juice
>
> ½ cup date molasses or brown rice syrup
>
> 1 teaspoon pure vanilla extract
>
> Pinch salt, or to taste
>
> 2 cups Banana Almond Granola or Banana, Date and Coconut Muesli (page 44)
>
> ½ batch Fruit Salad (page 37), or about 4 cups

TO MAKE THE BANANA CREAM:

1. Combine the tofu, bananas, lemon juice, date molasses, vanilla, and salt in a blender and puree until smooth and creamy. Chill at least 1 hour before serving.

TO ASSEMBLE THE PARFAIT:

2. Have ready four individual 6-ounce parfait glasses.
3. Spoon ¼ cup of the Banana Cream into the bottom of a parfait glass. Top with ¼ cup of the granola, followed by ¼ cup of the fruit salad. Repeat until you have filled the glass, then do the same with the remaining parfait glasses.

Cherry Pecan Granola Bars

THIS IS A perfect bar for breakfast on the go. Store these bars in an airtight container and they will keep for 3 or 4 days.

MAKES 12 BARS

2 cups rolled oats
½ cup dates, pitted and coarsely chopped
½ cup orange juice
¼ cup chopped pecans
1 cup fruit-sweetened dried cherries
½ teaspoon ground cinnamon
¼ teaspoon ground allspice
Pinch salt, or to taste

1. Preheat the oven to 325°F.
2. Spread the oats on a 13 x 18-inch baking sheet and bake for 10 minutes, or until they start to brown. Remove from the oven and place the oats in a large mixing bowl.
3. Combine the dates and orange juice in a small saucepan and cook over medium-low heat for about 15 minutes. Pour the mixture into a blender and process until smooth and creamy.
4. Add the date mixture to the bowl with the oats and add the pecans, dried cherries, cinnamon, allspice, and salt. Mix well.
5. Press the mixture into a nonstick 8 x 8-inch baking pan and bake for 20 minutes, or until the top is lightly golden. Let cool before slicing into bars.

Hot Cereals

Basic Oatmeal

THIS IS MY go-to quick and easy breakfast. Oatmeal is a filling meal, and it can be made with any number of additions—fresh or dried fruit, cinnamon or vanilla, toasted nuts, coconut, or any combination of those.

SERVES 2

> **1 cup rolled oats**
> **2 cups plant-based milk, or water**
> **Salt to taste**

Add the oats, plant-based milk, and salt to a small saucepan and bring to a boil. Reduce the heat to medium and cook for about 5 minutes, or until the oats become creamy.

Slow-Cooked Steel-Cut Oats

STEEL-CUT OATS MAKE a filling, healthy breakfast, but a stove top method requires cooking them 1½ hours before you want to eat. If you start this dish the night before in your slow cooker, breakfast will be ready when you are.

SERVES 2

> **1 cup steel-cut oats**
> **2 cups chopped dried apple**
> **1 cup dates, pitted and chopped**
> **1 cinnamon stick**

Combine the oats, dried apple, dates, cinnamon stick, and 4 cups of water in a 2- or 4-quart slow cooker. Cook for 8 hours, or until the oats are tender. Remove the cinnamon stick before serving.

Sweet Potato Pie Oatmeal

BRING YOUR OATMEAL to life with this recipe based upon my favorite pie. If you cook the sweet potato the night before, you'll be ready to make this recipe quickly in the morning.

SERVES 2

1 large sweet potato, peeled and diced

1 cup rolled oats

1 cup unsweetened almond milk

½ cup date molasses

½ teaspoon ground cinnamon

½ teaspoon ground ginger

¼ teaspoon orange zest

¼ teaspoon ground allspice

Pinch salt

Steam or boil the sweet potato until tender, about 10 minutes. Drain and mash it and add it to a small saucepan with the oats, almond milk, molasses, cinnamon, ginger, orange zest, allspice, and salt. Cook the mixture over medium heat until the oats are tender, 10 to 12 minutes.

Breakfast Quinoa with Apple Compote 📷

QUINOA IS A filling breakfast cereal and a nice change from the usual oatmeal. Make the compote the night before, and breakfast will be ready in less than 30 minutes the next morning.

SERVES 4

FOR THE QUINOA:

> 1½ cups quinoa, rinsed and drained
>
> 1 cinnamon stick
>
> Salt to taste

FOR THE APPLE COMPOTE:

> ½ cup date molasses
>
> 1 cup dates, pitted and chopped
>
> 4 Granny Smith apples, peeled, cored, and diced
>
> 1 teaspoon ground cinnamon
>
> Pinch ground nutmeg
>
> Zest and juice of 1 lemon

TO MAKE THE QUINOA:

1. Bring 3 cups of water to a boil over high heat. Add the quinoa, cinnamon stick, and salt. Cover the pot, bring the mixture back to a boil, reduce the heat to medium, and cook for 20 minutes, or until the quinoa is tender. Remove the cinnamon stick before serving.

TO MAKE THE APPLE COMPOTE:

2. Place the date molasses in a small saucepan and bring it to a boil over medium heat. Add the dates, apples, cinnamon, nutmeg, and lemon zest and juice and cook for 15 minutes, or until the apples are tender and start to break down.

3. To serve, divide the quinoa among 4 individual bowls and top with the apple compote.

Congee with Dates and Spices

A STAPLE BREAKFAST food in China, congee is similar to gruel or porridge, and it can be made either savory or sweet. This is a delicious way to use up leftover rice.

SERVES 4

4 cups cooked brown rice (see page 6)
½ cup dates, pitted and chopped
½ cup chopped unsulfured apricots (see page 9 for more about sulfites and sulfur dioxide)
1 large cinnamon stick
¼ teaspoon ground cloves
Salt to taste

Bring 2 cups of water to a boil in a large saucepan over medium heat. Add the rice, dates, apricots, cinnamon stick, and cloves. Cook over medium-low heat for 15 minutes, or until the mixture thickens. Season with salt. Remove the cinnamon stick before serving.

Brown Rice Breakfast Pudding

MY MOM USED to serve us a version of this for breakfast—cooked with milk, sugar, and a hint of cinnamon. It is still one of my favorite breakfasts, although now I make a more wholesome version with almond milk and chopped dates.

SERVES 4

3 cups cooked brown rice (see page 6)
2 cups unsweetened almond milk
1 cinnamon stick
⅛ to ¼ teaspoon ground cloves, to taste
1 cup dates, pitted and chopped
1 tart apple (such as Granny Smith), cored and chopped
¼ cup raisins
Salt to taste
¼ cup slivered almonds, toasted (see page 10)

Combine the rice, almond milk, cinnamon stick, cloves, and dates in a medium saucepan and cook over medium-low heat for 12 minutes, or until the mixture thickens. Add the apple, raisins, and salt. Remove the cinnamon stick before serving, and serve garnished with the toasted almonds.

Polenta with Dried Fruit Compote

THIS IS A perfect breakfast or a scrumptious dessert—you decide.

SERVES 4

> **1 cup dried unsulfured apricots (see page 9 for more about sulfites and sulfur dioxide)**
> **1 cup dried apple pieces or halves**
> **1 cup golden raisins**
> **½ cup brown rice syrup**
> **1 strip lemon rind**
> **1 cinnamon stick**
> **⅛ teaspoon ground cloves**
> **1 batch Basic Polenta (page 229), kept warm**

1. Combine the apricots, apples, raisins, brown rice syrup, lemon rind, cinnamon stick, and cloves in a medium saucepan. Add enough water to cover the fruit. Bring to a boil over medium-high heat, reduce the heat, and simmer until the fruit is tender, 15 to 20 minutes. Remove the lemon rind and cinnamon stick before serving.
2. To serve, divide the polenta among 4 individual bowls. Spoon the compote on top.

Polenta with Pears and Cranberries

USE THE RIPEST pears you can find in the market—Bosc, Asian, or D'Anjou—and fresh cranberries when they are in season (usually from October through December).

SERVES 4

> **½ cup brown rice syrup**
> **2 pears, peeled, cored, and diced**
> **1 cup fresh or dried cranberries**
> **1 teaspoon ground cinnamon**
> **1 batch Basic Polenta (page 229), kept warm**

1. Heat the brown rice syrup in a medium saucepan. Add the pears, cranberries, and cinnamon and cook, stirring occasionally, until the pears are tender, about 10 minutes.
2. To serve, divide the polenta among 4 individual bowls and top with the pear compote.

Fruited Barley

BARLEY IS A hearty, filling grain and takes on the flavor of anything cooked with it. In this recipe, it is combined with orange juice, currants, and apricots to make a creamy breakfast cereal.

SERVES 2

    1 to 1½ cups orange juice
    1 cup pearled barley
    2 tablespoons dried currants
    3 to 4 dried unsulfured apricots, chopped (see page 9 for more about sulfites and sulfur dioxide)
    1 small cinnamon stick
    ⅛ teaspoon ground cloves
    Pinch salt, or to taste

Bring 1 cup of water and 1 cup of the orange juice to a boil in a medium saucepan over medium heat. Add the barley, currants, apricots, cinnamon stick, cloves, and salt. Bring the mixture to a boil, cover, reduce the heat to medium-low, and cook for 45 minutes. If the barley is not tender after 45 minutes, add up to an additional ½ cup of orange juice and cook for another 10 minutes. Remove the cinnamon stick before serving.

Spelt Berry Hot Breakfast Cereal

SPELT IS AN ancient cousin of wheat, and it makes a hearty breakfast cereal. This recipe takes a little effort, but the flavor and health benefits make it well worth the time. You can cook the spelt berries the night before and finish the dish in about 15 minutes in the morning.

SERVES 2

    1 cup spelt berries
    ¼ teaspoon salt
    ⅛ teaspoon ground cinnamon
    ⅛ teaspoon ground cloves
    2 cups unsweetened almond milk
    ¾ cup dates, pitted and chopped
    ¼ teaspoon orange zest

1. Bring 2½ cups of water to a boil in a medium saucepan. Add the spelt, salt, cinnamon, and cloves. Cover the pot and bring the mixture to a boil. Reduce the heat to medium-low and cook for 45 to 50 minutes, or until the spelt is tender. Drain any excess water.
2. Add the almond milk, dates, and orange zest to the cooked spelt berries and simmer over medium-low heat for 10 to 12 minutes, or until heated through and creamy.

Hearty Breakfasts

Breakfast Scramble

THERE ARE MANY very good recipes for scrambles, but most call for tofu. In this recipe, cauliflower takes the place of the tofu—with delicious results. If you can find ackee, the national fruit of Jamaica with a taste similar to scrambled eggs, use it instead. It is the inspiration for this dish, but it is very hard to find outside of Jamaica. Serve this filling vegetable dish with Fruit Salad (page 37), or use it in Breakfast Rancheros (page 55).

SERVES 6

> 1 medium red onion, peeled and cut into ½-inch dice
> 1 medium red bell pepper, seeded and cut into ½-inch dice
> 1 medium green bell pepper, seeded and cut into ½-inch dice
> 2 cups sliced mushrooms (from about 8 ounces whole mushrooms)
> 1 large head cauliflower, cut into florets, or two 19-ounce cans Jamaican ackee,
>   drained and gently rinsed
> Salt to taste
> ½ teaspoon freshly ground black pepper
> 1½ teaspoons turmeric
> ¼ teaspoon cayenne pepper, or to taste
> 3 cloves garlic, peeled and minced
> 1 to 2 tablespoons low-sodium soy sauce
> ¼ cup nutritional yeast, optional

Place the onion, red and green peppers, and mushrooms in a medium skillet or saucepan and sauté over medium-high heat for 7 to 8 minutes, or until the onion is translucent. Add water 1 to 2 tablespoons at a time to keep the vegetables from sticking to the pan. Add the cauliflower and cook for 5 to 6 minutes, or until the florets are tender. Add the salt, black pepper, turmeric, cayenne pepper, garlic, soy sauce, and nutritional yeast (if using) to the pan and cook for 5 minutes more, or until hot and fragrant.

Breakfast Rancheros

THIS POPULAR MEXICAN dish can be served many ways: with or without corn tortillas, or with black beans or vegetarian refried beans (see page 206 for a homemade version). The choice is yours.

SERVES 6

> 1 medium yellow onion, peeled and diced small
>
> 4 cloves garlic, peeled and minced
>
> 1 jalapeño pepper, minced (for less heat, remove the seeds)
>
> 1 tablespoon minced oregano
>
> 2 large tomatoes, diced
>
> Salt to taste
>
> 6 corn tortillas
>
> 1 batch Breakfast Scramble (page 54)
>
> Chopped cilantro

1. Place the onion in a medium skillet or saucepan and sauté for 10 minutes, or until the onion is tender and starting to brown. Add water 1 to 2 tablespoons at a time to keep the onion from sticking to the pan. Add the garlic, jalapeño pepper, and oregano and cook for 2 more minutes. Add the tomatoes and cook until they start to fall apart, about 10 minutes. Season with salt.

2. While the sauce is cooking, heat the tortillas one at a time on a dry, nonstick skillet over medium heat, turning frequently, for a few minutes. Wrap the heated tortillas in a kitchen towel to keep them warm.

3. To serve, place a warm tortilla on a plate and spoon some of the sauce over it. Top with some of the Breakfast Scramble and garnish with the cilantro.

VARIATION

▶ To give this dish a southwestern twist, prepare the rancheros, but instead of serving on tortillas, place the breakfast scramble in a 9 x 13-inch baking dish lined with parchment paper, pour 1 batch of No-Cheese Sauce (page 29) over it, and bake in a 350°F oven for 30 minutes. Serve topped with the Breakfast Rancheros sauce and garnished with minced green onion and chopped cilantro.

Portobello Florentine 📷

GRILLED PORTOBELLO MUSHROOMS are served on a bed of wilted spinach with a cauliflower hollandaise—a wholly plant-based alternative to the classic Eggs Florentine.

SERVES 4

2 cups cauliflower florets (from ½ of a medium head)
¼ cup Vegetable Stock (page 23), or low-sodium vegetable broth
2 tablespoons fresh lemon juice
⅛ teaspoon cayenne pepper
1 pound fresh spinach
Salt and freshly ground black pepper to taste
1 batch Grilled Portobello Mushrooms (page 173)

1. Combine the cauliflower, vegetable stock, lemon juice, and cayenne pepper in a medium saucepan and bring to a boil over high heat. Reduce the heat to medium and cook until the cauliflower is tender, 8 to 10 minutes. Puree the mixture using an immersion blender, or transfer it to a blender with a tight-fitting lid and cover it with a towel, puree until creamy, and return the cauliflower hollandaise to the pan to keep warm.
2. Add the spinach to a large pot with ¼ cup of water. Cook, covered, over medium-low heat until the spinach wilts. Drain and season with salt and pepper.
3. To serve, place a Grilled Portobello Mushroom on each of four individual plates and divide the spinach among the mushrooms. Spoon the sauce over the spinach and serve hot.

Ful Medames (Egyptian Breakfast Beans)

THIS TRADITIONAL EGYPTIAN breakfast (pronounced *fool mudammis*) is almost always made with dried fava beans. They need to soak at least 8 hours before cooking, so start this dish the day before you want to serve it to let the beans soak overnight. Ful Medames is usually served with pita bread and a fried egg, but take some liberty and serve it over brown rice with fresh lemon instead.

SERVES 4

1½ pounds dried fava beans, soaked for 8 to 10 hours
1 medium yellow onion, peeled and diced small
4 cloves garlic, peeled and minced
1 teaspoon ground cumin
Zest and juice of 1 lemon
Salt to taste
1 lemon, quartered

1. Drain and rinse the beans and add them to a large pot. Cover with enough water to top the beans by 4 inches and bring to a boil over high heat. Reduce the heat to medium, cover, and cook until the beans are tender, 1½ to 2 hours.
2. While the beans are cooking, place the onion in a medium skillet or saucepan and sauté over medium heat for 8 to 10 minutes, or until the onion is tender and starting to brown. Add the garlic, cumin, and lemon zest and juice and cook for 5 minutes longer. Set aside until the beans are fully cooked.
3. When the beans are done cooking, drain all but ½ cup of the liquid from the pot and add the onion mixture to the beans. Mix well and season with salt. Serve garnished with the lemon quarters.

 *Grain Salads*

Curried Rice Salad

IN THIS SALAD the sweetness of the currants contrasts with the pungent curry flavor. If you don't have currants, use raisins, or any other dried fruit, and replace the lime zest and juice with orange zest and juice, plus a few orange segments. Serve this salad on a bed of greens—such as spinach, arugula, or field greens—for a nice lunch.

SERVES 4

> **2 cups brown basmati rice**
> **Zest and juice of 2 limes**
> **¼ cup brown rice vinegar**
> **¼ cup brown rice syrup**
> **½ cup dried currants**
> **6 green onions (white and green parts), finely chopped**
> **½ small red onion, peeled and minced**
> **1 jalapeño pepper, minced (for less heat, remove the seeds)**
> **1 tablespoon curry powder**
> **¼ cup chopped cilantro**
> **Salt and freshly ground black pepper to taste**

1. Rinse the rice under cold water and drain. Add it to a pot with 4 cups of cold water. Bring it to a boil over high heat, reduce the heat to medium, and cook, covered, for 45 to 50 minutes, or until the rice is tender.
2. While the rice is cooking, combine the lime zest and juice, brown rice vinegar, brown rice syrup, currants, green onions, red onion, jalapeño pepper, curry powder, cilantro, and salt and pepper in a large bowl and mix well. When the rice is finished cooking, add the rice to the bowl and mix well.

Warm Rice and Bean Salad

BASMATI RICE HAS a mild nutty flavor and is often toasted to enhance the "nuttiness." Be careful when toasting it in the oil-free skillet; it's easy to overdo, and at that point the rice will take a much longer time to cook.

SERVES 4

1½ cups brown basmati rice, toasted in a dry skillet over low heat for 2 to 3 minutes

2 cups cooked navy beans (see page 6), or one 15-ounce can, drained and rinsed

¼ cup plus 2 tablespoons balsamic vinegar

¼ cup brown rice syrup

Zest and juice of 1 lemon

1 cup thinly sliced green onion (white and green parts)

2 tablespoons minced tarragon

¼ cup minced basil

Salt and freshly ground black pepper to taste

4 cups packed baby spinach

1. Rinse the toasted rice under cold water and drain. Add it to a pot with 3 cups of cold water. Bring it to a boil over high heat, reduce the heat to medium, and cook, covered, for 45 to 50 minutes, or until the rice is tender.
2. While the rice is cooking, add the beans, balsamic vinegar, brown rice syrup, lemon zest and juice, green onion, tarragon, basil, and salt and pepper to a large bowl and mix well. When the rice is finished cooking, add it to the bowl and mix well. Divide the spinach among 4 plates and spoon the salad on top.

Rice Salad with Fennel, Orange and Chickpeas 📷

THE MILD ANISE-LIKE flavor of fennel is well balanced by the citrus in this hearty salad.

SERVES 4

1½ cups brown basmati rice (see page 6)

2 cups cooked chickpeas (see page 6), or one 15-ounce can, drained and rinsed

1 fennel bulb, trimmed and diced

1 orange, zested, peeled, and segmented (zest and segments reserved)

¼ cup plus 2 tablespoons white wine vinegar

½ teaspoon crushed red pepper flakes

¼ cup finely chopped parsley

1. Rinse the rice under cold water and drain. Add it to a pot with 3 cups of cold water. Bring it to a boil over high heat, reduce the heat to medium, and cook, covered, for 45 to 50 minutes, or until the rice is tender.
2. While the rice cooks, combine the chickpeas, fennel, orange zest and segments, white wine vinegar, crushed red pepper flakes, and parsley in a large bowl and mix well. When the rice is finished, add the rice to the bowl and mix well.

Quinoa Arugula Salad

THE MILD, NUTTY flavor of quinoa and the peppery bite of arugula are complemented by the sweet and tangy orange vinaigrette. This is a perfect one-dish meal in the early summer when arugula is everywhere at farmers' markets. This salad pairs well with Grilled Portobello Mushrooms (page 173) for a more substantial meal.

SERVES 4

1½ cups quinoa

Zest and juice of 2 oranges

Zest and juice of 1 lime

¼ cup brown rice vinegar

4 cups arugula

1 small red onion, peeled and thinly sliced

1 red bell pepper, seeded and cut into ½-inch cubes

2 tablespoons pine nuts, toasted (see page 10)

Salt and freshly ground black pepper to taste

1. Rinse the quinoa under cold water and drain. Bring 3 cups of water to a boil in a pot. Add the quinoa and bring the pot back to a boil over high heat. Reduce the heat to medium, cover, and cook for 15 to 20 minutes, or until the quinoa is tender. Drain any excess water, spread the quinoa on a baking sheet, and refrigerate until cool.
2. While the quinoa cools, combine the orange zest and juice, lime zest and juice, brown rice vinegar, arugula, onion, red pepper, pine nuts, and salt and pepper in a large bowl. Add the cooled quinoa and chill for 1 hour before serving.

Israeli Quinoa Salad

RECIPE BY JULIEANNA HEVER

THIS SALAD REPRESENTS the classic flavors of Middle Eastern cuisine—the earthiness of cumin and quinoa pairs with the crispy freshness of cucumber, lemon, and basil. It is an easy dish that can be served on the side or as a meal on its own. Try this dish with raw red pepper for an even fresher taste.

SERVES 4

½ **cup quinoa**
¼ **teaspoon ground cumin**
¼ **teaspoon turmeric**
1 **cup finely chopped tomatoes (from 1 to 2 medium tomatoes)**
1 **cup finely chopped cucumber (from about 1 medium cucumber, seeded)**
½ **cup finely chopped roasted red bell pepper (from about 1 medium pepper,**
  roasted and seeded—see page 8)
1 **tablespoon finely chopped basil**
Juice of 1 lemon
Salt and freshly ground black pepper to taste

1. Rinse the quinoa under cold water and drain. Bring 1¼ cups of water to a boil in a medium saucepan over high heat. Add the quinoa, cumin, and turmeric and bring to a boil over medium-high heat. Reduce the heat to low, cover, and cook for 10 to 15 minutes, or until all the water is absorbed, stirring occasionally. Remove the pan from the heat, fluff the quinoa with a fork, and allow it to cool for 5 minutes.
2. While the quinoa cools, combine the tomato, cucumber, red pepper, basil, and lemon juice in a medium bowl. Stir in the cooled quinoa and season with salt and pepper.

Quinoa Tabbouleh

THE MEDITERRANEAN GOES to South America when gluten-free quinoa stands in for the bulgur traditionally used in this dish. Adding chickpeas or edamame makes this a filling meal. Serve this salad on a bed of greens or in a lettuce wrap with Hummus (page 139).

SERVES 4

2½ **cups quinoa, cooked (see page 6) and cooled to room temperature**
Zest of 1 lemon and juice of 2 lemons, or to taste
3 **Roma tomatoes, diced**
1 **cucumber, peeled, halved, seeded, and diced**
2 **cups cooked chickpeas (see page 6), or one 15-ounce can, drained and rinsed**
8 **green onions (white and green parts), thinly sliced**
1 **cup chopped parsley**
3 **tablespoons chopped mint**
Salt and freshly ground black pepper to taste

Combine all ingredients in a large bowl. Chill for 1 hour before serving.

Spicy Asian Quinoa Salad 📷

YES, QUINOA IS from the Americas, not Asia, so you could certainly make this dish with brown rice, or even millet, to make it more authentically Asian. Authentic or not, the mild, nutty flavor of quinoa is a nice complement to the Asian flavors of the adzuki beans, fresh ginger, cilantro, and lime juice.

SERVES 4 TO 6

¼ cup plus 2 tablespoons brown rice vinegar

4 cloves garlic, peeled and minced

Zest and juice of 2 limes

1½ tablespoons grated ginger

1½ teaspoons crushed red pepper flakes

4 cups cooked quinoa (see page 6)

2 cups cooked adzuki beans (see page 6), or one 15-ounce can, drained and rinsed

¾ cup mung bean sprouts (see page 71)

½ cup finely chopped cilantro

6 green onions (white and green parts), thinly sliced

Salt to taste

4 cups spinach

Combine the brown rice vinegar, garlic, lime zest and juice, ginger, and crushed red pepper flakes in a large bowl and mix well. Add the quinoa, adzuki beans, mung bean sprouts, cilantro, green onions, and salt and toss to coat. Refrigerate for 30 minutes before serving on top of the spinach.

Quinoa, Corn and Black Bean Salad

IF CORN IS in season, use it fresh off the cob or roast the unhusked ears on the grill to add even more flavor to this great summer salad.

SERVES 4

2½ cups cooked quinoa (see page 6)

3 ears corn, kernels removed (about 2 cups)

1 red bell pepper, roasted (see page 8), seeded, and diced

½ small red onion, peeled and diced

2 cups cooked black beans (see page 6), or one 15-ounce can, drained and rinsed

1 cup finely chopped cilantro

6 green onions (white and green parts), thinly sliced

1 jalapeño pepper, minced (for less heat, remove the seeds)

Zest of 1 lime and juice of 2 limes

1 tablespoon cumin seeds, toasted (see page 10) and ground

Salt to taste

Combine all ingredients in a large bowl and mix well. Chill for 1 hour before serving.

Baby Lima Bean and Quinoa Salad

LIMA BEANS AND quinoa are both native to the Americas and, therefore, are a natural pairing in this dish.

SERVES 4

2 tablespoons brown rice syrup

¼ cup brown rice vinegar

Zest of 1 lime and juice of 2 limes

4 cups cooked quinoa (see page 6)

2 cups cooked baby lima beans (see page 6), or one 15-ounce can, drained and rinsed

1 cup shredded red cabbage

1 carrot, peeled and grated

½ cup chopped cilantro

Salt and freshly ground black pepper to taste

Place the brown rice syrup, brown rice vinegar, and lime zest and juice in a large bowl and whisk to combine. Add the quinoa, baby lima beans, red cabbage, carrot, cilantro, and salt and pepper and toss until well mixed. Refrigerate before serving.

Fruited Millet Salad

COOKING MILLET LIKE pasta—in a lot of water—keeps it from clumping as it cools. Serve this salad on a bed of arugula or mixed greens.

SERVES 4

1 cup millet

Zest and juice of 1 orange

Juice of 1 lemon

3 tablespoons brown rice syrup

½ cup dried unsulfured apricots, chopped (see page 9 for more on sulfites and sulfur dioxide)

½ cup dried currants

½ cup golden raisins

1 Gala apple, cored and diced

2 tablespoons finely chopped mint

1. Bring 2 quarts of lightly salted water to a boil over high heat and add the millet. Return to a boil, reduce the heat to medium, cover, and cook for 12 to 14 minutes. Drain the water from the millet, rinse it until cool, and set it aside.
2. Place the orange juice and zest, lemon juice, and brown rice syrup in a large bowl. Whisk to combine. Add the apricots, currants, raisins, apple, and mint and mix well. Add the cooked millet and toss to coat. Refrigerate before serving.

Bulgur, Cucumber and Tomato Salad

QUICK-COOKING BULGUR MAKES this a perfect summer dish—there's no long cooking in a hot kitchen. Use quinoa for a gluten-free version; it also cooks in less than 20 minutes.

SERVES 4

1½ cups bulgur

1 cup cherry tomatoes, halved

1 medium cucumber, halved, seeded, and diced

3 cloves garlic, peeled and minced

4 green onions (white and green parts), sliced

Zest and juice of 2 lemons

2 tablespoons red wine vinegar

1 teaspoon crushed red pepper flakes, or to taste

¼ cup minced tarragon

Salt and freshly ground black pepper to taste

Bring 3 cups of water to a boil in a medium pot and add the bulgur. Remove the pot from the heat, cover with a tight-fitting lid, and let it sit until the water is absorbed and the bulgur is tender, about 15 minutes. Spread the bulgur on a baking sheet and let cool to room temperature. Transfer the cooled bulgur to a bowl, add all the remaining ingredients, and mix well to combine. Chill for 1 hour before serving.

Autumn Wheat Berry Salad

WHEAT BERRIES ARE one of the heartiest grains, which gives them a long cooking time along with their exceptional health benefits. Use quinoa or millet for a gluten-free (and somewhat quicker-cooking) alternative.

SERVES 4

2½ cups wheat berries, soaked overnight

¼ cup plus 2 tablespoons apple cider vinegar

¼ cup brown rice syrup

2 celery stalks, thinly sliced

½ cup chopped green onion (white and green parts)

2 tablespoons minced tarragon

1 Bosc pear, cored and diced

½ cup fruit-sweetened dried cranberries

Salt and freshly ground black pepper to taste

1. Bring 5 cups water to a boil in a medium saucepan and add the wheat berries. Return to a boil over high heat, reduce the heat to medium, cover, and cook until the wheat berries are tender, about 1¾ hours. Drain the excess water from the pan and rinse the berries until cool.

2. Combine all the other ingredients in a large bowl. Add the cooled wheat berries and mix well. Chill for 1 hour before serving.

Bean Salads

Italian-Style Stuffed Tomatoes

THIS DISH MAKES a nice presentation for guests. If you keep pesto on hand—and I recommend that you do—then this is a very quick recipe to put together. Serve it with a green salad for a complete meal.

SERVES 6

> 4 cups cooked navy beans (see page 6), or two 15-ounce cans, drained and rinsed
>
> One 15-ounce can artichoke hearts (oil-free), drained and roughly chopped
>
> ½ medium yellow onion, peeled and diced small
>
> ½ cup Basil Pesto (page 24)
>
> 6 large tomatoes, such as beefsteak

1. Combine the beans, artichoke hearts, onion, and pesto in a small bowl and set aside.
2. Cut the top ½ inch off each tomato and scoop out the flesh, leaving a ½-inch shell. Divide the filling evenly among the prepared tomatoes and arrange them on a platter or among individual plates to serve.

White Bean Tomato Salad

SOUTHWESTERN FLAVORS ARE spicy and intense, so they make for good winter salads when it's cold and you need a little warmth. In cooler seasons, heat the beans and add them to the rest of the ingredients while they're still warm, and don't chill the salad before serving. During warmer months, serve the salad cold over a spicy green like arugula.

SERVES 4

> 4 cups cooked navy beans (see page 6), or two 15-ounce cans, drained and rinsed
>
> 2 large tomatoes, diced
>
> Zest and juice of 2 limes
>
> ¼ cup brown rice vinegar
>
> ½ cup chopped cilantro
>
> 6 green onions (white and green parts), thinly sliced
>
> 1 jalapeño pepper, minced (for less heat, remove the seeds)
>
> 4 cloves garlic, peeled and minced
>
> 1 tablespoon cumin seeds, toasted (see page 10) and ground
>
> Salt to taste

Combine all ingredients in a large bowl and mix well. Chill for 1 hour before serving, if desired.

Tomato, Corn and Bean Salad

IF YOU GET your corn at the farmers' market and it was picked just that morning, you can skip the cooking step—just add it directly into the salad and enjoy the sweet, fresh flavor it lends to the dish.

SERVES 4

> **6 ears corn**
> **3 large tomatoes, diced**
> **2 cups cooked navy beans (see page 6), or one 15-ounce can, drained and rinsed**
> **1 medium red onion, peeled and diced small**
> **1 cup finely chopped basil**
> **2 tablespoons balsamic vinegar**
> **Salt and freshly ground black pepper to taste**

1. Bring a large pot of water to a boil. Add the corn and cook for 7 to 10 minutes. Drain the water from the pot and rinse the corn under cold water to cool, then cut the kernels from the cob.
2. In a large bowl, toss together the corn, tomatoes, beans, onion, basil, balsamic vinegar, and salt and pepper. Chill for 1 hour before serving.

Mango Black Bean Salad

THE FIRST TIME I made a dish with mangoes, I threw several away before I realized that they all had a big seed in the center that you had to cut around. That was twenty years ago, though—long before there were YouTube videos showing how best to prepare one.

SERVES 4

> **4 cups cooked black beans (see page 6), or two 15-ounce cans, drained and rinsed**
> **2 mangoes, peeled, halved, pitted, and diced**
> **1 medium red bell pepper, seeded and diced small**
> **1 bunch green onions (white and green parts), thinly sliced**
> **½ cup finely chopped cilantro**
> **1 jalapeño pepper, minced (for less heat, remove the seeds)**
> **½ cup red wine vinegar**
> **Zest and juice of 1 orange**
> **Zest and juice of 1 lime**

Combine all ingredients in a large bowl and mix well. Chill for 1 hour before serving.

Grilled Vegetable and Black Bean Salad

THE NEXT TIME you make grilled vegetables for a cookout, reserve half of the recipe (or make extra!) and use the leftovers for this wholesome and delicious summer salad.

SERVES 4

½ batch Grilled Vegetable Kabobs (page 172), vegetables removed from the skewers

2 cups cooked black beans (see page 6), or one 15-ounce can, drained and rinsed

½ cup finely chopped cilantro

Zest of 1 lime and juice of 3 limes

1 jalapeño pepper, minced (for less heat, remove the seeds)

1 avocado, halved, pitted, peeled, and diced

Salt to taste

Combine all ingredients in a large bowl and mix well. Chill for 1 hour before serving.

Fava Bean Salad

ALSO KNOWN AS broad beans, fava beans are native to North Africa and parts of Asia. If you cook the dried bean, you have to remove the outer shell before eating them (so don't feel guilty about buying canned!). Fava beans are not as widely available as other beans, so if you can't find them, feel free to substitute lima beans or edamame.

SERVES 4

4 cups cooked fava beans (see page 6), or two 15-ounce cans, drained and rinsed

2 large tomatoes, chopped

4 green onions (white and green parts), sliced

1 large cucumber, peeled, halved, seeded, and diced

½ cup finely chopped cilantro

1 jalapeño pepper, minced (for less heat, remove the seeds)

Zest of 1 lemon and juice of 2 lemons

2 cloves garlic, peeled and minced

1 teaspoon cumin seeds, toasted (see page 10) and ground

Salt and freshly ground black pepper to taste

Combine all ingredients in a large bowl and mix well. Chill for 1 hour before serving.

Orange, Beet and Bean Salad

THE EARTHY SWEETNESS of beets is brightened by orange and fresh dill in this vibrant, healthy salad.

SERVES 4

> 4 to 6 medium beets (about 1½ pounds), washed and peeled
>
> 2 oranges, zested, peeled, and segmented
>
> 2 cups cooked navy beans (see page 6), or one 15-ounce can, drained and rinsed
>
> ¼ cup brown rice vinegar
>
> 3 tablespoons minced dill
>
> Salt to taste
>
> ½ teaspoon freshly ground black pepper
>
> 4 cups mixed salad greens
>
> 4 tablespoons slivered almonds, toasted (see page 10), optional

1. Place the beets in a saucepan and cover with water. Bring to a boil, cover, reduce the heat, and simmer for 20 minutes, or until the beets are tender. Drain the beets and set aside to cool.
2. Once the beets have cooled, cut them into wedges and place them in a large bowl. Add the orange zest and segments, beans, brown rice vinegar, dill, and salt and pepper to the beets. Toss lightly to combine.
3. To serve, divide the mixed salad greens among 4 individual plates. Top with the beet salad and garnish with the toasted almonds (if using).

Succotash Salad

WHEN I WAS a kid and my mom made succotash, I thought I was being punished with lima beans. How could such a good cook make something so unappealing unless she was mad at me? It was many years before I gained an appreciation for this lovely bean and realized that Mom never intended her succotash to be anything besides a nourishing and enjoyable dish for her family. This recipe is my version of her dish.

SERVES 4

> 1½ cups cooked baby lima beans (see page 6)
>
> 3 ears corn, kernels removed (about 2 cups)
>
> 2 large tomatoes, chopped
>
> 1 medium red onion, peeled and diced
>
> ¼ cup balsamic vinegar, or to taste
>
> ¼ cup chopped parsley
>
> Salt and freshly ground black pepper to taste

Combine all ingredients in a large bowl and mix well.

Lentil Salad with Lemon and Fresh Herbs

ONCE THE LENTILS are cooked, this salad comes together quickly. Mint and cilantro complement this dish well, but you could try basil and tarragon instead for a nice change.

SERVES 4

1½ cups green lentils, rinsed

3 cups Vegetable Stock (page 23), or low-sodium vegetable broth

Zest of 1 lemon and juice of 2 lemons

2 cloves garlic, peeled and minced

½ cup finely chopped cilantro

2 tablespoons finely chopped mint

4 green onions (white and green parts), finely chopped, plus more for garnish

Salt and freshly ground black pepper to taste

4 cups arugula

1. Place the lentils in a medium saucepan with the vegetable stock and bring to a boil over a high heat. Reduce the heat to medium, cover, and cook for 35 to 45 minutes, or until the lentils are tender but not mushy.
2. Drain the lentils and place them in a large bowl. Add the lemon zest and juice, garlic, cilantro, mint, green onions, and salt and pepper and mix well.
3. To serve, divide the arugula among 4 individual plates. Spoon the lentil salad on top of the greens and garnish with freshly chopped green onions.

Mung Bean Sprouts and Spinach Salad

RECIPE BY DARSHANA THACKER

THIS UNIQUE BLEND of greens with an Indian kick is as delicious as it is healthy.

SERVES 4

FOR THE SPROUTS:

½ cup whole mung beans

½ teaspoon turmeric

¼ teaspoon salt, or to taste, optional

FOR THE SALAD:

2 medium potatoes, skin on

½ cup finely chopped tomatoes

½ cup finely chopped spinach

¼ cup finely chopped avocado

¼ cup finely chopped cilantro

2 tablespoons finely chopped green onion

1 tablespoon fresh lime juice

1 teaspoon cayenne pepper

1 teaspoon ground cumin

1 teaspoon salt, or to taste

TO SPROUT THE MUNG BEANS:

1. Soak the mung beans in 1 cup of filtered water overnight. Spread a clean, damp cloth in a large bowl. Drain the water from the beans and spread them on the cloth. Fold the corners of the cloth over the beans to cover them. Place the bowl in a cool place away from sunlight. Dampen the cloth every 6 hours. The beans will sprout to about ½-centimeter sprouts in 12 hours.

2. Once the beans have sprouted, rinse them thoroughly in clean water. Boil the sprouts in 2 cups of water with the turmeric and salt for 10 minutes, or until the sprouts soften a little. Drain the sprouts and set them aside.

TO MAKE THE SALAD:

3. Cut the potatoes in half. Place in a medium saucepan and add enough water to cover. Bring to a boil, reduce the heat to medium, and cook for 10 minutes, or until tender when pierced with a fork. Drain the potatoes and let them cool, then peel and cut into ½-inch cubes. Place the potatoes in a large bowl and add the drained sprouts, tomatoes, spinach, avocado, cilantro, green onion, lime juice, cayenne pepper, cumin, and salt. Mix well and serve.

Orange, Fennel and White Bean Salad

THE SWEET, TANGY flavor of the orange balances the bright fennel in this dish very nicely. You could also serve this salad on a bed of spinach if you prefer a milder green.

SERVES 4

6 large oranges, peeled and segmented

2 tablespoons fresh lemon juice

2 tablespoons balsamic vinegar

1 medium fennel bulb, trimmed and thinly sliced

2 tablespoons minced fresh fennel fronds

2 cups cooked navy beans (see page 6), or one 15-ounce can, drained and rinsed

Salt to taste

Cayenne pepper to taste

4 cups arugula

1. Combine the orange sections, lemon juice, balsamic vinegar, fennel bulb and fronds, beans, salt, and cayenne pepper in a large bowl and mix well. Let sit for 1 hour before serving.
2. To serve, divide the arugula among 4 individual plates and spoon the salad on top of the greens.

Winter White Bean Salad 📷

YOU CAN BUY peeled and cubed squash in many supermarket produce departments. While it steams you can make the pesto and have dinner on the table in 30 minutes.

SERVES 4

> 1 pumpkin (about 2 pounds), or other similar winter squash, peeled and cut into ½-inch cubes
>
> 4 cups cooked cannellini or other white beans (see page 6), or two 15-ounce cans, drained and rinsed
>
> 1 medium red onion, peeled and diced small
>
> Salt and freshly ground black pepper to taste
>
> 1 batch Spicy Cilantro Pesto (page 24)

1. Steam the pumpkin in a double boiler or steamer basket for 10 to 12 minutes, or until tender. Drain and rinse the pumpkin until cool.
2. Once the pumpkin has cooled, add it to a medium bowl with the beans, onion, salt and pepper, and pesto. Mix well until combined.

Chickpea Avocado Salad

SERVE THIS FLAVORFUL salad on a bed of greens for a complete meal; I like arugula with this dish, but feel free to use your favorite.

SERVES 4

> 4 cups cooked chickpeas (see page 6), or two 15-ounce cans, drained and rinsed
>
> 1 small red onion, peeled and diced small
>
> 2 cloves garlic, peeled and minced
>
> Zest of 1 lime and juice of 4 limes
>
> 1 jalapeño pepper, minced (for less heat, remove the seeds)
>
> ½ cup chopped cilantro
>
> Salt to taste
>
> 1 avocado, halved, pitted, peeled, and coarsely chopped

Combine all ingredients in a medium bowl and mix well. Add the avocado just before serving.

Taco Salad with Cilantro-Lime Dressing 📷

RECIPE BY JULIEANNA HEVER

MILDLY SPICY, FRESH, and flavorful, this salad offers a southwestern flair that's versatile and colorful. Feel free to vary the salad ingredients to personalize it to your tastes.

SERVES 6

FOR THE SALAD:

    4 corn tortillas

    6 cups chopped romaine lettuce (or other salad greens)

    1½ cups seeded and chopped cucumber

    1½ cups seeded and chopped tomato

    1½ cups chopped broccoli florets

    One 15-ounce can black beans, drained and rinsed

    One 15-ounce can pinto beans, drained and rinsed

    3 ears corn, kernels removed (about 2 cups)

FOR THE DRESSING:

    One 15-ounce can cannellini beans, drained and rinsed

    2 cups cilantro, leaves and tender stems

    1 cup Italian parsley leaves

    ¼ cup tahini

    One 4-ounce can diced green chiles, drained

    2 tablespoons low-sodium soy sauce

    1 teaspoon chili powder

    ¼ teaspoon crushed red pepper flakes

    1 to 2 cloves garlic, peeled and minced, optional

    Zest and juice of 2 limes

TO MAKE THE SALAD:

1. Cut the corn tortillas into thin slices. Place the slices on a small baking sheet and toast in a toaster oven for 3 to 5 minutes, or until crispy.
2. Place the lettuce in the bottom of a large serving bowl. Add the cucumber, tomato, broccoli, black beans, pinto beans, and corn. Set aside.

TO MAKE THE DRESSING:

3. In a blender, combine the cannellini beans, cilantro, parsley, tahini, green chiles, soy sauce, chili powder, crushed red pepper flakes, garlic, lime zest and juice, and 1 cup of water. Blend on high until smooth.

TO SERVE:

4. Place the tortilla strips over the salad in the bowl and, if serving immediately, pour the dressing on top. Alternatively, if the entire salad will not be eaten at once, keep the dressing on the side to prevent the vegetables from wilting. You will have leftover dressing; store it in an airtight container for 4 to 6 days in the refrigerator and use it on another salad or as a dip for vegetables.

⚹ *Hearty Vegetable Salads with a Kick*

White Bean, Potato and Asparagus Salad

A SIMPLE POTATO salad becomes a meal when combined with beans. Make this salad for the first cookout of the season, when asparagus is still available at the farmers' market. If you are not serving this salad immediately, prepare the potatoes and asparagus and rinse until cool, refrigerate until ready to serve, and add the dressing just before serving.

SERVES 4

> 1 pound red-skin potatoes, scrubbed and cut into ½-inch dice
>
> ½ pound asparagus, trimmed and cut into ½-inch pieces
>
> 2 tablespoons brown rice vinegar
>
> 2 tablespoons Dijon mustard
>
> 2 cloves garlic, peeled and minced
>
> Salt and freshly ground black pepper to taste
>
> 2 cups cooked navy beans (see page 6), or one 15-ounce can, drained and rinsed
>
> 8 green onions (white and green parts), thinly sliced
>
> 3 tablespoons minced chives

1. Steam the potatoes in a double boiler or steamer basket for 10 minutes, or until tender, adding the asparagus during the last 3 minutes.
2. Combine the brown rice vinegar, mustard, garlic, and salt and pepper in a large bowl and whisk well. Add the warm potatoes and asparagus, beans, green onions, and chives and mix well.

VARIATION

▶ Leave out the Dijon mustard, brown rice vinegar, and chives and instead add up to ½ cup of Coriander Chutney (page 32).

Warm Black Bean Potato Salad with Arugula Pesto

BLACK BEANS MAKE this dish a filling meal, but it's also a great side dish for a summer picnic, as an alternative to the same old potato salad. Arugula makes an intense pesto, as its spicy flavor is heightened by pureeing it. You could also use cilantro in the pesto for more of a southwest flavor, or kick it up a notch further and use Spicy Cilantro Pesto (page 24) instead.

SERVES 4

2 pounds red-skin potatoes, scrubbed, trimmed, and diced

Salt to taste, optional

1 small red onion, peeled and diced small

Juice of 1 lemon

2 cups cooked black beans (see page 6), or one 15-ounce can, drained and rinsed

¾ cup Basil Pesto (page 24) made with arugula

Add the potatoes to a medium pot and add water to cover by 1 inch. Add salt if desired, bring to a boil, and cook over medium-low heat for about 10 minutes, or until the potatoes are tender. Drain the potatoes and add to a large bowl. Add the onion, lemon juice, beans, and pesto and mix well.

Purple Potato and Kale Salad with Cilantro-Tahini Dressing 📷

RECIPE BY DARSHANA THACKER

THIS IS A colorful and richly flavored salad that's fun to serve—the purple potatoes really give the dish a surprising look.

SERVES 4

5 to 6 small purple potatoes
2 cups chopped kale
½ cup chopped tomatoes
1¾ teaspoons fresh lime juice
1 cup chopped cilantro, plus more for garnish
1 clove garlic, peeled and chopped
¼ cup plus 2 tablespoons tahini
½ teaspoon salt, or to taste
1 teaspoon cayenne pepper

1. Place the potatoes in a medium saucepan and add enough water to cover. Bring to a boil, reduce the heat to medium, and cook for 10 minutes, or until tender when pierced with a fork. Drain the potatoes and let them cool. Once cooled, peel if desired and cut into ½-inch cubes.
2. Place the kale and tomatoes in a skillet or saucepan and sauté for 2 to 3 minutes, or until the kale has softened slightly. Add water 1 to 2 tablespoons at a time to keep the vegetables from sticking to the pan. Add ¼ teaspoon of the lime juice and let cool.
3. In a blender, combine the cilantro, garlic, tahini, salt, cayenne pepper, remaining 1½ teaspoons of lime juice, and 2 tablespoons of water. Blend until smooth.
4. To serve, prepare a bed of the cooked kale and tomatoes in a large salad bowl, top with the boiled potatoes, and spoon the dressing over the top. Garnish with chopped cilantro, if desired.

NOTE ▶ If you'd like an especially pretty salad, peel the potatoes; with the skins left on, the potatoes will be a bit harder to cut neatly but will still taste great.

Asian Vegetable Salad

THIS SALAD ALSO makes a great filling for spring rolls made with rice paper wrappers. Ponzu Sauce (page 35) works equally well as a dressing for this salad and as a dipping sauce for spring rolls.

SERVES 4

Zest of 1 lime and juice of 2 limes
¼ cup brown rice syrup
Low-sodium soy sauce to taste, optional
2 tablespoons brown rice vinegar
4 cups coarsely chopped Napa cabbage
1 red bell pepper, seeded and julienned
1 bunch green onions (white and green parts), finely sliced on the diagonal
1 cup mung bean sprouts (see page 71)
½ cup chopped cilantro
½ cup chopped basil
1 serrano chile, thinly sliced on the diagonal (for less heat, remove the seeds)
2 tablespoons chopped mint
Ponzu Sauce (page 35)

Combine the lime zest and juice, brown rice syrup, and soy sauce (if using) in a large bowl and whisk well. Add the brown rice vinegar, cabbage, pepper, green onions, sprouts, cilantro, basil, chile, and mint to the bowl and toss to mix well. Serve accompanied by the Ponzu Sauce.

Kale Salad with Maple-Mustard Dressing

RECIPE BY JULIEANNA HEVER | DRESSING INSPIRED BY CHEF AJ'S HOUSE DRESSING

ONE OF THE best ways to enjoy salad is with a rich and tasty dressing. This dressing is oil-free, but it's filled with flavor and can be whipped up in 5 minutes. It's a versatile dressing that can also be served over other types of salad, steamed veggies, baked potatoes, cooked whole grains, or legumes. Kale is delicious with the maple and mustard flavors in this dish, but free to vary the recipe to use any types or mixtures of greens you like.

SERVES 4 TO 6

FOR THE DRESSING:

> 1 cup cooked cannellini beans (see page 6)
>
> 2 tablespoons tahini
>
> 2 tablespoons stone-ground or Dijon mustard
>
> 2 tablespoons nutritional yeast
>
> 1 to 2 tablespoons low-sodium soy sauce, or Bragg Liquid Aminos
>
> 1 tablespoon 100% pure maple syrup
>
> Zest and juice of 1 lemon

FOR THE SALAD:

> 6 cups kale, ribs removed, then shredded
>
> 1 cup shredded red cabbage
>
> 1 cup shredded carrots (from 2 to 3 medium carrots, peeled)
>
> 1 cup finely chopped broccoli florets
>
> One 15-ounce can chickpeas, drained and rinsed

TO MAKE THE DRESSING:

1. In a blender, combine the cannellini beans, tahini, mustard, nutritional yeast, soy sauce, maple syrup, lemon zest and juice, and ¼ cup of water and blend on high until smooth. Add more water as needed to achieve a smooth consistency.

TO ASSEMBLE THE SALAD:

2. Place the kale, cabbage, carrots, broccoli, and chickpeas into a large bowl. Pour the dressing over and toss to combine.

Autumn Mixed Greens Salad

MAKE THIS SALAD when your favorite apples are in season. Honey Crisp and Gala apples contrast well with the tart cranberry vinaigrette. Cut the apples just before serving to maintain their color, or store them in water with a little lemon juice if you need to prepare them ahead of time. Serve this dish as is for a light lunch or with Pumpkin and Anasazi Bean Stew (page 120) for a heartier meal.

SERVES 4

6 tablespoons fruit-sweetened dried cranberries

¼ cup brown rice syrup

Zest and juice of 1 orange

2 tablespoons balsamic vinegar

1 teaspoon Dijon mustard

Pinch cayenne pepper

6 cups mixed salad greens

½ cup pecan halves, toasted (see page 10), optional

2 crisp apples, peeled, cored, and cut into ½-inch dice

1. Cover 3 tablespoons of the dried cranberries with 6 tablespoons of boiling water. Set aside to soak for about 15 minutes.
2. Blend the reconstituted cranberries, brown rice syrup, orange zest and juice, balsamic vinegar, mustard, and cayenne pepper in a blender until smooth. Set aside.
3. Add the salad greens to a large bowl with the pecans (if using), apples, and the remaining dried cranberries. Just before serving, add the dressing to the bowl and toss well.

Singles' Soup

RECIPE BY JULIEANNA HEVER

FOR THOSE TIMES when you're alone, hungry, and craving something nutritious and easy, this soup is perfect to whip up. Just throw everything in the pot, cook until ready, and voilà—dinner is served!

SERVES 1 TO 2

½ medium onion, peeled and chopped

1 to 2 cloves garlic, peeled and minced

4 cups Vegetable Stock (page 23), or low-sodium vegetable broth

2 medium carrots, peeled and chopped

3 celery stalks, chopped

7 small red-skin potatoes, scrubbed and chopped

1 large sweet potato, peeled and chopped

3 tablespoons low-sodium soy sauce, or to taste

1. In a medium saucepan over medium-high heat, sauté the onion and garlic in ½ cup of vegetable stock until the onion is translucent.
2. Add the carrots, celery, potatoes, sweet potato, and the remaining 3½ cups of vegetable stock and bring to a boil. Once the pot reaches a boil, lower the heat and simmer until the vegetables are soft, 25 to 30 minutes.
3. Add the soy sauce, stir to combine, and serve hot.

SOUPS

White Bean Gazpacho

GAZPACHO IS THE summer soup of choice—there's no cooking involved and there's not a lot of prep work. The beans make it a filling meal, but you can leave them out if you want to make a light side dish.

SERVES 4

6 large ripe tomatoes (about 4 pounds)

2 large cucumbers, peeled, halved, seeded, and diced

1 large red bell pepper, seeded and diced small

1 medium Vidalia onion, peeled and diced small

¼ cup red wine vinegar

Zest of 1 lemon

½ cup chopped basil

Salt and freshly ground black pepper to taste

2 cups cooked cannellini beans (see page 6), or one 15-ounce can, drained and rinsed

Coarsely chop 2 of the tomatoes and puree them in a blender. Transfer to a large bowl. Chop the remaining 4 tomatoes and add them to the bowl. Add the cucumbers, red pepper, onion, red wine vinegar, lemon zest, basil, salt and pepper, and beans and mix well. Chill for 1 hour before serving.

VARIATION

▶ Make a spicy version of this soup by adding 1 or 2 finely chopped jalapeño peppers, replacing the basil with chopped cilantro, and replacing the red wine vinegar with the zest and juice of 2 limes.

Summer Vegetable Soup

DURING THE SUMMER months, all of the vegetables in this soup can (and should!) be found fresh. Tomatoes, squash, and corn will be at their peak, and their fresh flavors will really shine through in this dish.

SERVES 6

1 large yellow onion, peeled and chopped

4 cloves garlic, peeled and minced

6 medium tomatoes, chopped

2 medium zucchini, diced

1 yellow squash, diced

3 ears corn, kernels removed (about 2 cups)

6 cups Vegetable Stock (page 23), or low-sodium vegetable broth

½ cup finely chopped basil

Zest and juice of 1 lemon

Salt and freshly ground black pepper to taste

Place the onion in a medium saucepan and sauté over medium heat for 7 to 8 minutes. Add water 1 to 2 tablespoons at a time to keep the onion from sticking to the pan. Add the garlic and sauté for another minute. Add the tomatoes and cook for 10 minutes, or until the tomatoes start to break down slightly. Add the zucchini, yellow squash, corn, and vegetable stock. Bring the pot to a boil over high heat, reduce the heat to medium, and cook until the vegetables are tender, about 15 minutes. Add the basil and lemon zest and juice. Season with salt and pepper.

Potato, Corn and Bean Soup

THIS IS A simple soup to put together, and it's best made when green beans and corn are ripe in the garden. Vegetables that are in season, fresh from the garden, taste far superior to those that travel across the country, or the world, to get to your table. If you don't have a garden, check out your local farmers' market instead. You will quickly become a fan of the remarkable difference in flavor.

SERVES 8

1 large yellow onion, peeled and diced

3 cloves garlic, peeled and minced

1 tablespoon minced thyme

8 cups Vegetable Stock (page 23), or low-sodium vegetable broth

1 pound red-skin potatoes (7 to 9 small), scrubbed and cut into ½-inch cubes

1 pound green beans, trimmed and cut into ½-inch pieces

6 ears corn, kernels removed (about 3½ cups)

4 cups cooked navy beans (see page 6), or two 15-ounce cans, drained and rinsed

Salt and freshly ground black pepper to taste

Place the onion in a large pot and sauté over medium heat for 10 minutes. Add water 1 to 2 tablespoons at a time to keep the onion from sticking to the pan. Add the garlic and thyme and cook for another minute. Add the vegetable stock, potatoes, green beans, and corn and cook, covered, over medium heat, for 15 minutes. Add the navy beans, season with salt and pepper, and cook for another 10 minutes, or until the vegetables are tender.

Navy Bean Soup with Lemon and Rosemary

LEMON ZEST AND rosemary add a little flair to what would be a good but otherwise plain bean soup. Here, the lemon flavor comes not from lemon juice (which adds a sour flavor to any dish), but rather from the zest, which brings out the true essence of the lemon.

SERVES 6

2 large leeks (white and light green parts), chopped and rinsed

1 celery stalk, chopped

3 cloves garlic, peeled and minced

2 teaspoons minced rosemary

1 pound Yukon Gold potatoes (about 3 medium), peeled and cubed

2 cups cooked navy beans (see page 6), or one 15-ounce can, drained and rinsed

6 cups Vegetable Stock (page 23), or low-sodium vegetable broth

Zest of 2 lemons

Salt and freshly ground black pepper to taste

Place the leeks and celery in a large pot and sauté over medium heat for 10 minutes. Add water 1 to 2 tablespoons at a time to keep the vegetables from sticking to the pan. Add the garlic and rosemary and cook for another minute, then add the potatoes, beans, and vegetable stock. Bring to a boil over high heat, reduce the heat to medium, and cook, covered, for 20 minutes, or until the potatoes are tender. Add the lemon zest, season with salt and pepper, and cook for another 5 minutes.

White Bean Caldo Verde

THIS SIMPLE BUT popular Portuguese soup is traditionally made with potatoes, onions, and kale. Adding beans is not normally done in this dish, but doing so makes it a filling meal. Think of this recipe also as a template for other pairings of root vegetables, greens, and beans—it works for a wide range of combinations, depending on what's most readily available, what you may already have on hand (especially if you're looking for a quick weeknight meal), and what you may be craving.

SERVES 4

> 1 large yellow onion, peeled and diced
> 6 cloves garlic, peeled and minced
> 4 cups Vegetable Stock (page 23), or low-sodium vegetable broth
> 2 large russet potatoes, peeled and diced
> 1 large bunch kale, ribs removed, chopped
> 2 cups cooked cannellini beans (see page 6), or one 15-ounce can, drained and rinsed
> Salt and freshly ground black pepper to taste

Place the onion in a large saucepan and sauté over medium heat for 10 minutes. Add water 1 to 2 tablespoons at a time to keep the onion from sticking to the pan. Add the garlic and cook for another minute, then add the vegetable stock, potatoes, kale, and cannellini beans and cook, covered, for 25 minutes. Season the soup with salt and pepper and cook, uncovered, for another 5 minutes.

Tomato and Red Pepper Soup

THIS SOUP IS a natural pairing of summer's freshest ingredients. For a richer dish, use Basil Pesto (page 24) in place of the basil chiffonade.

SERVES 4

> 2 medium yellow onions, peeled and coarsely chopped
> 2 large red bell peppers, seeded and coarsely chopped
> 3 large cloves garlic, peeled and minced
> 1 teaspoon thyme leaves
> 1 pound fresh tomatoes (about 3 medium), coarsely chopped
> Salt and freshly ground black pepper to taste
> ¼ cup basil chiffonade (see page 7)

Place the onions and red peppers in a large saucepan and sauté over medium heat for 10 minutes. Add water 1 to 2 tablespoons at a time to keep the vegetables from sticking to the pan. Add the garlic and thyme and cook for another minute, then add the tomatoes and cook, covered, for 20 minutes. Puree the soup using an immersion blender or in batches in a blender with a tight-fitting lid, covered with a towel. Season with salt and pepper and serve garnished with the basil.

Minestrone

ALTHOUGH THERE ARE as many versions of minestrone as there are of tomato sauce (it is simply a vegetable soup usually made with beans and pasta or rice), you'll quickly become a fan of this particular whole-foods recipe. For variation, try this recipe with spinach instead of kale, and turnips in place of potatoes. The nutritional yeast, while not traditional, is a great addition to any soup recipe for adding a deeper flavor to the dish.

SERVES 8 TO 10

1 large onion, peeled and chopped

2 large carrots, peeled and chopped

2 celery stalks, chopped

4 cloves garlic, peeled and minced

8 cups Vegetable Stock (page 23), or low-sodium vegetable broth

2 tablespoons nutritional yeast, optional

One 28-ounce can diced tomatoes

2 teaspoons oregano

2 medium red-skin potatoes, scrubbed and cubed

4 cups packed chopped kale, ribs removed before chopping

½ cup uncooked brown basmati rice

6 cups cooked cannellini beans (see page 6), or three 15-ounce cans, drained and rinsed

Salt and freshly ground black pepper to taste

1 cup finely chopped basil

Place the onion, carrots, and celery in a large saucepan over medium heat and sauté for 10 minutes. Add water 1 to 2 tablespoons at a time to keep the vegetables from sticking to the pan. Add the garlic and cook for another minute. Add the vegetable stock, nutritional yeast (if using), tomatoes, oregano, potatoes, kale, and rice. Bring the pot to a boil over high heat, reduce the heat to medium-low, and simmer for 30 minutes. Add the beans and simmer for 15 minutes, until the rice is tender. Season with salt and pepper and add the basil.

Creamy Asparagus Soup

MAKE THIS FRESH-FLAVORED soup in the spring when asparagus is in season. The bright green, tender stalks available in the warmer months really make this soup something special.

SERVES 6

> 1 large yellow onion, peeled and diced
>
> 2 teaspoons thyme
>
> 1 tablespoon minced tarragon
>
> 4 cups Vegetable Stock (page 23), or low-sodium vegetable broth
>
> 2 pounds fresh asparagus, trimmed and cut into ½-inch pieces
>
> Salt and freshly ground black pepper to taste

1. Place the onion in a large stockpot and sauté over medium heat for 10 minutes. Add water 1 to 2 tablespoons at a time to keep the onion from sticking to the pan. Add the thyme, tarragon, vegetable stock, and asparagus and cook over medium-low heat for 20 to 25 minutes, until the asparagus is very tender.
2. Puree the soup using an immersion blender or in batches in a blender with a tight-fitting lid, covered with a towel. Season with salt and pepper.

Spinach Vichyssoise 📷

THIS SOUP IS perfect in the late spring when spinach and dill are both in season. The cool freshness of the chilled soup is great for welcoming the warm months to come.

SERVES 6 TO 8

> 2 large leeks (white and light green parts), rinsed and diced
>
> 1 tablespoon chopped dill, or to taste
>
> 1 bay leaf
>
> 5 cups Vegetable Stock (page 23), or low-sodium vegetable broth
>
> 1½ pounds russet potatoes (4 to 5 medium), peeled and diced
>
> ½ pound spinach, chopped
>
> Zest of 1 lemon
>
> Salt and freshly ground black pepper to taste
>
> 1 cup unsweetened plain almond milk

1. Place the leeks in a large pot and sauté over medium heat until tender, about 5 minutes. Add water 1 to 2 tablespoons at a time to keep the leeks from sticking to the pan. Add the dill and bay leaf and cook for another minute. Add the vegetable stock and potatoes and bring to a boil. Cook for 15 to 20 minutes, or until the potatoes are tender.
2. Add the spinach and lemon zest and season with salt and pepper. Cook for another 5 minutes, or until the spinach is wilted. Puree the soup using an immersion blender or in batches in a blender with a tight-fitting lid, covered with a towel. Return the soup to a pot and add the almond milk. Let cool completely, then chill until ready to serve.

Zucchini Bisque

IF YOU GROW zucchini in your garden, then chances are you're always looking for another way to use this bountiful favorite. Get one taste of this soup and you'll wish you had fresh zucchini throughout the year!

SERVES 4

> 1 medium yellow onion, peeled and finely chopped
>
> 4 medium zucchini, finely chopped
>
> 2 cups Vegetable Stock (page 23), or low-sodium vegetable broth
>
> ½ teaspoon minced thyme
>
> ¼ teaspoon ground nutmeg
>
> ½ teaspoon lemon zest
>
> ½ to 1 cup unsweetened plain almond milk
>
> Salt and freshly ground black pepper to taste

1. Place the onion in a large saucepan and sauté over medium heat for 7 to 8 minutes, or until the onion is tender. Add water 1 to 2 tablespoons at a time to keep the onion from sticking to the pan. Add the zucchini, vegetable stock, thyme, nutmeg, and lemon zest and cook for 15 minutes, or until the zucchini is tender.
2. Puree the soup using an immersion blender or in batches in a blender with a tight-fitting lid, covered with a towel. Return the soup to the pot and add the almond milk. Season with salt and pepper and cook until heated through.

Cream of Broccoli Soup

PUREEING VEGETABLES INTENSIFIES their flavor, so you don't need to do much more than that to make a tasty soup. Use this recipe as a template to make any pureed vegetable soup you like, such as potato, carrot, or even celery root.

SERVES 6

> 3 large leeks (white parts only), sliced and rinsed
>
> 1 teaspoon thyme leaves
>
> 4 cups broccoli florets (from about 2 large heads)
>
> 4½ cups Vegetable Stock (page 23), or low-sodium vegetable broth, plus more as needed
>
> 3 tablespoons nutritional yeast, optional
>
> Salt and freshly ground black pepper to taste

1. Place the leeks in a large saucepan and sauté over medium heat for 10 minutes. Add water 1 to 2 tablespoons at a time to keep the leeks from sticking to the pan. Add the thyme and cook for another minute, then add the broccoli, vegetable stock, and nutritional yeast (if using). Bring to a boil over high heat, reduce the heat to medium, and cook, covered, until the broccoli is tender, about 10 minutes.
2. Puree the soup using an immersion blender or in batches in a blender with a tight-fitting lid, covered with a towel. Return the soup to the pot and season with salt and pepper.

Curried Cauliflower Bisque

PUREED CAULIFLOWER SOUPS make great bisques—the cauliflower becomes rich and creamy when pureed, and it takes on the flavor of whatever spices you add to it.

SERVES 4

1 large onion, peeled and diced

2 teaspoons grated ginger

1 jalapeño pepper, minced (for less heat, remove the seeds)

2 cloves garlic, peeled and minced

1½ teaspoons curry powder

1 large head cauliflower, cut into florets

4 cups Vegetable Stock (page 23), or low-sodium vegetable broth

Salt and freshly ground black pepper to taste

¼ cup chopped cilantro

4 green onions (white and green parts), thinly sliced

1. Place the onion in a large saucepan and sauté over medium heat for 10 minutes. Add water 1 to 2 tablespoons at a time to keep the onion from sticking to the pan. Add the ginger, jalapeño pepper, garlic, and curry powder and cook for 30 seconds. Add the cauliflower and vegetable stock and bring the pot to a boil over high heat. Reduce the heat to medium and cook, covered, for 20 to 25 minutes, or until the cauliflower is tender.

2. Puree the soup using an immersion blender or in batches in a blender with a tight-fitting lid, covered with a towel to avoid splatter. Return to the pot and season with salt and pepper. Serve garnished with the cilantro and green onions.

Curried Potato Soup with Corn and Red Pepper

THIS IS A hearty, healthy soup with the added warmth of curry spices.

SERVES 4

> 1 medium yellow onion, peeled and diced
>
> 1 large red bell pepper, seeded and diced
>
> 2 cloves garlic, peeled and minced
>
> 2 large Yukon Gold potatoes (about 1 pound), peeled and chopped
>
> 3 ears corn, kernels removed (about 2 cups)
>
> 4 cups Vegetable Stock (page 23), or low-sodium vegetable broth
>
> 1 tablespoon curry powder
>
> 1 batch No-Cheese Sauce (page 29)
>
> Salt and freshly ground black pepper to taste
>
> 4 green onions (white and green parts), sliced
>
> ½ cup chopped cilantro

Place the onion and red pepper in a large saucepan and sauté over medium-high heat for 7 to 8 minutes. Add water 1 to 2 tablespoons at a time to keep the vegetables from sticking to the pan. Add the garlic and cook for another minute. Add the potatoes, corn, vegetable stock, and curry powder and bring the mixture to a boil over high heat. Reduce the heat to medium and cook, covered, for 20 minutes, or until the potatoes are tender. Add the No-Cheese Sauce and cook over low heat for 5 minutes. Season with salt and black pepper and serve garnished with the green onions and cilantro.

"Cheesy" Potato Soup

A WARM, RICH, and creamy soup, this is a delicious, plant-based alternative to standard dairy-heavy, fat-laden cheese soups. Depending on your preference, you can puree all or part of this soup; it will taste great either way.

SERVES 4

1 medium yellow onion, peeled and diced

2 cloves garlic, peeled and minced

4 cups Vegetable Stock (page 23), or low-sodium vegetable broth

1 bay leaf

3 large Yukon Gold potatoes (about 1½ pounds), peeled and chopped

1 batch No-Cheese Sauce (page 29)

Salt and freshly ground black pepper to taste

4 green onions (white and green parts), sliced

2 tablespoons chopped parsley

1. Sauté the onion in a large saucepan over medium heat for 10 minutes. Add water 1 to 2 tablespoons at a time to keep the onion from sticking to the pan. Add the garlic and cook for another minute. Add the vegetable stock, bay leaf, and potatoes. Bring the mixture to a boil over high heat. Reduce the heat to medium and cook, covered, for 20 to 25 minutes, or until the potatoes are tender. Remove the bay leaf. Puree the soup using an immersion blender or in batches in a blender with a tight-fitting lid, covered with a towel.

2. Return the soup to the pot if necessary, add the No-Cheese Sauce, and season with salt and pepper. Cook over low heat, stirring frequently, for 5 minutes. Serve garnished with the green onions and parsley.

VARIATION

▶ For a southwestern version with a kick, sauté 2 minced jalapeño peppers along with the onion. With the garlic, add 1 tablespoon of cumin seeds, toasted (see page 10) and ground, and 1 tablespoon of ancho chile powder, toasted in a dry skillet. Add the zest and juice of 1 lime to the No-Cheese Sauce. Along with the green onions, garnish the soup with ¼ cup of chopped cilantro instead of parsley.

Corn Chowder

THIS IS A perfect soup for summer, when bell peppers, corn, and tomatoes are all fresh at the farmers' market.

SERVES 6

2 medium yellow onions, peeled and diced small

2 red bell peppers, seeded and finely chopped

3 ears corn, kernels removed (about 2 cups)

3 cloves garlic, peeled and minced

2 large russet potatoes, peeled and diced

1½ pounds tomatoes (4 to 5 medium), diced

6 cups Vegetable Stock (page 23), or low-sodium vegetable broth

¾ cup finely chopped basil

Salt and freshly ground black pepper to taste

1. Place the onions and peppers in a large saucepan and sauté over medium heat for 10 minutes. Add water 1 to 2 tablespoons at a time to keep the vegetables from sticking to the pan. Add the corn and garlic, and sauté for 5 more minutes. Add the potatoes, tomatoes, and vegetable stock. Bring the mixture to a boil over high heat. Reduce the heat to medium and cook, uncovered, for 25 minutes, or until the potatoes are tender.
2. Puree half of the soup in batches in a blender with a tight-fitting lid, covered with a towel. Return the pureed soup to the pot. Add the basil and season with salt and pepper.

VARIATION

▶ You can also make this with leeks instead of onions—substitute 2 leeks (white parts only), diced and rinsed.

Lotsa Vegetable Chowder 📷

RECIPE BY JUDY MICKLEWRIGHT

YOU MIGHT CALL this a "corny" chowder instead, because when I tell my two-year-old that I am making my "Heavenly and Heavily Herbaceous Cauliflower Crowded Chowder," she cracks up. We always have a large quantity of broccoli and cauliflower stalks hanging around from other recipes. I slice off the outer fibrous side of the stems (all the green part for the broccoli) and chop the stalks into ¼-inch chunks. If you do not have leftover stems available, you can add more celery at the end of the cooking process, about 10 minutes before the chowder is done, or you can add chayote, kohlrabi, turnips, yellow beets, or fennel. I find the more vegetables in this soup, the better it tastes. If you're caught with a bounty of fresh thyme and dill, this soup is also a great way of making use of them.

SERVES 4 TO 6

8 small Yukon Gold, white, or russet potatoes (about 2 pounds), cut into ½-inch chunks

½ small onion, peeled and chopped

3 ears fresh corn, kernels removed (about 1¾ cups), cobs reserved

2 medium carrots, peeled and diced

2 celery stalks, chopped

¼ cup chopped red bell pepper

1 cup chopped broccoli and cauliflower stalks, outer fibrous parts removed and discarded (about ½ pound)

1 clove garlic, peeled and minced

2 tablespoons chopped thyme

⅛ teaspoon white pepper

2 teaspoons ground cumin

3 tablespoons chopped dill

Salt to taste

1. In a large pot, combine the potatoes, onion, corn kernels and cobs, carrots, celery, red pepper, broccoli and cauliflower, garlic, thyme, white pepper, cumin, and 6 cups of water. Bring to a boil over high heat. Reduce the heat to medium-low and simmer for 30 minutes, or until the vegetables are tender.
2. Remove the corn cobs and let cool. Remove 1 cup of the soup and puree in a blender with a tight-fitting lid, covered with a towel. (If you like a thicker soup, puree 2 cups.) Return the pureed soup to the pot and add the dill. Scrape corn cobs with back of a knife to remove the creamy corn "milk" left over from the kernels, and add it to the pot. Stir well and season with salt.

Fall Harvest Vegetable Chowder

RECIPE BY JULIEANNA HEVER

SOOTHING AND SIMPLE, this soup is a great go-to recipe during the colder months for a warm pick-me-up.

SERVES 6

1 medium yellow onion, peeled and diced (about 1 cup)

3 celery stalks, diced (about 1 cup)

2 medium carrots, peeled and diced (about 1 cup)

6 cups Vegetable Stock (page 23), or low-sodium vegetable broth

2 small zucchini, diced

2 small yams, peeled and diced

4 bay leaves

2 tablespoons thyme

3 to 4 ears corn, kernels removed (about 2 cups)

4 cups packed spinach leaves

1. Place the onion, celery, carrots, and ½ cup of vegetable stock in a large soup pot and sauté over medium-high heat for 6 to 8 minutes, or until the onion is translucent.
2. Add the zucchini, yams, bay leaves, thyme, and the remaining broth and bring to a boil over high heat. Reduce the heat to medium-low and simmer for 20 to 30 minutes, or until the vegetables are tender.
3. Add half the corn and cook for 10 to 15 more minutes. Remove the bay leaves.
4. Puree the soup using an immersion blender or in batches in a blender with a tight-fitting lid, covered with a towel. Return the soup to the pot and add the remaining corn and spinach leaves. Cook for 5 more minutes, or until the spinach is wilted. Stir well and serve hot.

Sweet Potato Bisque

THIS SWEET AND savory soup could almost be a dessert soup, as ginger, nutmeg, and cinnamon are spices you find in many sweet potato and pumpkin pie recipes. The onion and garlic temper the sweetness, however, with a savory boost in this comforting recipe.

SERVES 6

1 large onion, peeled and diced
2 cloves garlic, peeled and minced
1 tablespoon grated ginger
1 tablespoon thyme
½ teaspoon ground nutmeg
1 teaspoon ground cinnamon
3 large sweet potatoes, peeled and diced
6 cups Vegetable Stock (page 23), or low-sodium vegetable broth
Zest and juice of 1 orange
1½ cups unsweetened plain almond milk
Salt and freshly ground black pepper to taste

1. Place the onion in a large saucepan and sauté over medium heat for 10 minutes. Add water 1 to 2 tablespoons at a time to keep the onion from sticking to the pan. Add the garlic, ginger, thyme, nutmeg, and cinnamon and cook for 1 minute. Add the sweet potatoes, vegetable stock, and orange zest and juice and bring the pot to a boil over high heat. Reduce the heat to medium and cook, covered, for 25 minutes, or until the sweet potatoes are tender.

2. Puree the soup using an immersion blender or in batches in a blender with a tight-fitting lid, covered with a towel. Return the soup to the pot and add the almond milk. Cook for an additional 5 minutes, or until heated through, and season with salt and pepper.

Savory Squash Soup

RECIPE BY DARSHANA THACKER

THIS DAIRY-FREE SOUP is nourishing, delicious, and surprisingly creamy.

SERVES 4

2½ cups butternut squash, peeled, halved, seeded, and diced (from about 1 medium)
1 large russet potato, diced (about 1 cup)
1 medium yellow onion, peeled and chopped (about ½ cup)
1 clove garlic, peeled and chopped
¼ teaspoon dried Italian herb mix, or a pinch each of oregano, basil, rosemary, and thyme
Pinch freshly ground black pepper, or to taste
¼ cup green peas
¼ teaspoon fresh lime juice
Finely chopped parsley

1. Bring 3 cups of water to boil in a large pot over high heat. Add the squash, potato, onion, garlic, herb mix, and pepper. Reduce the heat to medium and cook, covered, for 20 minutes, or until the vegetables are tender.
2. Puree the soup using an immersion blender or in a blender with a tight-fitting lid, covered with a towel. Return the soup to the pot and add the green peas and lime juice. Cook for an additional 5 to 7 minutes, or until the peas are tender. Serve hot, garnished with the parsley.

Curried Squash and Apple Soup

APPLES AND WINTER squash are the vegetables of the fall harvest, and the tart Granny Smith apple is a perfect balance for the earthy squash. Soup and a hearty salad make an easy, satisfying meal. Add dried cranberries and a few chopped walnuts to the salad for a beautiful, seasonal presentation.

SERVES 4

> 1 medium onion, peeled and diced small
>
> 1 large winter squash, acorn or butternut, peeled, halved, seeded, and cut into ½-inch dice (about 6 cups)
>
> 2 Granny Smith apples, peeled, cored, and diced
>
> 1 tablespoon curry powder
>
> 1 cup unsweetened apple cider
>
> 3 cups Vegetable Stock (page 23), or low-sodium vegetable broth
>
> Pinch cayenne pepper
>
> Salt to taste

Place the onion in a large saucepan and sauté over medium heat for 10 minutes, or until the onion is browned. Add water 1 to 2 tablespoons at a time to keep the onion from sticking to the pan. Add the squash, apples, curry powder, cider, vegetable stock, and cayenne pepper and bring to a boil over high heat. Reduce the heat to medium and cook, covered, for about 20 minutes, or until the squash is tender. Puree the soup using an immersion blender or in batches in a blender with a tight-fitting lid, covered with a towel. If necessary, return the soup to the pot to reheat. Season with salt.

Chestnut Soup

A FEW YEARS ago my friend Elizabeth served this soup for Christmas dinner, and she made it vegan for me. I thought I had died and gone to soup heaven! It was creamy without any dairy, and full of flavor without a lot of complicated ingredients. This is a recipe you have to try.

SERVES 4

> 1 medium yellow onion, peeled and finely chopped
>
> 1 stalk celery, finely chopped
>
> 1 medium carrot, peeled and finely chopped
>
> 1½ tablespoons minced sage
>
> 1 tablespoon minced thyme
>
> 1 bay leaf
>
> ⅛ teaspoon ground cloves
>
> 4 to 5 cups Vegetable Stock (page 23), or low-sodium vegetable broth
>
> One 15-ounce can chestnut puree
>
> Salt and freshly ground black pepper to taste
>
> 2 tablespoons finely chopped parsley

Place the onion, celery, and carrot in a large saucepan and sauté over medium heat for 15 minutes, or until the onion is tender and starting to brown. Add water 1 to 2 tablespoons at a time to keep the vegetables from sticking to the pan. Add the sage, thyme, bay leaf, cloves, and vegetable stock. Bring the pot to a boil over high heat and whisk in the chestnut puree. Season with salt and pepper and cook for another 5 minutes. Serve garnished with the chopped parsley.

Mushroom Barley Soup

PORCINI MUSHROOMS ADD an earthy richness to any dish—they're well worth their slight expense. If you can't find cremini mushrooms, use button mushrooms instead.

SERVES 4 TO 6

1 large yellow onion, peeled and chopped

2 medium carrots, peeled and diced

2 celery stalks, diced

8 ounces cremini mushrooms, sliced

2 cloves garlic, peeled and minced

2 tablespoons minced thyme

2 teaspoons minced rosemary

2 bay leaves

5 cups Vegetable Stock (page 23), or low-sodium vegetable broth

½ ounce dried porcini mushrooms, soaked for 30 minutes in 1 cup of water that has just been boiled

3 cups cooked barley (see page 6)

Salt and freshly ground black pepper to taste

Place the onion, carrots, celery, and cremini mushrooms in a large pot and sauté over medium heat for 10 minutes. Add water 1 to 2 tablespoons at a time to keep the vegetables from sticking to the pan. Add the garlic, thyme, rosemary, and bay leaves and cook for another minute. Add the vegetable stock and the porcini mushrooms and their soaking liquid and bring to a boil over high heat. Reduce the heat to medium-low and cook, covered, for about 20 minutes, until the mushrooms are cooked through. Add the cooked barley and cook for another 10 minutes. Season with salt and pepper.

Chipotle Black Bean Soup

TOASTED SPICES AND chipotle peppers give this soup its smoky flavor, and the orange juice and zest really brighten it up. Serve this soup with Whole-Grain Corn Muffins (page 228) and a salad.

SERVES 4

1 large yellow onion, peeled and diced

1 large green bell pepper, seeded and diced

3 cloves garlic, peeled and minced

1 tablespoon cumin seeds, toasted (see page 10) and ground

1 teaspoon dried Mexican oregano, toasted

1 teaspoon coriander seeds, toasted and ground

1 dried chipotle pepper, halved, toasted in a dry skillet for 2 to 3 minutes, soaked in cool water for 15 minutes, and chopped

1 cup orange juice

Zest of 1 orange

4 cups cooked black beans (see page 6), or two 15-ounce cans, drained and rinsed

Salt and freshly ground black pepper to taste

Place the onion and green pepper in a large pan and sauté over medium heat for 7 to 8 minutes. Add water 1 to 2 tablespoons at a time to keep the vegetables from sticking to the pan. Add the garlic, cumin, oregano, coriander, and chipotle pepper and cook for 2 minutes. Add the orange juice, orange zest, beans, and enough water to cover the beans by 3 inches. Bring the soup to a boil over high heat. Reduce the heat to medium and cook, covered, for 25 minutes. Season with salt and pepper.

Split Pea Soup

SWEET POTATO AND smoked paprika give a twist to this otherwise everyday split pea soup. The sweet potato almost melts into the soup, giving it a creamy texture, and the flavors are even better the next day. You could also add spinach or mustard greens to this recipe for even more whole-food health benefits.

SERVES 6

1 large yellow onion, peeled and diced

1 medium carrot, peeled and diced

1 celery stalk, diced

3 cloves garlic, peeled and minced

1 bay leaf

2 teaspoons minced rosemary

2 teaspoons thyme leaves

1 teaspoon smoked paprika

1 large sweet potato, peeled and diced

1½ cups split peas

6 cups Vegetable Stock (page 23), or low-sodium vegetable broth

Salt and freshly ground black pepper to taste

Place the onion, carrot, and celery in a large saucepan and sauté over medium heat for 10 minutes, or until the onion is translucent. Add water 1 to 2 tablespoons at a time to keep the vegetables from sticking to the pan. Add the garlic, bay leaf, rosemary, thyme, paprika, sweet potato, split peas, and vegetable stock and bring the pot to a boil over high heat. Reduce the heat to medium and cook until the peas are tender, about 50 minutes. Season with salt and pepper.

Lentil Soup with Cauliflower, Potatoes and Spinach

THIS SOUP HAPPENED by accident one day when I happened to be making two different soups at the same time: Lentil on one burner, and Cauliflower, Potato and Spinach on another. I added some ingredients meant for one soup into the other pot—but as so often happens with cooking "mistakes," it worked out well. The cauliflower, potatoes, and lentils all add a creaminess to the soup as it cooks, and the smooth texture is especially pronounced if you serve it the next day.

SERVES 8 TO 10

> 1 large onion, peeled and chopped
>
> 6 cloves garlic, peeled and minced
>
> 2 bay leaves
>
> 2 teaspoons curry powder, or to taste
>
> ½ teaspoon turmeric
>
> Pinch ground nutmeg
>
> One 15-ounce can diced tomatoes
>
> 1 cup green lentils, rinsed
>
> 2 large waxy potatoes, scrubbed and cut into ½-inch dice
>
> 1 small head cauliflower, cut into florets
>
> 6 cups finely chopped spinach leaves
>
> 2 tablespoons minced cilantro
>
> Zest and juice of 1 lemon
>
> Salt and freshly ground black pepper to taste

1. Place the onion in a large pot and sauté over medium for 10 minutes. Add water 1 to 2 tablespoons at a time to keep the onion from sticking to the pan. Add the garlic and cook for 1 minute. Add the bay leaves, curry powder, turmeric, and nutmeg and cook for 1 minute. Stir in the tomatoes and cook for 3 minutes. Add the lentils and 6 cups of water and bring to a boil over high heat. Reduce the heat to medium and cook, covered, for 30 minutes. Add the potatoes and cauliflower and cook until the lentils are tender, about 15 more minutes.

2. Stir in the spinach, cilantro, and lemon zest and juice. Season with salt and pepper.

Ful Nabed (Egyptian Fava Bean Soup)

THIS POPULAR EGYPTIAN bean soup is made with fava beans (also known as broad beans), which are native to North Africa. If you can't find them, use chickpeas or any other bean. The mint and lemon really bring the soup to life.

SERVES 4 TO 6

1 large yellow onion, peeled and diced

1 medium carrot, peeled and diced

1 celery stalk, thinly sliced

4 cloves garlic, peeled

2 teaspoons cumin seeds, toasted (see page 10) and ground

1 tablespoon sweet paprika

2 bay leaves

1 large tomato, finely chopped

6 cups Vegetable Stock (page 23), or low-sodium vegetable broth

3 cups cooked fava beans (see page 6)

¼ teaspoon cayenne pepper, or to taste

¼ cup finely chopped parsley

Zest and juice of 1 lemon

2 tablespoons finely chopped mint

Salt to taste

1. Place the onion, carrot, and celery in a large pot and sauté over medium heat for 10 minutes. Add water 1 to 2 tablespoons at a time to keep the vegetables from sticking to the pan. Add the garlic, cumin, paprika, bay leaves, and tomato and cook for 5 minutes. Add the vegetable stock and fava beans and cook, covered, for 20 minutes.
2. Add the cayenne pepper, parsley, lemon zest and juice, and mint. Cook for another 5 minutes and season with salt.

Miso Soup

THIS LIGHT SOUP, a standard in Japanese meals, comes together quickly. It makes an easy start to any meal, or a last-minute lunch if served with a salad.

SERVES 4

> **6 cups Kombu Broth (page 34)**
> **½ cup mellow white miso**
> **½ cup chopped green onion (white and green parts)**

Bring the kombu broth to a boil over high heat. Reduce the heat to medium-low and simmer for 2 minutes. Turn off the heat and transfer 1 cup of the broth to a small bowl. Add the miso to the bowl and whisk the mixture until is smooth and creamy. Add the miso mixture to the pot. Add the green onion and cook over low heat for another 2 minutes, or until heated through.

VARIATION
▶ Add 1½ cups of cooked spinach or 1½ cups of sliced mushrooms with the green onion.

Thai Noodle Soup 📷

ONCE THE INGREDIENTS are prepped for this soup, the dish comes together quickly. Sautéing the vegetables first shortens the stewing time, so there's no need to spend long hours over a soup pot. This is a great one-pot meal that makes serving dinner a snap.

SERVES 4

1 medium yellow onion, peeled and thinly sliced

1 medium carrot, peeled and julienned

6 ounces shiitake mushrooms, stems removed

3 cloves garlic, peeled and minced

1 tablespoon grated ginger

2 cups sliced bok choy

4 cups Vegetable Stock (page 23), or low-sodium vegetable broth

2 tablespoons low-sodium soy sauce

Zest and juice of 1 lime

1 serrano chile, stemmed and sliced into thin rounds (for less heat, remove the seeds)

6 ounces brown rice noodles, cooked according to package directions, drained, and kept warm

1 cup mung bean sprouts (see page 71)

½ cup chopped cilantro

1. Place the onion, carrot, and mushrooms in a medium pot and sauté for 7 to 8 minutes. Add water 1 to 2 tablespoons at a time to keep the vegetables from sticking to the pan. Add the garlic, ginger, bok choy, vegetable stock, soy sauce, lime zest and juice, and serrano chile. Bring to a boil over high heat. Reduce the heat to medium and simmer for 10 minutes.
2. To serve, divide the noodles among 4 individual bowls. Pour the broth over the noodles and garnish with the mung bean sprouts and cilantro.

Thai Vegetable Soup

RECIPE BY JUDY MICKLEWRIGHT

THIS PUNGENT THAI-STYLE soup is sweet, sour, and spicy. The vegetables in this dish create a soup rich in nutrients, flavor, and color. Added sweetener is generally an integral part of this soup, but this version is naturally sweetened by the yams and sweet potato. Cut the yams and potato into rather large chunks so that they do not fully break down into the soup. If you do not have fresh coconut, substitute unsweetened shredded coconut.

SERVES 4 TO 6

> Coconut water from 3 young coconuts, or about 3½ cups of your favorite coconut water
> Coconut meat scraped from ½ coconut (4 to 6 ounces), optional
> 1 sweet potato, peeled and cut into 1½-inch pieces
> 2 yams, peeled and cut into 1½-inch pieces
> 1 small butternut squash, peeled, halved, seeded, and cubed
> 2 small carrots, peeled and diced
> ¼ pound shiitake or cremini mushrooms, sliced
> 2 medium tomatoes, diced
> 3 stalks of lemongrass (bottom white part only), halved and cut into 2-inch pieces
> 2 jalapeño peppers, halved and seeded
> 3 kaffir lime leaves
> ½ medium onion, peeled and diced
> 1-inch piece ginger, peeled and scored
> 2 cloves garlic, peeled and minced
> Juice from 2 large limes (about ½ cup)
> 1½ tablespoons low-sodium soy sauce
> 1½ teaspoons ground coriander
> Pinch white pepper
> 3 cups spinach (about ½ pound), coarsely chopped
> 1½ cups snow peas, trimmed
> Chopped cilantro

1. Add the coconut water and coconut meat to a blender and puree on high.
2. In a large stockpot, combine the pureed coconut, sweet potato, yams, butternut squash, carrots, mushrooms, tomatoes, lemongrass, jalapeño pepper, kaffir lime leaves, onion, ginger, garlic, lime juice, soy sauce, coriander, and white pepper. Bring to a boil over high heat. Reduce the heat to medium-low and simmer for 20 minutes. Add the spinach and snow peas and cook for 1 minute.
3. Remove the pot from the heat. Remove and discard the lemongrass, ginger, lime leaves, and jalapeños. Garnish with cilantro and serve immediately (best served piping hot).

TIPS

▶ If you do not have both yams and a sweet potato on hand, one or the other will do, but you may need to adjust the potato or yam quantity to balance the sweetness and sourness of the soup. The soup will get sweeter as the potato melts into the soup, and yams give off more natural sugar than sweet potatoes. If you find the soup is not sour enough for your taste, just add more lime juice or, if you run out of lime juice, a small amount of rice wine vinegar will work. Since jalapeño peppers may vary in spiciness, start out with 1 jalapeño and add more according to your personal taste.

Tom Yum Goong (Thai Hot-and-Sour Soup)

TOM YUM GOONG is usually made with chicken stock and often includes both shrimp and a fish sauce called *nam pla*. Shopping for this soup takes more effort than preparing it, but it is well worth it. Many grocery stores have well-stocked Asian sections, but you can also order ingredients online or seek out Asian grocery stores. When possible, choose fresh lemongrass instead of jarred, and Thai basil instead of the standard Genovese you'll find in most American markets.

SERVES 4

4 cups Vegetable Stock (page 23), or low-sodium vegetable broth

4 thin slices fresh ginger

1 stalk lemongrass, cut into 1-inch pieces

2 tablespoons Thai red curry paste

3 tablespoons low-sodium soy sauce

Zest and juice of 2 limes

One 14-ounce can lite coconut milk

3 shallots, peeled and thinly sliced

2 Roma tomatoes, chopped

1 head baby bok choy, thinly sliced

1 small carrot, peeled and cut into matchsticks

1 cup mung bean sprouts (see page 71)

¼ cup chopped Thai basil

2 Thai red chiles, sliced into thin rounds

Cilantro sprigs

In a large saucepan, add the vegetable stock, ginger, lemongrass, curry paste, soy sauce, lime zest and juice, and coconut milk. Bring the pot to a boil over high heat. Stir in the shallots, tomatoes, bok choy, and carrot. Reduce the heat to medium-low and simmer until the vegetables are tender, about 25 minutes. Remove the ginger and lemongrass and add the mung bean sprouts, basil, and chiles. Serve garnished with cilantro.

Quick and Easy Thai Vegetable Stew 📷

THIS DELICIOUS STEW is a perfect dinner to serve to last-minute guests, but don't save it only for them—this will hit the spot anytime you're in the mood for Thai. The stew tastes great served over brown rice.

SERVES 4

1½ cups unflavored soy or rice milk

1 teaspoon arrowroot powder

½ teaspoon coconut extract

1 medium yellow onion, peeled and diced small

2 cloves garlic, peeled and minced

2 teaspoons grated ginger

2 teaspoons Thai red curry paste (see note), or to taste

Zest and juice of 1 lime

1 serrano chile, minced (for less heat, remove the seeds)

2 tablespoons low-sodium soy sauce, or to taste

1 cup Vegetable Stock (page 23), or low-sodium vegetable broth

3 cups mixed vegetables of your choice, such as edamame, water chestnuts, carrots, broccoli florets, or sugar snap peas

½ cup chopped cilantro

2 tablespoons minced mint

Mix the soy or rice milk, arrowroot powder, and coconut extract. Set aside. Place the onion in a large saucepan and sauté over medium-high heat for 7 to 8 minutes, or until the onion is tender and starting to brown. Add water 1 to 2 tablespoons at a time to keep the onion from sticking to the pan. Add the garlic, ginger, curry paste, lime zest and juice, and serrano chile and cook for 30 seconds. Add the soy sauce, soy/rice milk mixture, vegetable stock, and mixed vegetables, reduce the heat to medium, and cook for 10 minutes, or until the vegetables are tender. Stir in the cilantro and mint and serve.

NOTE ▶ Thai Kitchen's Red Curry Paste is widely available, and recommended, but any vegan curry paste will suit.

STEWS AND CHILIES

Spicy Thai Sweet Potato Stew

THIS THAI-INSPIRED STEW is a little sweet, a little tangy, and a little spicy—a common theme in Thai cooking. The trick is balancing those elements so that no one flavor dominates the dish.

SERVES 6

2 large yellow onions, peeled and diced

2 celery stalks, diced

2 medium carrots, peeled and diced

2 serrano chiles, seeded and minced

4 cloves garlic, peeled and minced

2 teaspoons grated ginger

1 tablespoon ground coriander

3 tablespoons Thai red chili paste

6 cups Vegetable Stock (page 23), or low-sodium vegetable broth

4 large sweet potatoes, peeled and cut into ½-inch pieces (about 8 cups)

Zest of 1 lime and juice of 2 limes

½ teaspoon cayenne pepper, optional

Salt and freshly ground black pepper to taste

½ cup chopped cilantro

Place the onions, celery, and carrots in a large saucepan and sauté over medium heat for 10 minutes. Add water 1 to 2 tablespoons at a time to keep the vegetables from sticking to the pan. Add the serrano chiles, garlic, ginger, coriander, red chili paste, and ½ cup of water. Whisk to combine well and cook 3 to 4 minutes. Add the vegetable stock and sweet potatoes and bring to a boil over high heat. Reduce the heat to medium and cook, covered, for 25 minutes, or until the potatoes are tender. Stir in the lime zest and juice and cayenne pepper (if using). Season with salt and pepper and serve garnished with cilantro.

Adzuki Bean Stew with Miso

ADZUKI BEANS ARE quick-cooking red beans with a taste and texture similar to black-eyed peas. They are often eaten as a dessert in eastern Asia, but here, they feature in a savory stew. The miso, coriander, and cilantro combine to give this dish a rich, earthy flavor.

SERVES 4

> 1 large yellow onion, peeled and diced small
>
> 1 large carrot, peeled and diced small
>
> 3 cloves garlic, peeled and minced
>
> 2 tablespoons ground coriander
>
> 2½ cups adzuki beans, soaked overnight (see page 6)
>
> 2 tablespoons mellow white miso
>
> 1 cup chopped cilantro
>
> 1 teaspoon crushed red pepper flakes
>
> Salt to taste

1. Place the onion and carrot in a large pot and sauté for 6 to 8 minutes over medium heat. Add water 1 to 2 tablespoons at a time to keep the vegetables from sticking to the pan. Add the garlic and coriander and sauté for another minute.
2. Add the beans and 8 cups water and bring the pot to a boil over high heat. Reduce the heat to medium, cover, and cook until the beans are tender, 50 to 60 minutes.
3. Transfer 1 cup of the cooking liquid to a small bowl and add the miso to it. Whisk the mixture until the miso is dissolved and add it to the pot. Add the cilantro and crushed red pepper flakes and season with salt.

VARIATION

▶ Add 1 bunch of chopped kale, stems removed, to the stew in the last 10 minutes of cooking.

Chilean Bean Stew

THIS BEAN AND squash stew is a summer staple in Chile. The fresh basil really stands out in an otherwise simple stew. Serve this dish with quinoa or brown rice and a green salad.

SERVES 4

1 large yellow onion, peeled and diced small

4 cloves garlic, peeled and minced

1 medium butternut squash (about 1 pound), peeled, halved, seeded, and cut into ½-inch pieces

2 cups cooked pinto beans (see page 6), or one 15-ounce can, drained and rinsed

6 ears corn, kernels removed (about 3½ cups)

Salt and freshly ground black pepper to taste

1 cup finely chopped basil

Place the onion in a large saucepan and sauté over medium heat for 10 minutes. Add water 1 to 2 tablespoons at a time to keep the onion from sticking to the pan. Add the garlic, squash, beans, corn, and 2 cups of water and cook for 25 minutes, or until the squash is tender. Season with salt and pepper and stir in the basil.

Spanish Chickpea Stew

THIS TRADITIONAL STEW from Catalonia, in northeastern Spain, is usually made with cumin, paprika, potatoes, and spinach or chard. Chorizo, a Spanish sausage, is often a main ingredient as well, but every house has its own approach to this popular dish. I add a little smoked paprika to my version and toast the cumin to give it a more pronounced flavor in the stew.

SERVES 4

- **1 medium onion, peeled and diced small**
- **1 green bell pepper, seeded and diced small**
- **2 cloves garlic, peeled and minced**
- **1 teaspoon cumin seeds, toasted (see page 10) and ground**
- **1 teaspoon sweet paprika**
- **½ teaspoon smoked paprika**
- **1 bay leaf**
- **1 large tomato, diced small**
- **3 medium Yukon Gold potatoes (about 1 pound), cut into ½-inch dice**
- **5 cups Vegetable Stock (page 23), or low-sodium vegetable broth**
- **2 cups cooked chickpeas (see page 6), or one 15-ounce can, drained and rinsed**
- **1 medium bunch Swiss chard, ribs removed, chopped**
- **Salt and freshly ground black pepper to taste**

Place the onion and pepper in a large pot and sauté over medium heat for 10 minutes. Add water 1 to 2 tablespoons at a time to keep the vegetables from sticking to the pan. Add the garlic, cumin, both kinds of paprika, and bay leaf and cook for 1 minute. Stir in the tomato and cook for 3 minutes. Add the potatoes, vegetable stock, and chickpeas and bring the pot to a boil over high heat. Reduce the heat to medium and cook, covered, for 20 minutes, or until the potatoes are tender. Add the Swiss chard, season with salt and pepper, and cook, covered, until the chard wilts, about 5 minutes.

Indian Zuppa with Tomatoes and Fava Beans

RECIPE BY DARSHANA THACKER

THIS IS A complete and nourishing meal in a bowl. Feel free to substitute your favorite greens for the spinach.

SERVES 4

1½ **cups cooked fava beans (see page 6)**
½ **cup uncooked quinoa**
Pinch fenugreek seeds
½ **cup leeks, finely chopped and rinsed**
½ **clove garlic, peeled and minced**
2 **medium tomatoes, chopped**
⅛ **teaspoon turmeric**
¼ **teaspoon ground cumin**
¼ **teaspoon salt, or to taste**
½ **cup spinach**
Freshly ground black pepper to taste

Add the fava beans, quinoa, and fenugreek seeds to a pot with 3 cups of water and bring to a boil over high heat. Add the leeks and garlic and cook on medium heat for 10 to 15 minutes. Add 1½ cups of water, the tomatoes, turmeric, cumin, and salt and cook for another 5 to 7 minutes on medium heat, or until the quinoa and fava beans are tender. Add the spinach and season with black pepper. Serve hot.

Pinto Bean Stew with Hominy and Spicy Cilantro Pesto

HOMINY IS MADE from dried corn that has been treated with lye, an acid which helps preserve the grain. It is used extensively in American Southern and Mexican cooking, either served whole in soups and stews, coarsely ground and served as grits, or ground more finely to make masa. In any preparation hominy has a mild flavor and takes on the flavor of whatever other ingredients it is cooked with. Ancho chiles can be found dried or canned in the Mexican section of most grocery stores. Toasting the dried chiles gives them a smoky flavor you don't quite get with the canned version, but both work for this dish. If you can't find either, use 1 tablespoon of ancho chile powder instead.

SERVES 6

> 1 large onion, peeled and chopped
> 1 medium red bell pepper, seeded and chopped
> 4 cloves garlic, peeled and minced
> 1 tablespoon cumin seeds, toasted (see page 10) and ground
> 1 dried ancho chile, toasted in a dry skillet for 3 minutes, soaked in warm water for 15 minutes, seeded, and pureed
> 2 cups cooked pinto beans (see page 6), or one 15-ounce can, drained and rinsed
> One 15-ounce can hominy, drained and rinsed
> One 28-ounce can tomatoes, drained and pureed
> 2 cups Vegetable Stock (page 23), or low-sodium vegetable broth
> Zest of 1 lime and juice of 2 limes
> Salt and freshly ground black pepper to taste
> Spicy Cilantro Pesto (page 24)

Place the onion and red peppers in a large saucepan and sauté over medium heat for 10 minutes. Add water 1 to 2 tablespoons at a time to keep the vegetables from sticking to the pan. Add the garlic, cumin, and ancho chile and cook for another minute. Add the beans, hominy, tomatoes, and vegetable stock and bring the soup to a boil over high heat. Reduce the heat to medium and cook, covered, for 30 minutes. Add the lime zest and juice and season with salt and pepper. Serve garnished with a dollop of Spicy Cilantro Pesto.

White Bean Stew with Saffron and Basil

THE WORLD'S MOST expensive spice meets one of the world's most popular herbs in this hearty soup. Saffron can be found in most grocery stores, but you may find it cheaper online. If you use the spice on a regular basis, buy it in bulk for even better savings.

SERVES 6

> 2 yellow onions, peeled and diced
>
> 2 celery stalks, chopped into medium dice
>
> 2 medium carrots, peeled and diced
>
> 3 cloves garlic, peeled and minced
>
> ½ cup white wine
>
> 2 large pinches saffron, crumbled and soaked for 15 minutes in ¼ cup of water that has just been boiled
>
> One 28-ounce can diced tomatoes
>
> 4 cups cooked cannellini beans (see page 6), or two 15-ounce cans, drained and rinsed
>
> 2 cups Vegetable Stock (page 23), or low-sodium vegetable broth
>
> 1 cup finely chopped basil
>
> Salt and freshly ground black pepper to taste

Place the onions, celery, and carrots in a large saucepan and sauté over medium heat for 10 minutes. Add water 1 to 2 tablespoons at a time to keep the vegetables from sticking to the pan. Add the garlic and cook for another minute. Add the wine and the saffron with its soaking liquid and bring the pot to a boil over high heat. Add the tomatoes, beans, and vegetable stock. Return the stew to a boil, then reduce the heat and simmer, covered, for 30 minutes. Add the basil, season with salt and pepper, and cook for another 5 minutes.

White Bean and Mushroom Stew

USE WHATEVER MUSHROOMS you have on hand for this stew, but keep in mind that mushrooms like cremini and shiitake have much more flavor than white button mushrooms. Serve this dish with Basic Polenta (page 229) and a salad.

SERVES 4

> 1 medium onion, peeled and diced
>
> 1 pound cremini mushrooms, halved
>
> 6 cloves garlic, peeled and chopped
>
> One 14-ounce can diced tomatoes
>
> ¼ cup minced basil
>
> 1 tablespoon minced thyme
>
> 2 teaspoons minced rosemary
>
> 1 bay leaf
>
> 4 cups cooked navy beans (see page 6), or two 15-ounce cans, drained and rinsed
>
> Salt and freshly ground black pepper to taste

Place the onion and mushrooms in a large saucepan and sauté over medium heat for 10 minutes. Add water 1 to 2 tablespoons at a time to keep the vegetables from sticking to the pan. Add the garlic and cook for 1 minute. Stir in the tomatoes, basil, thyme, rosemary, bay leaf, and beans and bring the pot to a boil over high heat. Reduce the heat to medium and cook, covered, for 15 minutes. Season with salt and pepper.

Lima Bean Stew

COOKING LIMA BEANS with aromatics like cloves, garlic, and bay leaves adds a depth of flavor to the already flavorful bean, the most underappreciated of the bean family. I never liked them as a kid because I, like most children, had a very sensitive texture palate. But after years of my avoiding them, one day a friend served them to me and the love affair began.

SERVES 6

1½ cups dried lima beans, soaked for 8 to 10 hours (or overnight) and drained
2 bay leaves
4 whole cloves
4 cloves garlic, peeled
1 large onion, peeled and chopped
2 celery stalks, chopped
2 medium carrots, peeled and chopped
1 green bell pepper, seeded and sliced
1 teaspoon thyme leaves
¼ cup tomato paste
Salt and freshly ground black pepper to taste

1. Place the soaked lima beans in a pot with 4 cups water and add the bay leaves, cloves, and garlic. Simmer for 1 hour, or until the beans are just tender, adding more water as needed to cover the beans well. Remove the bay leaves, cloves, and garlic.
2. While the beans are cooking, place the onion, celery, and carrots in a large saucepan and sauté over medium heat for 10 minutes. Add water 1 to 2 tablespoons at a time to keep the vegetables from sticking to the pan. Add the green pepper and thyme and cook for 4 minutes. Add the tomato paste and cook for 1 minute.
3. Add the vegetable mixture to the cooked beans and cook for 15 minutes over medium heat. Season with salt and pepper.

Tuscan Bean Stew

A TRADITIONAL COUNTRY soup from one of the world's culinary capitals, this soup is simple but very satisfying.

SERVES 6

3 large leeks (white and light green parts), diced and rinsed

2 celery stalks, diced

2 medium carrots, peeled and diced

2 cups chopped green cabbage

1 large russet potato, peeled and diced

6 cloves garlic, peeled and minced

3 cups cooked cannellini beans (see page 6)

6 cups Vegetable Stock (page 23), or low-sodium vegetable broth

½ cup chopped basil

Salt and freshly ground black pepper to taste

Place the leeks, celery, and carrots in a large saucepan and sauté for 10 minutes over medium heat. Add water 1 to 2 tablespoons at a time to keep the vegetables from sticking to the pan. Add the cabbage, potato, garlic, beans, and vegetable stock and bring the soup to a boil over high heat. Reduce the heat to medium and cook, uncovered, for 30 minutes, or until the potatoes are tender. Add the basil and season the soup with salt and pepper.

Pumpkin and Anasazi Bean Stew 📷

ANASAZI BEANS ARE similar to pinto beans but have a richer flavor. They are considered an heirloom bean and are not readily available in grocery stores. If you can't find them, use pinto beans instead.

SERVES 6 TO 8

> 1 large yellow onion, peeled and diced
>
> 2 large carrots, peeled and diced
>
> 2 celery stalks, diced
>
> 2 cloves garlic, peeled and minced
>
> 2 tablespoons cumin seeds, toasted (see page 10) and ground
>
> 2 tablespoons tomato paste
>
> 1 small pumpkin (about 1 pound), peeled, seeded, and cut into 1-inch cubes
>
> 4 cups cooked anasazi beans (see page 6), or two 15-ounce cans, drained and rinsed
>
> 6 cups Vegetable Stock (page 23), or low-sodium vegetable broth
>
> Salt and freshly ground black pepper to taste
>
> 6 green onions (white and green parts), thinly sliced

Place the onion, carrots, and celery in a large saucepan and sauté over medium heat for 10 minutes. Add water 1 to 2 tablespoons at a time to keep the vegetables from sticking to the pan. Add the garlic and cook for another minute. Add the cumin, tomato paste, pumpkin, beans, and vegetable stock and bring to a boil over high heat. Reduce the heat to medium and cook, covered, for 25 minutes, or until the pumpkin is tender. Season with salt and pepper and serve garnished with the green onions.

Tzimmes

THIS TRADITIONAL JEWISH stew is usually prepared for the Rosh Hashanah meal and usually contains meat and prunes, as well as other dried fruit. I am personally not a fan of prunes and have always prepared this dish with dried apples, although feel free to substitute prunes if you enjoy them. The inspiration for the cinnamon and allspice comes from my favorite carrot cake recipe. Tzimmes is best served over couscous or quinoa with a salad.

SERVES 4

4 large carrots, peeled and cut into 1-inch slices

3 large sweet potatoes, peeled and cut into ¾-inch cubes

1 cup dried unsulfured apricots (see page 9 for more on sulfites and sulfur dioxide)

1 cup dried chopped apples

½ cup golden raisins

2 tablespoons fresh lemon juice

½ cup unsweetened apple cider

¼ cup brown rice syrup

1½ teaspoons ground cinnamon

¼ teaspoon ground allspice

Salt to taste

1. Preheat the oven to 350°F.
2. Bring a large saucepan of water to a boil over high heat and add the carrots and sweet potatoes. Reduce the heat to medium and cook for 10 minutes, or until the vegetables are tender. Drain and rinse under cold water until cool.
3. Combine the drained carrots and sweet potatoes, apricots, apples, raisins, lemon juice, apple cider, brown rice syrup, cinnamon, and allspice in a 9 x 13-inch baking dish. Season with salt and cover with a lid or aluminum foil. Bake for 30 minutes, stirring gently every 10 minutes.

Creamy Sweet Potato and Vegetable Stew

RECIPE BY JUDY MICKLEWRIGHT

THIS RECIPE IS reminiscent of the aroma, taste, and comfort of my mama's traditional stew recipe, but my version is easier to make, healthier, and heartier. The potato, white bean cream, and Worcestershire sauce are some of the key elements in this dish—they give off flavors and textures similar to those that are achieved by braising (browning food in fat and then stewing). You can soak, cook, and store the white beans in the freezer in ½- to 1-cup portions, which are then readily at hand for thickening soups and sauces. Make sure you place the potatoes on the bottom of the pans so that they will be sure to cook within the suggested times.

SERVES 6 TO 8

FOR THE SWEET POTATO AND VEGETABLE MIXTURE:

> 1 large sweet potato, cut into 1½-inch slices
>
> 1 small onion, peeled and diced
>
> 2 medium carrots, peeled and cut into 1-inch slices
>
> 2 medium zucchini, cut into ½-inch slices
>
> 1 red bell pepper, seeded and cut into ¼-inch slices
>
> 2 cups cauliflower florets (from about one large head)
>
> ¼ pound green beans, trimmed
>
> 1 tablespoon thyme
>
> 1 bay leaf
>
> 3 cups Vegetable Stock (page 23), or low-sodium vegetable broth
>
> 2 cloves garlic, peeled and minced
>
> Salt and freshly ground black pepper to taste

FOR THE MASHED POTATO AND MUSHROOM MIXTURE:

> 8 small white, Yukon Gold, or russet potatoes, cut into ¼-inch cubes
>
> 2 cups Vegetable Stock (page 23), or low-sodium vegetable broth
>
> 8 ounces cremini mushrooms, sliced
>
> 2 shallots, peeled and minced
>
> 3 celery stalks, chopped
>
> ½ teaspoon celery seed
>
> ¼ teaspoon white pepper
>
> ½ teaspoon sage
>
> 2 cloves garlic, peeled and minced
>
> 1 tablespoon vegan Worcestershire sauce

FOR THE WHITE BEAN CREAM:

> 1 cup cooked cannellini or navy beans (see page 6)

1. Preheat the oven to 450°F.

TO MAKE THE SWEET POTATO AND VEGETABLE MIXTURE:

2. Place the sweet potato on the bottom of a large baking dish and top with the onion, carrots, zucchini, red pepper, cauliflower, green beans, thyme, bay leaf, vegetable stock, and garlic. Season with salt and black pepper. Cover with a lid or aluminum

foil. Place in the preheated oven and cook for 50 minutes, or until the sweet potatoes are tender. (Note that the dishes for both the Sweet Potato and Vegetable Mixture and the Mashed Potato and Mushroom Mixture should be placed in the oven at the same time.)

TO MAKE THE MASHED POTATO AND MUSHROOM MIXTURE:

3. Place the potatoes on the bottom of a large baking dish and top with the vegetable stock, mushrooms, shallots, celery, celery seed, white pepper, sage, garlic, and Worcestershire sauce. Cover with a lid or aluminum foil. Place in the preheated oven and bake for 50 minutes, or until the potatoes are tender. When the potatoes are tender, coarsely mash them in the baking dish with a potato masher.

TO MAKE THE WHITE BEAN CREAM:

4. Place the beans and 1 cup of water in a blender and process until creamy, adding more water as needed to achieve a smooth consistency.

TO ASSEMBLE THE STEW:

5. Pour the White Bean Cream into the Mashed Potato and Mushroom Mixture and mix well to combine. Spread on top of the Sweet Potato and Vegetable Mixture. Return the baking dish to the oven and bake for another 10 minutes.

Millet Stew

WHEN YOU NEED a change from rice, add millet to the menu. It's a healthy, gluten-free grain with a mild nutty flavor, and best of all, it's quick-cooking. Cooking the vegetable stock with cinnamon, ginger, and a bay leaf gives the soup a North African flavor. Add a pinch of saffron if you like. Like most grains, the longer the millet cooks in the soup, the more liquid it will absorb. Add more stock, or water, if needed, to thin the soup.

SERVES 4 TO 6

5 to 6 cups Vegetable Stock (page 23), or low-sodium vegetable broth
Two 1-inch pieces cinnamon stick
2 tablespoons grated ginger
1 bay leaf
1 large onion, peeled and cut into ¾-inch pieces
2 large carrots, peeled and cut into ½-inch slices
2 cloves garlic, peeled and minced
1 cup millet
1 large head cauliflower, cut into large florets
One 14.5-ounce can diced tomatoes
Salt and freshly ground black pepper to taste
½ cup chopped cilantro

1. In a small pot, combine the vegetable stock, cinnamon sticks, ginger, and bay leaf and cook over medium-high heat for 15 minutes. Remove from the heat, discard the spices, and set the vegetable stock aside.
2. Place the onion and carrots in a large saucepan over medium heat and sauté for 8 to 10 minutes, or until the vegetables are tender and starting to brown. Add water 1 to 2 tablespoons at a time to keep the vegetables from sticking to the pan. Add the garlic and cook for another minute. Add the prepared vegetable stock, millet, cauliflower, and tomatoes and bring to a boil over high heat. Reduce the heat to medium and cook, covered, for 12 to 15 minutes, or until the cauliflower and millet are tender. Season with salt and cook for another 5 minutes.
3. Serve garnished with cilantro.

Ethiopian Lentil Stew

THIS EXOTICALLY FLAVORFUL soup from the horn of Africa is made with a spice blend called *berbere* and the spiced, clarified butter known as Nitter Kibbeh (page 31). You can easily make your own Berbere Spice Blend (see below), or buy it in most spice stores. Its flavor is quite unique, so do not substitute curry powder; the minimal effort of finding or making the berbere spice is well worth it.

SERVES 4

¼ cup **Nitter Kibbeh (page 31)**

6 cloves **garlic, peeled and minced**

2 to 3 tablespoons **Berbere Spice Blend (see below)**

2 large **tomatoes, diced**

1½ cups **red lentils (about ½ pound), rinsed**

Salt and freshly ground black pepper to taste

Warm the nitter kibbeh, garlic, and berbere spice in a medium saucepan over medium-low heat for 5 minutes. Add the tomatoes and cook for 10 minutes, or until the tomatoes have started to break down. Add the lentils and 5 cups of water and bring the pan to a boil over high heat. Reduce the heat to medium and cook until the lentils are tender, about 20 minutes. Season with salt and pepper.

 Berbere Spice Blend

1 tablespoon **paprika**

1 teaspoon **ground allspice**

1 teaspoon **cayenne pepper**

1 teaspoon **ground cardamom**

1 teaspoon **ground cinnamon**

1 teaspoon **ground cloves**

1 teaspoon **ground coriander**

1 teaspoon **ground fenugreek**

1 teaspoon **ground ginger**

1 teaspoon **ground nutmeg**

1 teaspoon **turmeric**

Combine all ingredients in a small bowl and whisk well to blend. Store in an airtight container.

Autumn Vegetable Stew with North African Spices

THE SPICES IN this hearty soup are classic flavors of North African cooking—a mix of sweet, savory, bright, and earthy all in one dish. Saffron may be the world's most expensive spice, but this recipe, like most, calls for only a small amount. This dish also calls for sweet paprika, which usually refers to a milder form of the spice.

SERVES 6 TO 8

1 large onion, peeled and chopped

2 large carrots, peeled and chopped

2 celery stalks, cut into ½-inch slices

3 cloves garlic, peeled and minced

1 tablespoon grated ginger

1½ tablespoons sweet paprika

2 teaspoons ground cumin

1 tablespoon ground coriander

Two 1-inch pieces cinnamon stick

8 cups Vegetable Stock (page 23), or low-sodium vegetable broth

1 medium butternut squash (about 1 pound), peeled, halved, seeded, and cut into ¾-inch pieces

1 turnip, peeled and cut into ½-inch pieces

1 russet potato, peeled and cut into ½-inch pieces

One 15-ounce can crushed tomatoes

2 cups cooked chickpeas (see page 6), or one 15-ounce can, drained and rinsed

2 large pinches saffron, soaked for 15 minutes in ¼ cup warm water

2 tablespoons finely chopped mint

Salt and freshly ground black pepper to taste

½ cup finely chopped cilantro

Place the onion, carrots, and celery in a large pot and sauté for 10 minutes. Add water 1 to 2 tablespoons at a time to keep the vegetables from sticking to the pan. Add the garlic, ginger, paprika, cumin, coriander, and cinnamon sticks and cook for 3 minutes. Add the vegetable stock, squash, turnip, potato, tomatoes, and chickpeas and bring to a boil over high heat. Reduce the heat to medium-low and cook, uncovered, for 25 minutes. Add the mint and the saffron with its soaking water and season the stew with salt and pepper. Cook for 10 minutes more, or until the vegetables are tender. Serve garnished with the cilantro.

NOTE ▶ Other vegetables like celery root and cauliflower go well in this dish, so feel free to use whatever such vegetables you have on hand.

Brown Lentil Stew with Avocado Salsa

RECIPE BY DARSHANA THACKER

THIS DISH IS a delicious curried stew with a Latin flair. Serve it over brown rice or quinoa to make it a meal.

SERVES 4

FOR THE STEW:

1 cup brown lentils, rinsed

½ teaspoon salt, or to taste

½ teaspoon turmeric

1 medium green bell pepper, seeded and chopped (about ½ cup)

½ cup chopped celery

½ cup chopped tomato

½ teaspoon curry powder

½ teaspoon fresh lime juice

FOR THE AVOCADO SALSA:

½ avocado, halved, pitted, peeled and cut into ½-inch cubes (about ½ cup)

½ cup finely diced tomato

½ teaspoon finely chopped cilantro

½ teaspoon fresh lime juice

¼ teaspoon freshly ground black pepper

TO MAKE THE STEW:

1. Place the lentils, salt, turmeric, and 2 cups of water in a large saucepan. Cook, uncovered, over medium heat for 25 to 30 minutes. Add the green pepper, celery, tomato, and curry powder and cook for 10 minutes. Just before serving, add the lime juice.

TO MAKE THE AVOCADO SALSA:

2. Combine the avocado, tomato, cilantro, lime juice, and black pepper in a medium bowl. Mix well to combine.

3. Serve the stew hot and top with the avocado salsa.

Lentil Chili

RECIPE BY JULIEANNA HEVER

THIS HEARTY CHILI is robust and satisfying. Enjoy with a Whole-Grain Corn Muffin or two (page 228) and even a dollop of No-Cheese Sauce (page 29). Keep this recipe on standby for anytime you want a warm, easy, and soothing meal.

SERVES 6 TO 8

3 medium yellow onions, peeled and chopped (about 1½ cups)

1½ cups chopped celery

2 medium carrots, peeled and sliced (about 1 cup)

2 medium bell peppers, seeded and chopped (about 1 cup)

1 to 2 cloves garlic, peeled and minced

6 cups Vegetable Stock (page 23), or low-sodium vegetable broth

1½ tablespoons chili powder

1 teaspoon ground cumin

1 teaspoon paprika

½ teaspoon chipotle powder or smoked paprika

½ teaspoon cayenne pepper

2 cups red lentils, rinsed

One 28-ounce can crushed tomatoes

One 15-ounce can kidney beans, drained and rinsed

Zest and juice of 1 lime

Salt and freshly ground black pepper to taste

1. Place the onions, celery, carrots, bell peppers, garlic, and 1 cup of the vegetable stock in a large pot over medium-high heat. Cook, stirring occasionally, until the vegetables soften, 5 to 7 minutes. Add the chili powder, cumin, paprika, chipotle powder, and cayenne pepper and cook for an additional minute, stirring well.

2. Add the lentils, tomatoes, kidney beans, and the remaining vegetable stock to the pot. Cover and bring to a boil over high heat. Reduce the heat to medium-low and simmer, stirring occasionally, until the lentils are soft, about 45 minutes. Add the lime zest and juice and season with salt and pepper.

Bean and Mushroom Chili

I HAD GIVEN up on chili until I went to work at my first restaurant job and tasted their chili. This is my re-creation of that recipe. Mushrooms, fennel, and a hint of cocoa make this stew stand out from the crowd—the mushrooms give the soup an earthy flavor, the fennel adds a surprising brightness, and the unsweetened cocoa is a classic ingredient in Mexican sauces and stews.

SERVES 6

> **1 large onion, peeled and chopped**
> **1 pound button mushrooms, chopped**
> **6 cloves garlic, peeled and minced**
> **1 tablespoon ground cumin**
> **1 tablespoon ancho chile powder**
> **4 teaspoons ground fennel**
> **½ teaspoon cayenne pepper, or to taste**
> **1 tablespoon unsweetened cocoa powder**
> **One 28-ounce can diced tomatoes**
> **4 cups cooked pinto beans (see page 6), or two 15-ounce cans, drained and rinsed**
> **Salt to taste**

Place the onion and mushrooms in a large saucepan and sauté over medium heat for 10 minutes. Add water 1 to 2 tablespoons at a time to keep the vegetables from sticking to the pan. Add the garlic, cumin, chile powder, fennel, cayenne pepper, and cocoa powder and cook for 3 minutes. Add the tomatoes, beans, and 2 cups of water and simmer, covered, for 25 minutes. Season with salt.

White Bean Chili with Jalapeño and Lime

I GREW UP with chili for dinner at least twice a week and swore I would never eat it as an adult. Then I learned that there are several ways to make chili, and I can prepare it any way I want to. I often use whatever beans I have on hand, and I like to vary the flavor of what I usually call my mom's All-American Chili by adding lime and fresh cilantro, or even cinnamon or allspice, which is popular in Cincinnati-style chili. Vary the spice level to your taste by increasing or decreasing the jalapeño pepper, or by adding chipotle powder for more kick and a little smoky flavor. I like the lime zest more than I like the juice; you can use both or just one or the other.

SERVES 6

1 large yellow onion, peeled and diced

1 large green pepper, seeded and diced

3 jalapeño peppers, seeded and minced

6 cloves garlic, peeled and minced

2 tablespoons cumin seeds, toasted (see page 10) and ground

One 28-ounce can diced tomatoes

4 cups cooked navy or other white beans (see page 6), or two 15-ounce cans, drained and rinsed

3 cups Vegetable Stock (page 23), or low-sodium vegetable broth

Zest of 1 lime and juice of 2 limes

1 cup finely chopped cilantro

Salt to taste

Place the onion, green pepper, and jalapeño peppers in a large saucepan and sauté over medium heat for 7 to 8 minutes. Add water 1 to 2 tablespoons at a time to keep the vegetables from sticking to the pan. Add the garlic and cumin and cook for 2 minutes. Add the tomatoes, beans, and vegetable stock and bring to a boil over high heat. Reduce the heat to medium and cook, covered, for 25 minutes. Add the lime zest and juice and cilantro and season with salt.

Lettuce Wraps

Lettuce wraps are the ideal food for picnics, parties, and hot days when you may not be hungry for more than crisp, fresh lettuce wrapped around a savory filling. This section includes several variations on the theme. The recipes call for romaine lettuce; be sure to buy a leafy head, not the packaged hearts, which are not flexible enough for easy wrapping. If you prefer Bibb lettuce—or any other type of large leafy green—feel free to substitute it for the romaine in any of these wraps.

Hummus and Tabbouleh Lettuce Wraps

QUINOA TABBOULEH, HUMMUS, and Spicy Cilantro Pesto come together for a party in your mouth. If you don't like cilantro, use Basil Pesto (page 24) instead.

SERVES 4

> **½ cup Spicy Cilantro Pesto (page 24)**
> **8 romaine lettuce leaves**
> **2 cups Hummus (page 139)**
> **2 cups Quinoa Tabbouleh (page 62)**

Spread 1 tablespoon of pesto on one of the lettuce leaves. Top with 2 tablespoons of hummus and 2 tablespoons of the tabbouleh. Fold the leaf in from the sides and roll it up like a cigar. Repeat for the remaining lettuce leaves.

Stir-Fried Veggie Lettuce Wraps with Hummus and Fresh Herbs

MAKE BASIC VEGETABLE stir-fries with whatever you have on hand, or the freshest produce at the market, and use the leftovers for these lettuce wraps.

SERVES 4

> **1 batch Hummus (page 139)**
> **8 romaine lettuce leaves**
> **1 batch Basic Vegetable Stir-Fry (page 169)**
> **1 cup chopped herbs, such as chives, basil, or cilantro**

Spoon 3 tablespoons hummus into one of the lettuce leaves. Top with some of the stir-fried vegetables and garnish with the fresh herbs. Fold the leaf in from the sides and roll it up like a cigar. Repeat for the remaining lettuce leaves.

Portobello Wraps

MAKE EXTRA GRILLED Portobello Mushrooms (page 173) when you have the grill fired up, and you'll have a quick and easy meal ready to go later in the week. Use any pesto you have on hand for these wraps, or try something unusual, like Pineapple Chutney (page 33).

SERVES 4

½ cup Spicy Cilantro Pesto (page 24) or Coriander Chutney (page 32)
8 romaine lettuce leaves
2 cups cooked brown rice (see page 6)
1 batch Grilled Portobello Mushrooms (page 173), cut into ¾-inch-wide strips

Spread 1 tablespoon of the pesto in the bottom of one of the lettuce leaves and top with ¼ cup of the rice and about half of a grilled mushroom. Roll the lettuce leaf up around the filling. Repeat for the remaining lettuce leaves.

Samosa Lettuce Wraps

SAMOSAS ARE LIKE India's burrito—a delicious, flavorful filling wrapped up in a savory, crispy dough. Samosas as lettuce wraps are certainly not the norm, but they are just as delicious in a lettuce wrap as they are in fried dough, *and* a lot healthier. For the filling, make the Potato Samosa Filling as directed in Potato Samosa–Stuffed Chard (page 200).

SERVES 4 TO 6

1 batch Potato Samosa Filling (see page 200)
8 romaine lettuce leaves
3 cups cooked brown rice (see page 6)
Coriander Chutney (page 32)

Place some of the samosa filling on the bottom of one of the lettuce leaves. Top with some brown rice and a spoonful of the coriander chutney. Roll the leaf up around the filling. Repeat for the remaining lettuce leaves.

Black Bean and Rice Wraps

I LOVE THIS wrap. It is like eating a taco in a lettuce shell. If you like, add a little chopped tomato and fresh diced onion for a more authentic "taco" wrap.

SERVES 6

> **1 batch Black Beans and Rice (page 202)**
> **1 large head romaine lettuce, leaves separated**
> **1 batch Not-So-Fat Guacamole (page 27)**

Place some of the black beans and rice into the center of one of the lettuce leaves. Top with some of the guacamole. Fold the leaf in from the sides and roll it up like a cigar. Repeat for any remaining lettuce leaves until the beans and rice and guacamole are used up.

Baba Ghanoush Wraps with Marinated Tomatoes 📷

BABA GHANOUSH IS a Middle Eastern dish similar to Hummus (page 139), but made with roasted eggplant instead. It is commonly used as a hearty condiment or a savory filling, as in these wraps.

SERVES 4

FOR THE BABA GHANOUSH:

1 large eggplant, stemmed

4 cloves garlic, peeled and coarsely chopped

½ tablespoon cumin seeds, toasted (see page 10) and finely ground

½ tablespoon roasted tahini, optional

2 tablespoons fresh lemon juice

Zest of 1 lemon

Salt to taste

Cayenne pepper to taste, optional

FOR THE MARINATED TOMATOES:

2 large tomatoes, diced

1 clove garlic, peeled and minced

2 tablespoons minced basil

2 to 3 tablespoons balsamic vinegar

Salt and freshly ground black pepper to taste

8 romaine lettuce leaves

TO MAKE THE BABA GHANOUSH:

1. Preheat the oven to 400°F. Prick the eggplant all over with a fork and place on a baking sheet. Bake for 1 hour, or until the eggplant is shriveled and tender. Let the eggplant cool, cut it in half, and scrape the flesh from the skin. Add the flesh to the bowl of a food processor with the garlic, cumin, tahini (if using), lemon juice, lemon zest, salt, and cayenne pepper (if using) and puree until smooth and creamy.

TO MAKE THE MARINATED TOMATOES:

2. Combine the tomatoes, garlic, basil, and balsamic vinegar in a large bowl and mix well. Season with salt and pepper.

TO ASSEMBLE THE WRAPS:

3. Spoon some of the baba ghanoush onto the bottom of one of the lettuce leaves. Top with some of the marinated tomatoes. Roll the leaf up and over the filling. Repeat for the remaining lettuce leaves.

Fava Bean Wraps

FAVA BEAN SPREAD, similar to Hummus (page 139) but thinner, is often served warm. It can also be eaten as a soup, or used a sauce for pasta. It works in this recipe as a thicker spread that will hold up to the lettuce, so use only a small amount of water when making the spread.

SERVES 4

> 1½ cups Fava Bean Spread (page 140)
> 8 romaine lettuce leaves
> 1 batch Tomato, Cucumber and Mint Salad (see below)

Place some of the fava bean spread in the center of one of the lettuce leaves. Top with some of the tomato salad. Fold the leaf in from the sides and roll it up like a cigar. Repeat for the remaining lettuce leaves.

Tomato, Cucumber and Mint Salad

> 2 large tomatoes, diced
> 2 large cucumbers, peeled, halved, seeded, and diced
> 2 green onions (white and green parts), thinly sliced
> ¼ cup balsamic vinegar
> 3 tablespoons finely chopped mint
> Salt and freshly ground black pepper to taste

Combine the tomatoes, cucumbers, green onions, balsamic vinegar, and mint in a bowl and mix well. Season with salt and pepper. Let sit for 30 minutes before serving.

Thai Portobello Wraps

THIS VERSION OF a popular Thai street food is made with minced mushrooms, stir-fried with shallots, and combined with many traditional Thai ingredients—mint, cilantro, ginger, soy sauce, and lime. You can also substitute cremini mushrooms if portobello mushrooms aren't available.

SERVES 4

1 tablespoon grated ginger

2 cloves garlic, peeled and minced

Zest and juice of 1 lime

3 tablespoons low-sodium soy sauce

1 teaspoon crushed red pepper flakes

2 large shallots, diced small

1 pound portobello mushrooms, stemmed and finely chopped

½ cup coarsely chopped cilantro

3 tablespoons finely chopped mint

4 green onions (white and green parts), thinly sliced

4 large romaine lettuce leaves or 8 small ones

1. Combine the ginger, garlic, lime zest and juice, soy sauce, and crushed red pepper flakes in a small bowl and set aside.
2. Heat a large skillet over high heat. Add the shallots and mushrooms and stir-fry for 3 to 4 minutes. Add water 1 to 2 tablespoons at a time to keep the vegetables from sticking to the pan. Add the ginger mixture and cook for another minute. Add the cilantro, mint, and green onions and remove from the heat.
3. To serve, place some of the mushroom mixture on the bottom of one the lettuce leaves and fold the lettuce over the filling. Repeat for the remaining lettuce leaves.

Tortilla Wraps

Easy Bean and Rice Wraps

A HEALTHY MEAL gets no easier than this, especially if you use leftover rice. Make it even healthier by serving it on mixed greens or in a lettuce wrap. Feel free to adjust the heat of the salsa used in this recipe to your taste.

SERVES 4

> 2 cups cooked brown rice (see page 6)
> 2 cups cooked black beans (see page 6), or one 15-ounce can, drained and rinsed
> ⅔ cup Fresh Tomato Salsa (page 26)
> 3 tablespoons fresh lime juice
> ½ teaspoon salt, or to taste
> 1 clove garlic, peeled and minced
> 3 tablespoons finely chopped cilantro
> 4 whole wheat tortillas

1. Combine the rice, beans, salsa, lime juice, salt, garlic, and cilantro in a large bowl.
2. Place 1 heaping cup of the rice mixture in the center of one of the tortillas. Fold the sides in over the filling and roll the tortilla up like a cigar. Repeat for the remaining tortillas.

Portobello Mushroom Tacos 📷

GRILLED MUSHROOMS MAKE a great filling for any number of wraps or tacos, and they're so flavorful that you don't need a lot to accompany them.

SERVES 4

> 12 corn tortillas
> 1 batch Grilled Portobello Mushrooms (page 173), cut into ¾-inch-wide strips
> 1 batch Salsa Verde (page 26)
> Diced red onion
> Shredded romaine lettuce

1. Heat the tortillas one at a time on a dry, nonstick skillet over medium heat, turning frequently, until they are soft and pliable.
2. To serve, put a few of the mushroom strips in the center of a tortilla and top with some of the salsa verde. Garnish with the red onion and romaine lettuce. Fold the tortilla in half over the filling. Repeat for the remaining tortillas.

Veggie Fajitas

WHEN I MAKE fajitas I always feel like I've won a prize. They taste "special" without taking all day in the kitchen. Cooking the vegetables in a dry pan over high heat really brings out the grilled flavor of the vegetables.

SERVES 4

12 corn tortillas

1 small red onion, peeled and thinly sliced

1 medium red bell pepper, seeded and julienned

1 batch Grilled Portobello Mushrooms (page 173), cut into ¾-inch-wide strips

½ teaspoon ground cumin

1 jalapeño pepper, seeded and diced small

3 cloves garlic, peeled and minced

¼ cup chopped cilantro

2 tablespoons fresh lime juice

½ teaspoon salt, or to taste

Not-So-Fat Guacamole (page 27)

Tofu Sour Cream (page 28)

Fresh Tomato Salsa (page 26)

1. Wrap the tortillas in aluminum foil and place in a 350°F oven while you prepare the remaining ingredients.
2. Sauté the onion and red pepper in a large skillet over high heat for 5 minutes. Add water 1 to 2 tablespoons at a time to keep the vegetables from sticking to the pan. Add the grilled mushroom strips, cumin, jalapeño pepper, garlic, cilantro, lime juice, and salt and cook for another minute. Remove from the heat.
3. Serve the fajita mixture with the warmed tortillas, guacamole, tofu sour cream, and salsa.

Spreads

Roasted Red Pepper Spread

I OFTEN MAKE this spread with tofu, but white beans are lower in fat and provide more fiber. This spread is great in lettuce wraps with fresh sprouts and chopped green onion.

MAKES 2 CUPS

> 2 cups cooked great northern beans (see page 6), or one 15-ounce can, drained and rinsed
>
> 1 red bell pepper, roasted (see page 8), seeded, and coarsely chopped
>
> 3 cloves garlic, peeled and minced
>
> 3 tablespoons finely chopped dill
>
> Zest and juice of 1 lemon
>
> Salt to taste
>
> Pinch cayenne pepper

Combine all ingredients in the bowl of a food processor and puree until smooth and creamy.

Hummus

HUMMUS IS A classic condiment and spread from the Middle East, and it goes well with many dishes. Although it's often made with oil, this healthy version uses only lemon juice and garlic to spark up the texture of the chickpeas.

MAKES 1½ CUPS

> 2 cups cooked chickpeas (see page 6), or one 15-ounce can, drained and rinsed
>
> 4 cloves garlic, peeled and chopped
>
> Zest and juice of 1 lemon
>
> 1 teaspoon cumin seeds, toasted (see page 10) and ground
>
> Salt to taste

Combine all ingredients in the bowl of a food processor and puree until smooth and creamy. Add water as needed to achieve a smooth consistency.

Fava Bean Spread

THIS RECIPE IS similar to Hummus (page 139), but the silky texture of the fava beans provides a creamier spread than you can achieve with most other beans.

MAKES ABOUT 3½ CUPS

>   4 cups cooked fava beans (see page 6), or two 15-ounce cans, drained and rinsed
>   8 cloves garlic, peeled and chopped
>   Zest of 1 lemon and juice of 2 lemons
>   1 teaspoon cumin seeds, toasted (see page 10) and ground
>   Salt to taste

Combine the fava beans, garlic, lemon zest and juice, cumin, salt, and 1 cup of water in the bowl of a food processor and puree until smooth and creamy. Add more water as needed to achieve a smooth consistency.

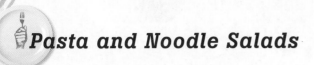

Pasta and Noodle Salads

Spring Pasta Salad

LET THIS BE the first pasta salad of the spring when asparagus and sugar snap peas are fresh in the farmers' market. Use fresh chives from the garden if you have them.

SERVES 4

> ½ pound asparagus, trimmed and cut into ½-inch pieces
> ½ pound sugar snap peas, trimmed
> 12 ounces whole-grain penne, cooked according to package directions, drained, and rinsed until cool
> One 15-ounce can artichoke hearts (oil-free), drained and quartered
> 4 green onions (white and green parts), thinly sliced
> ¼ cup finely chopped chives
> ¼ cup plus 2 tablespoons balsamic vinegar
> 1 tablespoon Dijon mustard
> Salt and freshly ground black pepper to taste

1. Prepare an ice bath by filling a large bowl with ice and cold water. Bring a 2-quart pot of water to a boil, add the asparagus and sugar snap peas, and cook for 3 minutes, then drain the vegetables and plunge them into the ice bath. Drain the vegetables again and combine them with the cooked pasta, artichoke hearts, green onions, and chives.
2. In a small bowl, combine the balsamic vinegar, Dijon mustard, and salt and pepper.
3. Pour the dressing over the pasta mixture and toss well.

Creamy Basil Pasta Salad

THIS PASTA DISH is my grown-up version of macaroni salad. The fresh basil and toasted pine nuts give it zing, and best of all, the homemade mayonnaise makes the dish creamy without the guilt.

SERVES 4

> 12 ounces whole-grain penne, cooked according to package directions, drained, and rinsed until cool
> One 15-ounce can artichoke hearts (oil-free), drained and halved
> 1 pint cherry or grape tomatoes, halved if large
> ¼ cup pine nuts, toasted (see page 10), optional
> 1 cup Mayonnaise (page 28)
> 1½ cups finely chopped basil
> Salt and freshly ground black pepper to taste

Combine everything except the salt and pepper in a large bowl and mix well. Season with salt and pepper and chill for 1 hour before serving.

Macaroni Salad

THE ALL-AMERICAN PASTA salad gets a healthy makeover with homemade mayonnaise. Take this dish to any picnic and don't tell a soul how healthy it is—no one will know the difference.

SERVES 4

3 cups (12 ounces) whole-grain elbow macaroni, cooked according to package directions, drained, and rinsed until cool
3 celery stalks, thinly sliced
1 large red bell pepper, seeded and diced
1 medium red onion, peeled and diced
1 cup Mayonnaise (page 28)
1½ tablespoons prepared mustard
Salt and freshly ground black pepper to taste

In a large bowl, combine the cooked macaroni, celery, red pepper, and red onion. Add the mayonnaise and mustard to the pasta mixture and toss well to coat. Season with salt and black pepper. Chill for 1 hour before serving.

VARIATION

▶ Add 2 cups of cherry tomatoes, 1 large cucumber (peeled, halved, seeded, and thinly sliced), and ¼ cup of chopped dill to the pasta mixture before adding the mayonnaise and mustard.

Ponzu Noodle Salad 📷

PONZU IS A soy and citrus sauce popular in Japanese cooking. Use it to dress up simple vegetable and rice dishes, or use it as a sauce for stir-fries. Make this dish in the spring when snow peas and cilantro are in season. Brown rice noodles can be found in most grocery stores, natural food stores, or online.

SERVES 4

1 pound brown rice noodles
½ pound snow peas, trimmed and cut into matchsticks
3 medium carrots, peeled and cut into matchsticks
3 green onions (white and green parts), cut into ¾-inch pieces
½ cup coarsely chopped cilantro
½ cup Ponzu Sauce (page 35)
½ teaspoon crushed red pepper flakes, optional

Cook the brown rice noodles according to package directions, adding the snow peas and carrots during the last minute of cooking. Drain and rinse the mixture until cooled and place it in a large bowl. Add the green onions, cilantro, ponzu sauce, and crushed red pepper flakes (if using). Mix well before serving.

Indonesian Noodle Salad

COOL VEGETABLES MEET a hot and spicy chili sauce in this fresh salad. Serve this alongside mixed greens for a filling meal.

SERVES 4

12 ounces brown rice noodles, cooked according to package directions, drained, and rinsed until cool

2 medium cucumbers, peeled, halved, seeded, and sliced thinly on the diagonal

2 heads baby bok choy, trimmed and thinly sliced

1 cup snow peas, trimmed and sliced in half on the diagonal

4 green onions (white and green parts), trimmed and thinly sliced

¼ cup fresh lime juice

½ cup chopped cilantro

¼ cup finely chopped mint

3 tablespoons sambal oelek (see note), or to taste

2 tablespoons low-sodium soy sauce, or to taste

Combine all ingredients in a large bowl and mix well.

NOTE ▶ Sambal oelek is an Indonesian chili sauce available in the Asian section of most supermarkets.

Mango Pasta Salad

EASTERN FLAVORS COME to the West in this unusual pasta salad made with fresh mango and mango chutney. The chutney, Thai red chili paste, and Thai chiles give this dish lots of kick, while the fresh mango and red bell pepper cool it down.

SERVES 4

1 pound whole-grain rotini, cooked according to package directions, drained, and rinsed until cool

1 medium red bell pepper, seeded and diced small

2 mangoes, peeled, seeded, and chopped

6 green onions (white and green parts), thinly sliced

1 cup chopped cilantro

½ cup Mayonnaise (page 28)

½ cup Mango Chutney (page 32)

1 Thai red pepper, thinly sliced

2 teaspoons Thai red curry paste, dissolved in 2 tablespoons hot water

Combine all ingredients in a large bowl and mix well. Chill until ready to serve.

Grilled Vegetable Pasta Salad with Pineapple Chutney

THE PINEAPPLE CHUTNEY (page 33) makes an unusual but delicious dressing for this salad.

SERVES 6

> 1 batch Grilled Vegetable Kabobs (page 172), skewers removed, vegetables cooled to room temperature
>
> 1 cup Pineapple Chutney (page 33), or to taste
>
> 12 ounces whole-grain penne, cooked according to package directions, drained, and rinsed until cool
>
> ½ cup chopped cilantro
>
> 4 green onions (white and green parts), thinly sliced

Place the vegetables in a large bowl. Add the pineapple chutney, cooked pasta, cilantro, and green onions and mix well.

Kimchi Noodle Salad 📷

KIMCHI IS A fermented condiment that can be made from any number of vegetables. In this recipe, I like to use a very spicy cabbage kimchi, and I recommend you do, too. Taste your kimchi first and use less of it if you want a milder salad, and certainly feel free to add more if you want to give the dish more kick. Kimchi is often made with shellfish or other animal ingredients, so be sure to look for a vegan brand for this recipe. Both kimchi and gochujang (Korean chile paste) are available in the Asian section of grocery stores or online.

SERVES 4

> 1 pound brown rice noodles, cooked according to package directions, drained, and rinsed until cool
>
> 2½ cups chopped cabbage kimchi
>
> 3 to 4 tablespoons gochujang
>
> 1 cup mung bean sprouts (see page 71)
>
> 4 green onions (white and green parts), thinly sliced
>
> 1 medium cucumber, halved, seeded and thinly sliced
>
> 2 tablespoons sesame seeds, toasted (see page 10)

1. Place the rice noodles, kimchi, gochujang, and mung bean sprouts in a large bowl and mix well.
2. To serve, divide the mixture among 4 individual plates and garnish each with the green onions, cucumber slices, and sesame seeds.

Banana Granola Parfait
(page 46)

Breakfast Quinoa with Apple Compote (page 50)

CLOCKWISE FROM THE LEFT: Very Berry Smoothie (page 38), **Chunky Monkey Smoothie** (page 40) and **Mean Green Smoothie** (page 37)

Portobello Florentine
(page 56)

Rice Salad with Fennel, Orange and Chickpeas
(page 60)

Spicy Asian Quinoa Salad
(page 63)

Winter White Bean Salad (page 73)
with **Spicy Cilantro Pesto** (page 24)

**Purple Potato and Kale Salad with
Cilantro-Tahini Dressing** (page 77)

Taco Salad with Cilantro-Lime Dressing (page 74)

Spinach Vichyssoise (page 88)

Lotsa Vegetable Chowder
(page 94)

Thai Noodle Soup (page 106)

**Quick and Easy Thai Vegetable
Stew** (page 109)

Pumpkin and Anasazi Bean Stew (page 120)

Baba Ghanoush Wraps with Marinated Tomatoes (page 134)

Portobello Mushroom Tacos (page 137)
with **Salsa Verde** (page 26)

Ponzu Noodle Salad (page 142)

Kimchi Noodle Salad (page 144)

Mushroom Stroganoff (page 152)

Soba Noodles in Kombu Broth (page 162)

Stir-Fried Vegetables with Miso and Sake (page 170), served with quinoa

Vegetable White Bean Hash (page 182)

Eggplant Rollatini (page 196)

Millet-Stuffed Chard Rolls (page 199)
with **Roasted Red Pepper Sauce** (page 25)

Hearty Nachos
(page 205), with
baked tortilla chips

Chana Saag
(page 213)

Curried Millet Cakes with Red Pepper Coriander Sauce (page 238),
topped with **Coriander Chutney** (page 32)

Barley and Sweet Potato Pilaf (page 245)

Southwestern Mac and "Cheese"
(page 252)

Eggplant Polenta Casserole (page 258)

Nutty Raspberry Thumbprint Cookies
(page 271), **Almond Anise Biscotti** (page 275)
and **Apricot Fig Squares** (page 280)

FROM LEFT TO RIGHT: Whole Wheat Berry Muffins (page 289), **Ginger Peach Muffins** (page 287) and **Double Chocolate Cupcakes** (page 285) with **Fudgy Chocolate Frosting** (page 286)

Bursting with Berries Cobbler (page 298)

Cold Soba Noodles with Orange Miso Dressing

SOBA NOODLES ARE thin Japanese noodles made from buckwheat and served in cold salads, with a dipping sauce, or in a hot broth. This recipe comes together in less than 20 minutes, most of which are spent cooking the noodles. While you wait, cut up and steam a head of broccoli to serve alongside.

SERVES 4

3 tablespoons mellow white miso

Zest of 1 orange and juice of 2 oranges

3 tablespoons grated ginger

½ teaspoon crushed red pepper flakes, or to taste

1 pound soba noodles, cooked according to package directions, drained, and rinsed until cool

¼ cup chopped cilantro

4 green onions (white and green parts), chopped

Place the miso, orange zest and juice, ginger, and crushed red pepper flakes in a large bowl and whisk well to combine. Add water as needed to make a pourable sauce. Add the cooked noodles and mix well. Serve garnished with the cilantro and green onions.

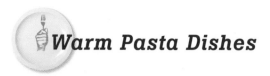 *Warm Pasta Dishes*

Spaghetti with No-Cook Tomato Sauce

THIS IS A perfect summer dish when tomatoes and basil are in season, and with no long-cooking sauce, you spend little time in a hot kitchen.

SERVES 4

Zest and juice of 2 lemons

6 cloves garlic, peeled and minced

1 cup finely chopped basil

3 medium tomatoes, chopped

3 ears corn, kernels removed (about 2 cups)

1 pound spaghetti, cooked according to package directions, drained, and kept warm

Salt and freshly ground black pepper to taste

Combine the lemon zest and juice, garlic, basil, tomatoes, and corn in a large bowl. Add the cooked pasta and toss well. Season with salt and pepper.

Penne with Chickpeas and Spinach

WHITE WINE, SUN-DRIED tomatoes, and fresh dill make an otherwise ordinary pasta dish really special.

SERVES 4

1 medium yellow onion, peeled and diced

4 cloves garlic, peeled and minced

½ cup dry white wine

6 sun-dried tomatoes, soaked for 15 minutes in hot water, drained, and chopped

½ pound baby spinach

¼ cup chopped dill

2 cups cooked chickpeas (see page 6), or one 15-ounce can, drained and rinsed

12 ounces whole-grain penne, cooked according to package directions, drained, and kept warm

Salt and freshly ground black pepper to taste

Place the onion in a large skillet or saucepan and sauté over medium heat for 10 minutes. Add water 1 to 2 tablespoons at a time to keep the onion from sticking to the pan. Add the garlic and cook for 3 minutes. Add the white wine and sun-dried tomatoes and cook until almost all the liquid has evaporated. Add the spinach, dill, and chickpeas and cook until the spinach is wilted. Remove from the heat. Add the cooked pasta, mix well, and season with salt and pepper.

Penne with Broccoli Rabe

BROCCOLI RABE, ALSO known as rapini, is a popular vegetable in southern Italian cooking, often sautéed with garlic and crushed red pepper flakes. Toasted pine nuts are a great addition to many dishes and golden raisins add a contrasting sweetness to the bite of the vegetable.

SERVES 4

1 medium yellow onion, peeled and thinly sliced

1 pound broccoli rabe, trimmed and cut into 1-inch pieces

4 cloves garlic, peeled and minced

Zest and juice of 2 lemons

½ teaspoon crushed red pepper flakes

¼ cup golden raisins

¼ cup nutritional yeast, optional

1 pound whole-grain penne, cooked according to package directions, drained, and kept warm,
 ¼ cup cooking liquid reserved

Salt and freshly ground black pepper to taste

¼ cup pine nuts, toasted (see page 10)

½ cup chopped basil

Place the onion in a large skillet over medium-high heat and sauté for 10 minutes, or until the onion starts to brown. Add water 1 to 2 tablespoons at a time to keep the onion from sticking to the pan. Add the broccoli rabe and cook, stirring frequently, until the rabe is tender, about 5 minutes. Add the garlic, lemon zest and juice, crushed red pepper flakes, raisins, nutritional yeast (if using), and the cooked pasta and reserved cooking water. Remove from the heat. Mix well and season with salt and pepper. Serve garnished with the pine nuts and basil.

Pesto Pasta with White Beans

THIS QUICK AND easy pasta dish takes only about as long to put together as it takes to cook the pasta itself. White beans make it a more filling dish, but you could use steamed asparagus in place of the beans for a lighter version. One of my favorite pesto recipes is one made with equal parts basil, tarragon, and arugula, so feel free to try that variation as well for an unusual twist on the classic sauce.

SERVES 4

> 12 ounces whole-grain spaghetti, cooked according to package directions, drained, and kept warm,
>   ½ cup cooking liquid reserved
> 1 cup Basil Pesto (page 24)
> 2 cups cooked cannellini beans (see page 6), or one 15-ounce can, drained and rinsed

Place the cooked spaghetti in a large bowl and add the pesto. Add enough of the reserved cooking liquid to achieve a creamy sauce. Add the beans and toss well.

Rigatoni Antipasti

KALAMATA OLIVES HAVE much more flavor than canned black olives, and many grocery stores now have olive bars where you can choose from a variety of olives, from Niçoise to garlic-stuffed. You could almost make this dish from an Italian antipasto bar, except this version doesn't contain all the additional oil.

SERVES 4

> 5 cloves garlic, peeled and minced
> 2 tablespoons tomato paste
> 2 large tomatoes, diced small
> ½ cup dry white wine
> 1 tablespoon oregano
> 1 cup kalamata olives, pitted and halved
> One 15-ounce can artichoke hearts (oil-free), drained and halved
> 1 pound whole-grain rigatoni, cooked according to package directions, drained, and kept warm
> Salt and freshly ground black pepper to taste
> Chopped parsley

Place the garlic in a large skillet or saucepan and sauté over low heat for 5 minutes. Add water 1 to 2 tablespoons at a time to keep the garlic from sticking to the pan. Raise the heat to medium and add the tomato paste, tomatoes, white wine, and oregano and cook for 12 to 15 minutes, or until the liquid is reduced by half. Add the olives, artichokes, and cooked pasta, mix well, and cook for another 5 minutes. Season with salt and pepper. Serve garnished with the parsley.

Penne with Roasted Red Pepper Sauce

ROASTING AND THEN pureeing red peppers intensifies their flavor, which makes them really stand out in this bright pasta dish. The Roasted Red Pepper Sauce and fresh basil are a natural pairing, but you could also use herbs like tarragon or fresh dill.

SERVES 4

- **1 large yellow onion, peeled and cut into ½-inch half-rings**
- **1 large head broccoli, cut into florets**
- **3 cloves garlic, peeled and minced**
- **Salt and freshly ground black pepper to taste**
- **1 pound penne, cooked according to package instructions, drained, and kept warm**
- **1½ cups Roasted Red Pepper Sauce (page 25)**
- **½ cup basil chiffonade (see page 7)**

1. Place the onion and broccoli in a large skillet and sauté over medium-high heat for 7 to 8 minutes. Add water 1 to 2 tablespoons a time to keep the vegetables from sticking to the pan.
2. Add the garlic to the onion mixture and season with salt and pepper. Add the pasta and the red pepper sauce to the pan and mix well, stirring until heated through. Serve garnished with the basil chiffonade.

Penne with Spicy Eggplant

I LIKE TO peel the eggplants for this dish so that the vegetable cooks down into the sauce. If you want firm pieces of eggplant in your dish, leave them unpeeled.

SERVES 4

- **1 medium yellow onion, peeled and diced**
- **2 medium eggplants (about 1½ pounds), stemmed, peeled, quartered, and cut into ½-inch pieces**
- **6 cloves garlic, peeled and minced**
- **2 teaspoons minced oregano**
- **1 teaspoon crushed red pepper flakes, or to taste**
- **One 28-ounce can diced tomatoes**
- **2 tablespoons red wine vinegar**
- **Salt to taste**
- **1 pound penne, cooked according to package directions, drained, and kept warm**
- **½ cup chopped basil**

Place the onion in a large saucepan and sauté over medium heat for 10 minutes. Add water 1 to 2 tablespoons at a time to keep the onion from sticking to the pan. Add the eggplant and cook, stirring constantly, for 5 minutes, adding water only when the eggplant starts to stick to the pan. Add the garlic, oregano, and crushed red pepper flakes and cook for 30 seconds. Add the tomatoes and red wine vinegar and cook, covered, for 10 minutes. Season with salt. Remove from the heat, add the pasta, and toss well. Garnish with the basil.

Penne with Tomato "Alfredo" Sauce

I'VE MADE THIS dish in the spring, when dill is fresh in the garden, and in the summer, when basil is abundant. It is delicious no matter what herbs you choose.

SERVES 4

> 2 large shallots, peeled and minced
> 3 cloves garlic, peeled and minced
> 3 large tomatoes, peeled (see page 7), seeded, and diced
> 1 batch No-Cheese Sauce (page 29)
> 1 pound whole-grain penne, cooked according to package directions, drained, and kept warm
> ½ cup finely chopped herbs, such as chives, tarragon, basil, or dill
> Salt and freshly ground black pepper to taste

1. Place the shallots in a large saucepan and sauté over medium heat for 7 minutes. Add water 1 to 2 tablespoons at a time to keep the shallots from sticking to the pan. Add the garlic and cook for 4 minutes. Add the tomatoes and cook for 10 to 12 minutes, or until they start to release their juices. Add the No-Cheese Sauce and cook until heated through.
2. Place the cooked pasta in a large bowl with the fresh herbs. Add the warm sauce and toss well. Season with salt and pepper.

Penne with Spinach Béchamel

HERE'S A GREAT way to get two vegetables on the dinner table in a way that no one will object to. The béchamel sauce, made with pureed cauliflower, is worth the effort it takes to cook and puree. I bet that if you don't tell anyone this "cream" sauce is actually a vegetable, they won't know the difference.

SERVES 4

1 large head cauliflower, cut into florets

Unsweetened plain almond milk, as needed

¼ cup nutritional yeast, optional

¼ teaspoon ground nutmeg

Salt and freshly ground black pepper to taste

1 medium yellow onion, peeled and diced small

2 cloves garlic, peeled and minced

2 teaspoons minced thyme

¼ cup finely chopped basil

4 cups chopped spinach, cooked until wilted

1 pound penne, cooked according to package directions, drained, and kept warm

1. Add the cauliflower to a large pot and add enough water to cover. Bring to a boil over high heat and cook until the cauliflower is very tender, about 10 minutes. Drain the excess water from the pan and puree the cauliflower using an immersion blender or in a blender with a tight-fitting lid, covered with a towel, in batches if necessary. Add almond milk 1 tablespoon at a time, as needed, to achieve a creamy consistency. Add the nutritional yeast (if using), nutmeg, and salt and pepper. Set the puree aside.

2. Place the onion in a large saucepan and sauté over medium heat for 10 minutes. Add water 1 to 2 tablespoons at a time to keep the onion from sticking to the pan. Add the garlic, thyme, and basil and cook for another minute. Add the spinach and cooked pasta and cook for 5 minutes, or until heated through.

3. To serve, divide the pasta mixture among 4 plates and top with the warm cauliflower puree.

Mushroom Stroganoff 📷

STROGANOFF ORIGINATED IN Russia as a beef dish served in a rich sour cream sauce. And though there are many versions of the original recipe, I prefer this plant-based one, made with earthy porcini mushrooms and lots of fresh herbs.

SERVES 4

2 large shallots, peeled and minced

4 cloves garlic, peeled and minced

2 teaspoons minced thyme

Salt and freshly ground black pepper to taste

1 teaspoon minced rosemary

1 pound portobello mushrooms, stemmed and cut into large pieces

1 ounce porcini mushrooms, soaked for 30 minutes in 1 cup of water that has just been boiled, and roughly chopped

½ cup dry white wine

1 cup Tofu Sour Cream (page 28)

1 pound whole-grain fettuccine, cooked according to package directions, drained, and kept warm

Chopped parsley

1. Place the shallots in a large skillet and sauté over a medium heat for 8 minutes. Add water 1 to 2 tablespoons at a time to keep the shallots from sticking to the pan. Add the garlic and thyme and cook for another minute. Stir in the salt and pepper, rosemary, and portobello mushrooms and cook for 10 minutes, stirring occasionally. Add the porcini mushrooms and their soaking liquid. Add the wine, stir, and cook over medium-low heat for 20 minutes.

2. When the stroganoff is finished cooking, stir in the sour cream. Add the cooked noodles and toss well. Serve garnished with the parsley.

Cauliflower-Cream Pasta

PUREED CAULIFLOWER MAKES one of my favorite "cream" sauces. Not only is it a fat-free option, but it is also full of flavor, adapts well to whatever seasonings you add to it, and adds another serving of vegetables to the dish.

SERVES 4

1 medium head cauliflower, cut into florets

2 cups Vegetable Stock (page 23), or low-sodium vegetable broth

1 medium yellow onion, peeled and diced

1 medium red bell pepper, seeded and diced

4 cloves garlic, peeled and minced

4 minced sage leaves

1 small butternut squash (about 1 pound), peeled, halved, seeded, and cut into ½-inch cubes

1 pound whole-grain penne, cooked according to package directions, drained, and kept warm

Salt and freshly ground black pepper to taste

1. Combine the cauliflower and vegetable stock in a medium saucepan and bring it to a boil. Cook over medium heat for 10 minutes, or until the cauliflower is very tender. Remove from the heat and puree the sauce using an immersion blender or in a blender with a tight-fitting lid, covered with a towel, until smooth and creamy. Set aside.

2. Place the onion and red pepper in a large saucepan and sauté over medium heat for 7 to 8 minutes. Add water 1 to 2 tablespoons at a time to keep the vegetables from sticking to the pan. Add the garlic, sage, and squash and cook for 5 to 6 minutes, or until the squash is tender. Add the cauliflower puree, stirring until heated through, then add the cooked pasta. Toss well to combine. Season with salt and pepper.

VARIATION

▶ To turn this into a six-vegetable pasta dish—or if butternut squash is not in season—in place of the sage and squash, with the garlic add 1 head of broccoli, cut into florets, and cook for 5 minutes. Add 1 medium zucchini, diced, and the corn kernels from 3 ears (about 2 cups). Cook until the broccoli is tender, about 5 minutes. Add the cauliflower puree and cooked pasta, toss to combine, and season with salt and pepper.

Rigatoni with Peas and Curried Cream Sauce

CAULIFLOWER MAY BECOME your new favorite vegetable, no longer the leftover pile on the crudités tray at parties. It makes a delicious sauce, taking on the flavor of whatever you add to it. If you don't believe me, also try the Spinach and Sweet Potato Lasagna (page 267) or Moussaka (page 264).

SERVES 4

1 large head cauliflower, cut into florets

2 cups Vegetable Stock (page 23), or low-sodium vegetable broth

2 large shallots, peeled and diced small

2 cloves garlic, peeled and minced

1 tablespoon curry powder

1 teaspoon crushed red pepper flakes

Salt to taste

2 cups peas

1 pound whole-grain rigatoni, cooked according to package directions, drained, and kept warm

½ cup chopped cilantro

1. Combine the cauliflower and vegetable stock in a medium saucepan and bring to a boil. Cook for 10 minutes, or until the cauliflower is very tender. Remove from the heat and puree the sauce using an immersion blender or in a blender with a tight-fitting lid, covered with a towel, in batches if necessary, until smooth and creamy.

2. Place the shallots in a large saucepan and sauté over medium heat for 7 to 8 minutes. Add water 1 to 2 tablespoons at a time to keep the shallots from sticking to the pan. Add the garlic and cook for 4 minutes. Add the curry powder and crushed red pepper flakes and cook for another minute, then season with salt. Add the pureed cauliflower and the peas and cook until heated through, about 5 minutes. Add the cooked pasta to the pan and toss well. Serve garnished with the cilantro.

Penne with Swiss Chard, Olives and Currants

SALTY, PUNGENT OLIVES and sweet currants contrast with each other in this dish while mild, earthy chard pulls it all together.

SERVES 4

4 large shallots, peeled and diced small

2 bunches Swiss chard, ribs removed and chopped, leaves chopped

4 cloves garlic, peeled and minced

2 teaspoons minced thyme

1 pound whole-grain penne, cooked according to package directions, drained, and kept warm,
   ½ cup cooking liquid reserved

Salt and freshly ground black pepper to taste

½ cup kalamata olives, pitted and coarsely chopped

½ cup dried currants

Place the shallots and chard ribs in a large saucepan and sauté over medium heat for 5 minutes. Add water 1 to 2 tablespoons at a time to keep the vegetables from sticking to the pan. Add the garlic and thyme and cook for another minute. Add half of the chard leaves and a few tablespoons of the reserved pasta cooking liquid and cook until the leaves start to wilt, adding more leaves as the chard cooks down, until all the leaves are wilted, about 10 minutes. Season with salt and pepper and add the olives, currants, and cooked pasta. Toss well before serving.

Sicilian Cauliflower Linguine

TRADITIONAL VERSIONS OF this dish are made with extra virgin olive oil—lots of it—and anchovies. This version is far healthier, but still packed with flavor. Plus, with a little bit of flavor-packed miso, you won't miss the fish.

SERVES 4

1 large head cauliflower, cut into florets

2 medium red onions, peeled, halved, and thinly sliced

4 cloves garlic, peeled and minced

2 tablespoons tomato paste

1 tablespoon mellow white miso, dissolved in 3 tablespoons hot water

½ cup golden raisins

Large pinch saffron, soaked for 10 minutes in water that has just been boiled

1 pound whole-grain linguine, cooked according to package directions, drained, and kept warm, ½ cup cooking liquid reserved

3 tablespoons pine nuts, toasted (see page 10)

Chopped parsley

1. Steam the cauliflower in a double boiler or steamer basket for 6 minutes, or until tender. Drain and rinse until cool. Set aside.
2. Place the red onions in a large saucepan and sauté over medium-high heat for 8 to 10 minutes, or until the onions are browned. Add water 1 to 2 tablespoons at a time to keep the onions from sticking to the pan. Add the garlic and tomato paste and cook for another minute. Add the dissolved miso, raisins, and saffron with its soaking liquid. Simmer the mixture for 2 minutes. Add the steamed cauliflower, stirring until heated through, and then add the cooked linguine. Toss well, adding reserved pasta cooking water as needed if the mixture is too thick. Serve garnished with the pine nuts and parsley.

Spaghetti with Squash Sauce

PUREED VEGETABLES MAKE great sauces. They are creamy without the cream, and full of flavor. Butternut squash is readily available all year long, but look for other varieties of this popular autumn vegetable when it's in season, especially at farmers' markets. Acorn, kabocha, and Hubbard are all interesting varieties and worth trying as well.

SERVES 4

1 medium butternut squash, peeled, halved, seeded, and cubed (about 3 cups)

Salt and freshly ground black pepper to taste

1 pound whole-grain spaghetti

2 large shallots, peeled and minced

3 tablespoons minced sage

¼ cup dry white wine

Unsweetened plain almond milk, as needed

Chopped parsley

1. Preheat the oven to 350°F.
2. Cut the squash in half lengthwise and scoop out the pulp and seeds. Line a baking sheet with parchment paper. Season the cut side of the squash with salt and pepper and place the squash, cut side down, on the prepared baking sheet. Bake for 50 to 60 minutes, or until the squash is tender. Remove the squash from the oven and let it cool. When the squash has cooled enough to handle, scoop out the flesh and place it in the bowl of a food processor. Process until smooth. Set it aside.
3. While the squash is baking, cook the pasta according to package directions. Drain and keep warm.
4. Place the shallots in a large skillet or saucepan and sauté over medium heat for 7 to 8 minutes. Add water 1 to 2 tablespoons at a time to keep the shallots from sticking to the pan. Add the sage and white wine and cook until the liquid is almost evaporated. Add the pureed squash and mix well. If the sauce is too thick, add almond milk a few tablespoons at a time to achieve the desired consistency. Season with salt and pepper.
5. To serve, divide the cooked pasta among 4 individual plates. Spoon some of the sauce over the pasta and garnish with the parsley.

Spaghetti with Lentil Ragu

RAGU IS USUALLY a richly flavored meat sauce served with pasta. This far healthier version, made with lentils, captures the all the flavor of the traditional sauce without the heaviness of a meat-based sauce.

SERVES 4

1 medium yellow onion, peeled and diced small

1 large carrot, peeled and diced small

1 large celery stalk, diced small

6 cloves garlic, peeled and minced

1 tablespoon minced rosemary

1 tablespoon minced thyme

1 cup green lentils, rinsed

3 cups Vegetable Stock (page 23), or low-sodium vegetable broth

1 bay leaf

2 large tomatoes, diced small

Salt and freshly ground black pepper to taste

1 pound whole-grain spaghetti, cooked according to package directions, drained, and kept warm

Chopped parsley

1. Place the onion, carrot, and celery in a large saucepan and sauté over medium heat for 10 minutes. Add water 1 to 2 tablespoons at a time to keep the vegetables from sticking to the pan. Add the garlic, rosemary, and thyme and cook for another minute.
2. Add the lentils, vegetable stock, and bay leaf. Increase the heat to high and bring the pan to a boil. Reduce the heat to medium, cover, and cook for 35 minutes.
3. Add the tomatoes to the lentil mixture and season with salt and pepper. Cook for 10 minutes, or until the lentils are tender.
4. Serve the lentil ragu over the cooked spaghetti and garnish with the parsley.

Spaghetti and "Meatballs"

THE CLASSIC ITALIAN-AMERICAN dish gets a healthy makeover with millet standing in for the meat. Make sure to shape these into balls immediately after mixing the millet with the onion mixture, since millet loses its binding power as it cools. Add the "meatballs" just before serving, as they fall will apart if left in the warm sauce too long.

SERVES 4

2 cups Vegetable Stock (page 23), or low-sodium vegetable broth

1 cup millet

½ teaspoon salt, or to taste

1 large yellow onion, peeled and diced small

6 cloves garlic, peeled and minced

½ cup minced basil

½ teaspoon freshly ground black pepper, or to taste

¼ cup tomato puree

2 tablespoons arrowroot powder or cornstarch

1 pound whole-grain spaghetti, cooked according to package directions, drained, and kept warm

2 cups Tomato Sauce (page 25), heated

1. Preheat the oven to 350°F.
2. Bring the vegetable stock to a boil in a medium saucepan. Add the millet and salt and bring the mixture back to a boil over high heat. Reduce the heat to medium and cook, covered, for 20 minutes, or until the millet is tender. Drain any excess water and keep warm.
3. Place the onion in a large saucepan and sauté over medium heat for 7 to 8 minutes. Add water 1 to 2 tablespoons at a time to keep the onion from sticking to the pan. Add the garlic, basil, and pepper and cook for another minute. Add the tomato puree and ¼ cup of water and cook until the liquid is almost evaporated, about 3 minutes.
4. Line a baking sheet with parchment paper.
5. Add the cooked millet and the arrowroot power to the onion mixture and mix well. Using an ice-cream scoop, shape the millet mixture into 2-inch balls and place on the prepared baking sheet. Bake for 10 to 12 minutes.
6. To serve, divide the spaghetti among 4 individual plates. Top with some of the "meatballs" and pour some of the tomato sauce over the prepared plates.

Penne with White Wine Mushroom Sauce

ADD CHOPPED FRESH dill to this dish for a little variation, or use shiitake or any other wild mushrooms in place of the button mushrooms. If you are not a mushroom lover, try this dish with fresh spinach or asparagus instead.

SERVES 4

½ **medium yellow onion, peeled and diced small**

1 **pound cremini or button mushrooms, thinly sliced**

3 **cloves garlic, peeled and minced**

1 **tablespoon minced thyme**

½ **teaspoon ground nutmeg**

1 **cup dry white wine**

Zest and juice of 1 lemon

Salt and freshly ground black pepper to taste

1 **batch No-Cheese Sauce (page 29)**

1 **pound whole-grain penne, cooked according to package directions, drained, and kept warm**

1. Place the onion and mushrooms in a large saucepan and sauté over medium heat for 7 to 8 minutes. Add water 1 to 2 tablespoons at a time to keep the onion from sticking to the pan. Add the garlic, thyme, and nutmeg and cook for 2 minutes. Reduce the heat to medium-low, add the wine and lemon zest and juice, and simmer until the liquid is reduced by half. Season with salt and pepper.
2. Add the No-Cheese Sauce and simmer for 5 minutes. Toss with the cooked pasta.

Warm Noodle Dishes

Stir-Fried Noodles with Spring Vegetables

GARLIC CHIVES ARE a gardener's favorite springtime herb, and they taste of both garlic *and* chives, just as the name implies. If you don't grow them and can't find them in your local market, use regular chives instead.

SERVES 4

½ medium yellow onion, peeled and thinly sliced

1 medium carrot, peeled and cut into matchsticks

½ pound asparagus, trimmed and cut into 1-inch pieces

1½ cups snow peas, trimmed

1 batch Chinese Brown Sauce (page 35)

½ pound brown rice noodles, cooked according to package directions, drained, and kept warm

½ cup chopped garlic chives

Freshly ground black pepper to taste

Heat a large skillet over high heat. Add the onion and stir-fry for 4 minutes, adding water 1 to 2 tablespoons at a time to keep the onion from sticking to the pan. Add the carrot, asparagus, and snow peas and cook for 3 minutes. Add the Chinese brown sauce and cook until heated through, about 2 minutes. Add the rice noodles and garlic chives, toss well, and cook for another minute. Season with pepper.

VARIATION

▶ For a Thai variation, replace the Chinese brown sauce with a sauce made with ¼ cup of Chinese Brown Sauce (page 35), 3 tablespoons of sweet chili sauce, and 3 table-spoons of fresh lime juice. Instead of the garlic chives, substitute 2 tablespoons of finely chopped mint leaves and ½ cup of chopped cilantro.

Soba Noodles in Kombu Broth 📷

NOODLES ARE VERY popular in Japanese cooking, whether served cold with dipping sauces or warmed in broth, like in this dish. The shiitake mushrooms and leeks in this recipe add richness to the broth, so if you can't find fresh shiitake mushrooms, use dried ones and soak them in warm water for about 15 minutes to reconstitute them. For a gluten-free option, seek out soba made from 100 percent buckwheat flour, or use brown rice noodles instead.

SERVES 4

> 12 cups Kombu Broth (page 34)
> 8 ounces shiitake mushrooms, thinly sliced
> 3 leeks (white and light green parts), thinly sliced and rinsed
> 1 carrot, peeled and cut into matchsticks
> ¼ cup low-sodium soy sauce, or to taste
> One 10- to 12-ounce package soba noodles, cooked according to package directions, drained, and
>   kept warm
> 1 bunch watercress, trimmed and chopped
> 4 green onions (white and green parts), thinly sliced on the diagonal

1. Bring the kombu broth to a boil in a large pot. Add the mushrooms, leeks, carrot, and soy sauce, reduce the heat, and simmer for 10 minutes.
2. To serve, divide the noodles and watercress evenly among 4 individual bowls. Pour the broth over the noodles and garnish with the green onions.

Vegetable Lo Mein

AS A KID I used to visit my mom after work and she would take me to eat at a Chinese restaurant near her office. Lo mein noodles were my favorite dish on the menu, but it was nearly twenty years before I learned to make them at home. They are worth the effort.

SERVES 2

> 2 tablespoons low-sodium soy sauce
> 2 tablespoons brown rice syrup
> 1 clove garlic, peeled and minced
> 1 medium yellow onion, peeled and thinly sliced
> 2 carrots, peeled and julienned
> 1 medium red bell pepper, seeded and julienned
> 1½ cups snow peas, trimmed
> 1 cup mung bean sprouts (see page 71)
> 8 ounces brown rice noodles, cooked according to package directions, drained, and kept warm

1. Combine the soy sauce, brown rice syrup, and garlic in a small bowl and set aside.
2. Heat a large skillet over high heat. Add the onion, carrots, and red pepper and stir-fry for 3 minutes. Add water 1 to 2 tablespoons at a time to keep the vegetables from sticking to the pan. Add the snow peas and stir-fry another 2 minutes. Add the mung bean sprouts, brown rice noodles, and soy sauce mixture and toss until heated through.

Peanut Noodles with Broccoli

RECIPE BY JULIEANNA HEVER

FOR A QUICK and satisfying meal, try this sweet and spicy entrée. You can also add more vegetables in addition to the broccoli depending on what you have in your fridge. Coconut water is the liquid found in young fresh coconuts, which can be extracted by driving a nail through the "eyes" of the coconut and letting the water drain out. You can also buy it in many grocery stores or just use water instead. Peanut butter is the classic ingredient in this dish, but feel free to try it with your favorite nut or seed butter.

SERVES 2

> **8 ounces brown rice noodles**
> **4 cups broccoli florets (from about 2 large heads)**
> **1 cup coconut water**
> **3 tablespoons peanut butter**
> **2 tablespoons 100% pure maple syrup**
> **2 tablespoons low-sodium soy sauce**
> **1 tablespoon minced fresh ginger**
> **½ teaspoon crushed red pepper flakes, or to taste**

1. In a medium pot, bring 6 to 8 cups water to a boil over medium-high heat. Once boiling, add the rice noodles and cook according to package instructions—usually 4 to 5 minutes, or until tender. Add the broccoli florets to the cooking water and cook for an additional minute. Drain the noodles and broccoli and set aside.
2. In a large pot over low heat, combine the coconut water, peanut butter, maple syrup, soy sauce, ginger, and crushed red pepper flakes. Stir continuously and cook until smooth, 8 to 10 minutes.
3. Add the noodle and broccoli mixture to the peanut sauce. Use tongs to mix well.

Indonesian "Fried" Noodles

THIS DISH IS another great example of a "fried" food that can taste great without all the oil and fat.

SERVES 3 TO 4

> 3 tablespoons low-sodium soy sauce
>
> 2 tablespoons date molasses or brown rice syrup
>
> 1 tablespoon tomato paste
>
> 1 to 2 tablespoons sambal oelek (see note on page 15), or to taste
>
> 3 cloves garlic, peeled and minced
>
> 1 medium yellow onion, peeled and cut into ½-inch slices
>
> 1 cup shredded cabbage
>
> 1 medium carrot, peeled and cut into matchsticks
>
> 12 ounces brown rice noodles, cooked according to package directions, drained, and kept warm
>
> 1 cup mung bean sprouts (see page 71)
>
> 4 green onions (white and green parts), thinly sliced

1. Combine the soy sauce, molasses, tomato paste, sambal oelek, and garlic in a small bowl and set aside.
2. Heat a large skillet over high heat. Add the onion, cabbage, and carrot and stir-fry for 2 to 3 minutes. Add water 1 to 2 tablespoons at a time to keep the vegetables from sticking to the pan. Add the soy sauce mixture and cook for 1 minute. Add the cooked noodles and mung bean sprouts and toss well. Serve garnished with the green onions.

Udon Noodle Stir-Fry

UDON NOODLES, A Japanese pasta made from wheat, have a different texture from soba noodles, which are made from buckwheat. Because of textural differences, soba noodles are not an ideal replacement for udon, but if you'd like to make the recipe gluten-free you can substitute brown rice noodles.

SERVES 4

> 1 medium yellow onion, peeled and cut into ½-inch slices
>
> 1 cup snow peas, trimmed and halved
>
> 2 cups fresh shiitake mushrooms, stems removed and thinly sliced
>
> ½ cup Chinese Brown Sauce (page 35)
>
> 1 pound udon or brown rice noodles, cooked according to package directions, drained, and kept warm
>
> 1 cup mung bean sprouts (see page 71)
>
> 6 green onions (white and green parts), cut into ½-inch pieces

Heat a large skillet over high heat. Add the onion and stir-fry for 2 to 3 minutes. Add water 1 to 2 tablespoons at a time to keep the onion from sticking to the pan. Add the snow peas and mushrooms and cook for 3 minutes. Stir in the Chinese brown sauce and cook for 1 minute. Add the cooked noodles and mung bean sprouts and toss well. Serve garnished with the green onions.

Singapore Noodles

MY VERSION HAS all of the flavor, but none of the unwanted fat, of this Chinese-restaurant favorite.

SERVES 2

1 small yellow onion, peeled and cut into ½-inch slices

2 medium carrots, peeled and cut into matchsticks

1 medium red bell pepper, seeded and cut into ½-inch slices

8 ounces shiitake mushrooms, stems removed

½ cup Vegetable Stock (page 23), or low-sodium vegetable broth

4 teaspoons low-sodium soy sauce, or to taste

1 tablespoon grated ginger

2 cloves garlic, peeled and minced

1 tablespoon curry powder, or to taste

4 ounces brown rice noodles, cooked according to the package directions, drained, and kept warm

Freshly ground black pepper to taste

Heat a large skillet over high heat. Add the onion, carrots, red pepper, and mushrooms and stir-fry for 3 to 4 minutes. Add water 1 to 2 tablespoons at a time to keep the vegetables from sticking to the pan. Add the vegetable broth, soy sauce, ginger, garlic, and curry powder and cook for 3 to 4 minutes. Add the cooked noodles, toss well, and season with black pepper.

Noodles with Curried Red Lentil Sauce

RED LENTILS COOK quickly and have more flavor than most lentils. Their creamy texture makes them an ideal ingredient in pasta sauces. The brown rice noodles I use here are gluten-free, and like other gluten-free noodles and pastas, they tend to get mushy if they sit around in a warm sauce, so be sure to add the sauce just before serving. There are many types of curry powder on the market, so use your favorite in this dish.

SERVES 4

> 3 cups Vegetable Stock (page 23), or low-sodium vegetable broth
> 1 cup red lentils, rinsed
> 1 medium red onion, peeled and diced small
> 2 tablespoons plus 2 teaspoons curry powder, or to taste
> 6 cups packed baby spinach
> Zest and juice of 2 lemons
> ½ teaspoon crushed red pepper flakes, optional
> Salt and freshly ground black pepper to taste
> 1 pound brown rice noodles, cooked according to package directions, drained, and kept warm
> Finely chopped cilantro

1. Bring the vegetable stock to a boil in a medium saucepan over medium-high heat. Add the lentils and cook for 20 to 25 minutes, or until the lentils are tender but not mushy.
2. Place the onion in a large skillet and stir-fry over medium heat for 7 to 8 minutes, or until the onion starts to brown. Add water 1 to 2 tablespoons at a time to keep the onion from sticking to the pan. Stir in the curry powder and spinach and cook until the spinach wilts, about 5 minutes. Add the cooked lentils, lemon zest and juice, and crushed red pepper flakes (if using) and season with salt and pepper.
3. To serve, divide the noodles among 4 individual plates. Spoon some of the lentil sauce over the noodles and garnish with the cilantro.

Five-Spice Noodles

CHINESE FIVE SPICE powder is a popular seasoning for any number of meat or vegetable dishes. Made from star anise, cinnamon, Szechuan pepper, fennel, and cloves, a little of this pungent spice goes a long way.

SERVES 3 TO 4

½ cup Chinese Brown Sauce (page 35)

¾ teaspoon Chinese five-spice powder

¼ teaspoon crushed red pepper flakes

2 medium carrots, peeled and cut into matchsticks

1 medium onion, peeled and thinly sliced

1 medium head broccoli, cut into florets

1 cup snow peas, trimmed

2 cloves garlic, peeled and minced

½ pound brown rice noodles, cooked according to package directions, drained, and kept warm

1. In a small bowl, combine the Chinese brown sauce, five-spice powder, and crushed red pepper flakes. Set aside.
2. Heat a large skillet over high heat. Add the carrots and onion to the pan and stir-fry for 2 to 3 minutes. Add water 1 to 2 tablespoons at a time to keep the vegetables from sticking to the pan. Add the broccoli and snow peas and cook for 2 minutes, stirring frequently. Add the garlic and the sauce mixture and cook for 3 minutes longer. Remove from the heat and toss with the cooked noodles.

Pad Thai

THIS POPULAR NOODLE dish has as many variations as there are versions of pizza—and, like most pizzas, many of them are full of fat. My version is a healthy variation on one I used to eat at a hole-in-the-wall Thai restaurant in my hometown; when you ordered it vegan there, they added fresh basil and tomatoes, and the end result was perfection. Tamarind paste can be found in Asian grocery stores and online. If you can't find it, substitute a jar of prune baby food and a tablespoon of fresh lemon or lime juice.

SERVES 2

> 2 tablespoons low-sodium soy sauce
>
> 2 dates, pitted
>
> 1 tablespoon tamarind paste
>
> 1 medium yellow onion, peeled and diced small
>
> 2 teaspoons grated ginger
>
> 1 clove garlic, peeled and minced
>
> 6 green onions (white and green parts), sliced
>
> 1 tablespoon Asian hot chili sauce, or to taste
>
> 1 cup mung bean sprouts (see page 71)
>
> ¼ cup finely chopped Thai basil leaves
>
> 8 ounces brown rice noodles, cooked according to package directions, drained, and kept warm
>
> ¼ cup peanuts, toasted (see page 10) and coarsely chopped
>
> 1 lime, quartered
>
> 1 ripe tomato, cut into small wedges

1. Place the soy sauce, dates, tamarind paste, and ½ cup of water in a blender and process to a smooth paste. Add a more water, as needed, to achieve a creamy paste. Set it aside.
2. Heat a large skillet over high heat. Add the onion and stir-fry for 2 minutes. Add water 1 to 2 tablespoons at a time to keep the onion from sticking to the pan. Add the ginger, garlic, and green onions and cook for another 30 seconds. Add the date mixture, chili sauce, mung bean sprouts, and basil and cook for 30 seconds longer. Toss the sauce with the cooked noodles, remove from the heat, and garnish with the peanuts. Serve with fresh lime and tomato wedges.

Basic Vegetable Stir-Fry

STIR-FRY DISHES CAN be as easy and uncomplicated as this one, which features broccoli and snow peas. Feel free to use as many different vegetables as you like, but maintain the ratio of vegetables to sauce. Keep a batch of the Chinese Brown Sauce and your favorite vegetables on hand, and you can make stir-fries at a moment's notice.

SERVES 2

> 1 medium yellow onion, peeled and cut into ½-inch slices
> 1 large head broccoli, cut into florets
> 1 cup snow peas, trimmed
> One 6-ounce can sliced water chestnuts, drained
> ¼ cup plus 2 tablespoons Chinese Brown Sauce (page 35)
> ¼ cup cashews, toasted (see page 10)

Heat a large skillet over high heat. Add the onion, broccoli, snow peas, and water chestnuts and stir-fry for 4 to 5 minutes. Add water 1 to 2 tablespoons at a time to keep the vegetables from sticking to the pan. When the broccoli is crisp-tender, add the Chinese brown sauce and cook until thickened, about 3 minutes. Serve garnished with the toasted cashews.

VARIATION

▶ Cabbage is one of those vegetables that benefits from being cooked with salt and pepper, and it doesn't need much else. It does very well, though, in any stir-fry dish. To use it in this recipe, make the following adjustments: In place of the broccoli and snow peas, use 1 celery stalk, thinly sliced; 1 medium green pepper, seeded and cut into ½-inch dice; 1½ cups of chopped green cabbage (about 1-inch pieces); and 1 head of baby bok choy, thinly sliced. Season with ¼ teaspoon of black pepper, or to taste, and replace the cashews with 4 green onions (white and green parts), thinly sliced.

Stir-Fried Vegetables with Miso and Sake 📷

MISO AND SAKE are good friends in many Japanese dishes. They make a flavorful sauce for this dish with not much effort. Serve this dish over brown rice or your favorite grain.

SERVES 4

¼ **cup mellow white miso**
½ **cup Vegetable Stock (page 23), or low-sodium vegetable broth**
¼ **cup sake**
1 medium yellow onion, peeled and thinly sliced
1 large carrot, peeled, cut in half lengthwise, and then cut into half-moons on the diagonal
1 medium red bell pepper, seeded and cut into ½-inch strips
1 large head broccoli, cut into florets
½ **pound snow peas, trimmed**
2 cloves garlic, peeled and minced
½ **cup chopped cilantro, optional**
Salt and freshly ground black pepper to taste

1. Whisk together the miso, vegetable stock, and sake in a small bowl and set aside.
2. Heat a large skillet over a high heat. Add the onion, carrot, red pepper, and broccoli and stir-fry for 4 to 5 minutes. Add water 1 to 2 tablespoons at a time to keep the vegetables from sticking to the pan. Add the snow peas and stir-fry for another 4 minutes. Add the garlic and cook for 30 seconds. Add the miso mixture and cook until heated through.
3. Remove the pan from the heat and add the cilantro (if using). Season with salt and pepper.

Miso-Glazed Squash with Spinach

THE EARTHY FLAVOR of squash pairs nicely with the tangy, salty flavor of miso. This is great served over either cooked pasta or brown rice.

SERVES 4

1 large winter squash, such as butternut or acorn, peeled, halved, seeded, and cubed

1 batch Easy Miso Sauce (page 34)

6 cups packed baby spinach

1. Preheat the oven to 375°F.
2. Steam the squash in a double boiler or steamer basket for 10 to 12 minutes, or until tender. Place it in a large bowl and toss it with the miso sauce. Spread the squash mixture in a 9 x 13-inch baking dish and bake for 15 to 20 minutes.
3. While the squash bakes, steam the spinach in a large pot for 4 to 5 minutes, or until wilted.
4. To serve, divide the spinach among 4 individual plates and top with the glazed squash.

Grilled Vegetable Kabobs

NOTHING SAYS SUMMER like grilling, but this popular outdoor sport is not just for burgers. Vegetables really come to life on the grill and make even the simplest dinners into a special event. Serve these vegetables over your favorite cooked grain.

SERVES 6

½ cup balsamic vinegar

3 cloves garlic, peeled and minced

1½ tablespoons minced rosemary

1½ tablespoons minced thyme

Salt and freshly ground black pepper to taste

1 green bell pepper, seeded and cut into 1-inch pieces

1 red bell pepper, seeded and cut into 1-inch pieces

1 pint cherry tomatoes

1 medium zucchini, cut into 1-inch rounds

1 medium yellow squash, cut into 1-inch rounds

1 medium red onion, peeled and cut into large chunks

1. Prepare the grill.
2. Soak 12 bamboo skewers in water for 30 minutes.
3. Combine the balsamic vinegar, garlic, rosemary, thyme, and salt and pepper in a small bowl.
4. Skewer the vegetables, alternating between different-colored vegetables for a nice presentation. Place the skewers on the grill and cook, brushing the vegetables with the vinegar mixture and turning every 4 to 5 minutes, until the vegetables are tender and starting to char, 12 to 15 minutes.

NOTE ▶ If it's inconvenient to grill the skewers, they can be cooked under the broiler for 10 to 12 minutes instead. Baste and turn the skewers every 3 to 4 minutes, as you would on the grill.

Grilled Portobello Mushrooms

PORTOBELLO MUSHROOMS ARE probably my favorite vegan burger. They are easy to prepare and they take on the flavor of whatever marinade you choose. You could serve these on whole-grain buns for a cookout, but for a wholesome, easy meal at home, serve them on a bed of grains with a salad.

SERVES 4

3 tablespoons low-sodium soy sauce

3 tablespoons brown rice syrup

3 cloves garlic, peeled and minced

1 tablespoon grated ginger

Freshly ground black pepper to taste

4 large portobello mushrooms, stemmed

1. Combine the soy sauce, brown rice syrup, garlic, ginger, and pepper in a small bowl and mix well.
2. Place the mushrooms stem side up on a baking dish. Pour the marinade over the mushrooms and let marinate for 1 hour.
3. Prepare the grill.
4. Pour the excess marinade off the mushrooms, reserving the liquid, and place the mushrooms on the grill. Grill each side for 4 minutes, brushing with the marinade every few minutes.

VARIATION

▶ During the last few minutes of grilling, brush the mushrooms with Barbecue Sauce (page 36).

Grilled Cauliflower "Steaks" with Spicy Lentil Sauce

CAULIFLOWER HOLDS UP well on the grill, and like many vegetables, it takes on the flavor of whatever marinade or sauce it meets. The mild flavor of the "steaks" is a perfect balance for the spicy lentil sauce. Serve them over brown rice or on a bed of fresh or wilted spinach. If you don't have access to a grill, broiling or baking the cauliflower in a conventional oven yields good results, too.

SERVES 4

> **2 medium heads cauliflower**
> **2 medium shallots, peeled and minced**
> **1 clove garlic, peeled and minced**
> **½ teaspoon minced sage**
> **½ teaspoon ground fennel**
> **½ teaspoon crushed red pepper flakes**
> **½ cup green lentils, rinsed**
> **2 cups Vegetable Stock (page 23), or low-sodium vegetable broth**
> **Salt and freshly ground black pepper to taste**
> **Chopped parsley**

1. Cut each of the cauliflower heads in half through the stem of the vegetable (the stem holds the "steak" together), and then trim each half so that you have a 1-inch-thick cutlet. Place each piece on a baking sheet. Save the extra cauliflower florets for other uses.
2. Place the shallots in a medium saucepan and sauté over medium heat for 10 minutes. Add water 1 to 2 tablespoons at a time to keep the shallots from sticking to the pan. Add the garlic, sage, fennel, crushed red pepper flakes, and lentils and cook for 3 minutes. Add the vegetable stock and bring the mixture to a boil over high heat. Reduce the heat to medium and cook, covered, for 45 to 50 minutes, or until the lentils are very tender. Add water as needed to keep the mixture from drying out.
3. Puree the lentil mixture using an immersion blender or in a blender with a tight-fitting lid, covered with a towel. Return the puree to the pan if necessary and season with salt and pepper. Keep warm.
4. Prepare the grill.
5. Place the "steaks" on the grill and cook each side for about 7 minutes.
6. To serve, place the grilled "steaks" on a plate and spoon the sauce over them. Garnish with chopped parsley.

VARIATIONS

▶ Instead of serving with the spicy lentil sauce, make a marinade with ½ cup of Ponzu Sauce (page 35), 2 teaspoons of ground coriander, a pinch of cayenne pepper, and salt to taste. Marinate the cauliflower for 1 hour before grilling. During the grilling, brush each side with any remaining marinade once or twice. Serve on a bed of rice or quinoa pilaf with a salad.

▶ Brush the cauliflower "steaks" with Barbecue Sauce (page 36), or Easy Miso Sauce (page 34) in the last 3 to 4 minutes of grilling. Serve on a bed of rice or quinoa pilaf with a salad.

NOTE ▶ The spicy lentil sauce makes a great topping for baked potatoes, too.

Grilled Eggplant "Steaks"

EGGPLANT WAS BORN to be grilled. The skin holds it together while the flesh inside becomes almost creamy as it cooks, and, of course, it adapts well to whatever marinade you have on hand. Serve this dish over your favorite grains or a bed of wilted greens like spinach or arugula.

SERVES 4

> **3 tablespoons balsamic vinegar**
> **Juice of 1 lemon**
> **2 tablespoons low-sodium soy sauce**
> **Freshly ground black pepper to taste**
> **1 large eggplant, stemmed and cut into ¾-inch slices**

1. Prepare the grill.
2. Combine the balsamic vinegar, lemon juice, soy sauce, and pepper in a small bowl.
3. Brush both sides of the eggplant slices with the marinade.
4. Place the eggplant on the hot grill and cook on each side for 4 to 5 minutes, brushing periodically with additional marinade.

Ratatouille

SUMMER'S PERFECT STEW gets an oil-free makeover without losing flavor. Serve this over your favorite cooked grain or pasta.

SERVES 4

1 medium red onion, peeled and diced

1 medium red bell pepper, seeded and diced

1 medium eggplant, about 1 pound, stemmed and diced

1 small zucchini, diced

4 cloves garlic, peeled and minced

½ cup chopped basil

1 large tomato, diced

Salt and freshly ground black pepper to taste

Place the onion in a medium saucepan and sauté over medium heat for 10 minutes. Add water 1 to 2 tablespoons at a time to keep the onion from sticking to the pan. Add the red pepper, eggplant, zucchini, and garlic. Cook, covered, for 15 minutes, stirring occasionally. Stir in the basil and tomato and season with salt and pepper.

VARIATION

▶ To make this into Ratatouille Lasagna, which will serve 6 to 8, cook 1 pound of whole-grain or Jerusalem artichoke–flour lasagna noodles according to the package directions, drain, and rinse until cool. Prepare 3 cups of Tomato Sauce (page 25) and 3 cups of No-Cheese Sauce (page 29; about 1½ batches). Preheat the oven to 375°F. Spread 1 cup of tomato sauce on the bottom of a 9 x 13-inch baking pan. Place a layer of cooked noodles over the sauce. Spread half of the ratatouille on top of the noodles, then drizzle another cup of tomato sauce over the ratatouille. Add another layer of noodles, then the remaining ratatouille, and then the remaining cup of tomato sauce. Top with one more layer of lasagna noodles and the No-Cheese Sauce. Bake for 30 minutes, until the lasagna is bubbly. Let sit for 10 minutes before serving.

Spicy Sweet-and-Sour Eggplant

EGGPLANT AND BELL peppers are cooked in a spicy pineapple sweet-and-sour sauce. Serve this dish with brown rice. If you aren't able to use fresh pineapple, make sure to use pineapple canned in juice, not syrup.

SERVES 4

> 1 large yellow onion, peeled and chopped
> 1 medium red bell pepper, seeded and chopped
> 1 medium green pepper, seeded and chopped
> 1 large eggplant, stemmed and cut into ½-inch dice
> 2 cloves garlic, peeled and minced
> 2 teaspoons crushed red pepper flakes
> 2 cups pineapple chunks, or one 20-ounce can, drained
> 1 batch Pineapple Sweet-and-Sour Sauce (page 33)

Place the onion, red and green peppers, and eggplant in a large skillet and sauté over medium-high heat for 8 to 9 minutes, or until the vegetables are tender. Add water 1 to 2 tablespoons at a time to keep the vegetables from sticking to the pan. Add the garlic, crushed red pepper flakes, pineapple, and sweet-and-sour sauce and cook for 5 minutes.

Eggplant Dengaku Stir-Fry

DENGAKU IS A traditional Japanese broiled dish, but one night I threw together some leftover stir-fried vegetables and sauce and found that the flavor combination was similar to the original broiled version. Making my version from scratch is just about as easy as throwing leftovers together. This dish is excellent served over brown rice.

SERVES 4

> 1 medium yellow onion, peeled and thinly sliced
> 1 medium red bell pepper, seeded and cut into ½-inch strips
> 1 large eggplant, stemmed and cut into 1-inch pieces
> 1 cup Easy Miso Sauce (page 34)
> 3 green onions (white and green parts), chopped

Heat a large skillet over high heat and add the onion and pepper and stir-fry for 2 to 3 minutes. Add water 1 to 2 tablespoons at a time to keep the vegetables from sticking to the pan. Add the eggplant and cook for 5 to 6 minutes longer, stirring frequently, or until the eggplant is tender. Add the miso sauce and cook until thickened, about 3 minutes. Serve garnished with the green onions.

Indian Spiced Eggplant

THE ORIGINAL VERSION of this recipe has almost ½ cup of oil in it. This version is far healthier, but maintains all of the flavor with fresh vegetables and toasted spices. Serve this over brown rice for a complete meal.

SERVES 4

2 medium onions, peeled and diced

1 large red bell pepper, seeded and diced

2 medium eggplants, stemmed, peeled, and cut into ½-inch dice

2 large tomatoes, finely chopped

3 tablespoons grated ginger

2 teaspoons cumin seeds, toasted (see page 10) and ground

1 teaspoon coriander seeds, toasted and ground

½ teaspoon crushed red pepper flakes

Pinch cloves

Salt to taste

½ bunch cilantro, leaves and tender stems, finely chopped

Place the onions and red pepper in a large saucepan and sauté over medium heat for 10 minutes. Add water 1 to 2 tablespoons at a time to keep the vegetables from sticking to the pan. Add the eggplant, tomatoes, ginger, cumin, coriander, crushed red pepper flakes, and cloves and cook until the eggplant is tender, about 15 minutes. Season with salt and serve garnished with the cilantro.

Aloo Gobi (Potato and Cauliflower Curry)

MOST VERSIONS OF this potato and cauliflower curry call for frying the vegetables and spices in plenty of oil. Here the potatoes and cauliflower are first steamed and then cooked with the spices just enough to bring out their flavors. Serve this dish over brown rice or your favorite grain.

SERVES 4

1 medium yellow onion, peeled and diced

1 tablespoon grated ginger

2 cloves garlic, peeled and minced

½ jalapeño pepper, seeded and minced

2 medium tomatoes, diced

1 medium head cauliflower, cut into florets

1 pound Yukon Gold or other waxy potatoes, cut into ½-inch dice

1 teaspoon ground cumin

1 teaspoon ground coriander

1 teaspoon crushed red pepper flakes

½ teaspoon turmeric

¼ teaspoon ground cloves

2 bay leaves

1 cup green peas

¼ cup chopped cilantro or mint

1. Place the onion in a large saucepan and sauté over medium heat for 7 to 8 minutes. Add water 1 to 2 tablespoons at a time to keep the onion from sticking to the pan. Add the ginger, garlic, and jalapeño pepper and cook for 3 minutes. Add the tomatoes, cauliflower, potatoes, cumin, coriander, crushed red pepper flakes, turmeric, cloves, and bay leaves and cook, covered, for 10 to 12 minutes, until the vegetables are tender. Add the peas and cook for 5 minutes longer.
2. Remove the bay leaves and serve garnished with the cilantro or mint.

Spiced Green Peas and Yams

RECIPE BY DARSHANA THACKER

THIS IS A sweet and spicy dish that goes well with a salad, as a filling in a wrap, or as a side with lentil soup and rice. Asafetida, a spice used often in Indian cooking, smells very pungent raw but has a milder earthy flavor when cooked. There are as many versions of garam masala, a spice blend used in Indian cooking, as there are curries, and its flavor tends to be pungent but not necessarily hot.

SERVES 4

3 medium white yams, cut into ½-inch dice (about 2 cups)
½ cup green peas
¾ teaspoon cumin seeds, toasted (see page 10)
1 pinch asafetida, optional
¼ teaspoon cayenne pepper
¼ teaspoon garam masala
½ teaspoon ground coriander
½ teaspoon ground cumin
½ teaspoon salt, or to taste
½ tablespoon fresh lime juice
½ tablespoon finely chopped cilantro

1. Steam the yams in a double boiler or steamer basket for 5 to 7 minutes, or until tender. Set aside.
2. In a small saucepan, bring 1 cup of water to a boil, add the peas, and cook for 5 to 10 minutes, until the peas are soft. Drain and set aside.
3. In a large skillet over medium heat, place the cumin seeds, asafetida, white yams, peas, cayenne pepper, garam masala, coriander, cumin, and salt. Add 2 tablespoons of water, mix well, and cook for another 2 to 3 minutes, or until the water has evaporated. Stir in the lime juice and mix well. Serve garnished with the cilantro.

Braised Red Cabbage with Beans

BRAISED CABBAGE IS often served as a side dish with pork, but it is equally good as a main course when cooked with beans. You can substitute any kind of white beans and your favorite type of apple, but make sure you pick a tart variety; the apples and red wine are what give the dish its pleasant sweet-and-sour flavor.

SERVES 4

1 large yellow onion, peeled and diced

2 large carrots, peeled and diced

2 celery stalks, diced

2 teaspoons thyme

1½ cups red wine

2 tablespoons Dijon mustard

1 large head red cabbage, cored and shredded

4 cups cooked navy beans (see page 6), or two 15-ounce cans, drained and rinsed

2 tart apples (such as Granny Smith), peeled, cored, and diced

Salt and freshly ground black pepper to taste

Place the onion, carrots, and celery in a large saucepan and sauté over medium heat for 7 to 8 minutes. Add water 1 to 2 tablespoons at a time to keep the vegetables from sticking to the pan. Add the thyme, red wine, and mustard and cook until the wine is reduced by half, about 10 minutes. Add the cabbage, beans, and apples. Cook, covered, until the cabbage is tender, about 20 minutes. Season with salt and pepper.

Vegetable White Bean Hash 📷

MAKING HASH IS a great way to use whatever vegetables you have left over from the night before; just dice up any combination of vegetables and sauté them until they become tender (starting with those that take the longest to cook). This particular recipe, though, is tasty enough to be worth a trip to the grocery store if you don't have leftovers on hand.

SERVES 4

1 leek (white part only), finely chopped

1 red bell pepper, seeded and diced

3 cloves garlic, peeled and minced

2 teaspoons minced rosemary

1 large turnip, peeled and diced

1 medium sweet potato, peeled and diced

Zest and juice of 1 orange

2 cups cooked white beans (see page 6), or one 15-ounce can, drained and rinsed

1 cup chopped kale

Salt and freshly ground black pepper to taste

1. Place the leek and red pepper in a large saucepan and sauté over medium heat for 8 minutes. Add water 1 to 2 tablespoons at a time to keep the vegetables from sticking to the pan.
2. Add the garlic and rosemary and cook for another minute. Add the turnip, sweet potato, orange juice and zest, and the beans and cook for 10 minutes, or until the vegetables are tender. Add the kale, season with salt and pepper, and cook until the kale is tender, about 5 minutes.

Mixed Winter Vegetables with Spicy Poppy Seed Sauce

RECIPE BY DARSHANA THACKER

THIS IS A nourishing dish showcasing the rich taste of Indian curry—it's perfect when paired with steamed rice. The word *curry* comes from the southern Indian word *kari*, which means "sauce"—and if you're used to cooking with store-bought curry powder, you'll be amazed by the flavor in this homemade sauce.

SERVES 4 TO 6

1 cup green beans, trimmed, cut into ¼-inch pieces

2 carrots, peeled and sliced

1 medium potato, chopped (about 1 cup)

1 cup cauliflower florets

½ teaspoon cumin seeds

3 tablespoons white poppy seeds

1 small yellow onion, peeled and finely chopped

1 clove garlic, peeled and minced

½ teaspoon grated ginger

⅛ teaspoon ground cloves

⅛ teaspoon ground cinnamon

Pinch ground cardamom

¼ teaspoon freshly ground black pepper, or to taste

½ teaspoon turmeric

1 medium tomato, chopped (about 1 cup)

1 teaspoon salt, or to taste

2 tablespoons raw cashews, finely ground (see tip)

½ tablespoon fresh lime juice

1 tablespoon chopped cilantro

1. Steam the green beans, carrots, potato, and cauliflower in a double boiler or steamer basket for 8 to 10 minutes, or until tender. Set aside.
2. In a dry skillet over medium-low heat, toast the cumin seeds for 2 minutes. Add the poppy seeds and toast for another 2 to 3 minutes until the poppy seeds begin to brown. Remove from the heat and let cool. Combine the toasted seeds, onion, garlic, ginger, cloves, cinnamon, cardamom, pepper, and turmeric in a blender and process into a thick paste. Add the paste to a large skillet and cook on medium heat for 5 to 7 minutes.
3. Add the tomato to the blender and puree until smooth. Add the tomato puree and salt to the onion paste in the skillet and cook for another 2 to 3 minutes. Add the cashew powder and cook for 2 minutes. Add the steamed vegetables, lime juice, and 1½ cups of water and bring the mixture to a boil. Remove the pan from the heat and serve garnished with the cilantro.

TIP
▶ Use a spice grinder to grind the raw cashew nuts into a fine powder.

Baked Spaghetti Squash with Swiss Chard

SPAGHETTI SQUASH IS nature's noodle—easy to prepare, full of flavor, and chock-full of nutrients. Also try it topped with your favorite pasta sauce, or try it simply prepared with just salt and pepper as a side dish.

SERVES 4

2 small spaghetti squash (about 1 pound each), halved

Salt and freshly ground black pepper to taste

1 large bunch red-ribbed Swiss chard

1 medium yellow onion, peeled and diced small

1 red bell pepper, seeded and diced small

4 cloves garlic, peeled and minced

2 teaspoons ground cumin

2 teaspoons ground coriander

½ teaspoon paprika

½ teaspoon crushed red pepper flakes

Zest and juice of 1 lemon

1. Preheat the oven to 350°F.
2. Season the cut sides of the squash with salt and pepper. Place the squash halves, cut side down, on a rimmed baking sheet. Add ½ cup of water to the pan and bake the squash for 45 to 55 minutes, or until very tender (the squash is done when it can be easily pierced with a knife).
3. While the squash is baking, remove the stems from the chard and chop them. Chop the leaves into bite-size pieces and set them aside. Place the onion, red pepper, and chard stems in a large saucepan and sauté over medium heat for 5 minutes. Add water 1 to 2 tablespoons at a time to keep the vegetables from sticking to the pan. Add the garlic, cumin, coriander, paprika, and crushed red pepper flakes and cook for 3 minutes. Add the chard leaves and lemon zest and juice. Season with salt and pepper and cook until the chard is wilted, about 5 minutes. Remove from the heat.
4. When the squash is finished baking, scoop out the flesh (it should come away looking like noodles) and stir it into the warm chard mixture.

VARIATION

▶ Baked spaghetti squash also pairs well with pesto. Prepare and cook 2 spaghetti squash as directed above, but bake for about 40 minutes, until it is tender but not overcooked. Gently turn the squash over and carefully spread ¾ cup of Basil Pesto (page 24) over each squash half. Return to the oven and cook for another 10 minutes. Serve the squash halves on individual serving plates with a salad.

STUFFED AND BAKED VEGETABLES

Baked Spaghetti Squash with Spicy Lentil Sauce

SPAGHETTI SQUASH IS much like pasta in that it adapts well to almost any sauce. A fun way to serve this dish is to spoon the lentil sauce right into the shell with the cooked squash and serve one half to each of your guests.

SERVES 4

2 small spaghetti squash (about 1 pound each), halved

Salt and freshly ground black pepper to taste

1 medium yellow onion, peeled and diced small

3 cloves garlic, peeled and minced

2 teaspoons crushed red pepper flakes, or to taste

¼ cup tomato paste

1 cup cooked green lentils (see page 6)

1 cup Vegetable Stock (page 23), or low-sodium vegetable broth, plus more as needed

Chopped parsley

1. Preheat the oven to 350°F.
2. Season the cut sides of the squash with salt and pepper. Place the squash halves, cut-side down, on a baking sheet, and bake them for 45 to 55 minutes, or until the squash is very tender (it is done when it can be easily pierced with a knife).
3. While the squash bakes, place the onion in a large saucepan and sauté over medium heat for 5 minutes. Add water 1 to 2 tablespoons at a time to keep the onion from sticking to the pan. Add the garlic, crushed red pepper flakes, tomato paste, and ½ cup of water and cook for 5 minutes. Add the lentils to the pan and cook until heated through. Season with additional salt. Puree the lentil mixture using an immersion blender or in a blender with a tight-fitting lid, covered with a towel, until smooth and creamy. Add some of the vegetable stock, as needed, to make a creamy sauce.
4. To serve, scoop the flesh from the spaghetti squash (it should come away looking like noodles) and divide it among 4 plates. Top with some of the lentil sauce and garnish with the parsley.

Bulgur-Stuffed Tomatoes

QUICK-COOKING GRAINS SUCH as bulgur (and quinoa, as in the variation below) are perfect summertime options when you don't want to spend hours in a hot kitchen. Tomatoes, zucchini, corn, and basil, all fresh from the garden, are also summertime standbys.

SERVES 4

4 large tomatoes (about 2 pounds)

2 leeks (white and light green parts), diced small and rinsed

1 clove garlic, peeled and minced

1 medium zucchini, diced small

3 ears corn, kernels removed (about 1½ cups)

1 cup bulgur, cooked in 2 cups Vegetable Stock (page 23), or low-sodium vegetable broth

½ cup finely chopped basil

Zest and juice of 1 lemon

Salt and freshly ground black pepper to taste

1. Preheat the oven to 350°F.
2. Cut the tops off the tomatoes and scoop out the flesh, leaving a ½-inch wall. Set the tomatoes aside while you prepare the filling.
3. Place the leeks in a large saucepan and sauté over medium heat for 7 to 8 minutes. Add the garlic and cook for 3 minutes longer. Stir in the zucchini and corn and cook for 5 minutes. Add the cooked bulgur, basil, and lemon zest and juice. Season with salt and pepper. Remove from the heat.
4. Divide the bulgur mixture among the prepared tomatoes and arrange them in a baking dish. Cover the dish with aluminum foil and bake for 30 minutes.

VARIATION

▶ Using 2 cups of cooked quinoa in place of the bulgur makes this dish gluten-free. For an extra flavorful variation, omit the corn and add ½ cup of Basil Pesto (page 24) with the quinoa.

Quinoa-Stuffed Tomatoes with Spicy Cilantro Pesto

THE FILLING FOR this dish tastes great baked in a ripe, juicy tomato, as in this recipe. Feel free to try the filling for burritos, too, as it tastes great with the quinoa standing in for the usual rice.

SERVES 4

4 large tomatoes (about 2 pounds)
½ yellow onion, peeled and diced small
½ red bell pepper, seeded and diced small
2 cloves garlic, peeled and minced
2 ears corn, kernels removed (about 1 cup)
2 cups cooked black beans (see page 6), or one 15-ounce can, drained and rinsed
2 cups cooked quinoa (see page 6)
Salt and freshly ground black pepper to taste
¾ cup Spicy Cilantro Pesto (page 24)

1. Preheat the oven to 350°F.
2. Cut the tops off of the tomatoes and scoop out the flesh, leaving a ½-inch wall. Set the tomatoes aside while you prepare the filling.
3. Place the onion and red pepper in a large saucepan and sauté over medium heat for 10 minutes. Add water 1 to 2 tablespoons at a time to keep the vegetables from sticking to the pan. Add the garlic and cook for 2 minutes, then add the corn, black beans, and cooked quinoa. Season with salt and pepper and cook for 5 minutes. Remove from the heat. Add the cilantro pesto to the pan and mix well.
4. Divide the quinoa mixture evenly among the prepared tomatoes and arrange them in a baking dish. Cover the dish with aluminum foil and bake for 30 minutes.

Yellow Bell Pepper Boats

RECIPE BY DARSHANA THACKER

YELLOW BELL PEPPERS are stuffed with potatoes and corn and complemented by a homemade hot sauce. Serve this dish as a beautiful appetizer or as a colorful side dish.

SERVES 6

FOR THE BELL PEPPER BOATS:

> **2 medium potatoes, halved**
>
> **1 ear corn, kernels removed (about ½ cup)**
>
> **½ small onion, peeled and finely chopped**
>
> **1 small green bell pepper, seeded and finely chopped (about ¼ cup)**
>
> **¼ teaspoon grated ginger**
>
> **½ clove garlic, peeled and minced**
>
> **½ teaspoon minced serrano chile, or to taste (for less heat, remove the seeds)**
>
> **½ teaspoon salt, or to taste**
>
> **1 teaspoon fresh lime juice**
>
> **2 yellow bell peppers**
>
> **¼ cup sunflower seeds, toasted (see page 10)**

FOR THE HOT SAUCE:

> **1 large tomato, chopped (about 2 cups)**
>
> **½ teaspoon cayenne pepper**
>
> **½ teaspoon salt, or to taste**
>
> **½ clove garlic, peeled and mashed to a paste**
>
> **½ tablespoon finely chopped cilantro**

TO MAKE THE BELL PEPPER BOATS:

1. Preheat the oven to 350°F.
2. Boil the potatoes in a saucepan of water for 15 minutes over medium heat, until tender. Remove from the heat, drain, and let cool. Mash the potatoes in a mixing bowl.
3. Place the corn and 1 cup of water in a small pan. Cook on medium heat until the corn is tender, 5 to 7 minutes. Drain and add to the potatoes along with the onion, green pepper, ginger, garlic, serrano chile, salt, and lime juice. Mix well.
4. Cut the yellow peppers into 3 long, boat-shaped slices each and remove the seeds. Divide the potato mixture among the slices and sprinkle with sunflower seeds. Bake, covered, for 30 to 35 minutes, until the yellow peppers are soft when poked with a fork.

TO MAKE THE HOT SAUCE:

5. Puree the tomato in a blender. Add the puree to a saucepan with the cayenne pepper, salt, and garlic, bring to a boil, and cook for 5 minutes. Reduce the heat to low and simmer for 5 more minutes.
6. To serve, spread the hot sauce on top of the baked bell peppers. Garnish with cilantro.

Poblano Peppers with Chipotle Black Bean Sauce

IN THIS DISH, roasted peppers are stuffed with Spinach, Mushroom and Quinoa Pilaf (page 241) and served with a smoky black bean sauce. You can use a canned chipotle in adobo sauce in place of the dried chipotle pepper, but look carefully at the label: some brands contain oil or other additives. Add about a teaspoon of the adobo sauce (more or less to taste) along with the pepper if you use this substitution.

SERVES 3

> **6 poblano peppers, roasted (see page 8)**
> **1 batch Spinach, Mushroom and Quinoa Pilaf (page 241)**

FOR THE CHIPOTLE BLACK BEAN SAUCE:

> **½ medium yellow onion, peeled and diced small**
> **2 cloves garlic, peeled and minced**
> **1 teaspoon cumin seeds, toasted (see page 10) and ground**
> **2 cups cooked black beans (see page 6), or one 15-ounce can, drained and rinsed**
> **1 chipotle pepper, halved, seeded, and soaked in warm water for 20 minutes**
> **Salt to taste**

1. Preheat the oven to 350°F.
2. Cut the tops off the peppers and carefully remove the cores and seeds. Fill each of the roasted poblano peppers with pilaf and arrange the stuffed peppers in a baking dish. Bake for 15 minutes, or until warmed through.

TO MAKE THE CHIPOTLE BLACK BEAN SAUCE:

3. Place the onion in a medium skillet and sauté over medium heat for 7 to 8 minutes. Add water 1 to 2 tablespoons at a time to keep the onion from sticking to the pan. Add the garlic and cumin and cook for another minute.
4. Add the black beans and the chipotle pepper to a blender and process until smooth, adding water as needed to achieve a smooth consistency. Add the bean mixture to the pan with the onion mixture. Add ½ to ¾ cup of water, as needed, and whisk until creamy. Cook over low heat until warmed through, then season with salt and serve over the warm poblano peppers.

"Cheesy" Broccoli Baked Potatoes

EVEN THOUGH THE potatoes take a little while to bake, the rest of this dish comes together almost effortlessly, making this recipe a great option for a healthy weeknight dinner.

SERVES 4

4 large russet potatoes, scrubbed
1 batch No-Cheese Sauce (page 29)
2 cups broccoli florets

1. Preheat the oven to 350°F.
2. Pierce each potato with a fork a few times so that it will release steam during baking. Place the pierced potatoes on a baking sheet and bake for 60 to 75 minutes, or until tender.
3. Combine the No-Cheese Sauce and the broccoli in a saucepan and cook over medium heat for 8 to 10 minutes, or until the broccoli is tender.
4. When the potatoes are cool enough to handle, pierce each with a fork in a dotted line across the top. Squeeze each potato at either end of the dotted line to force it open. To serve, place 2 potato halves on each plate and spoon some of the warm broccoli mixture into the halves.

Southwestern Twice-Baked Potatoes

TWICE-BAKED POTATOES HAVE a notorious reputation as a decadent side dish, topped with bacon, cheese, and sour cream. No longer! This version makes a hearty, healthy meal, filled with black beans, corn, and spices.

SERVES 6

6 large russet potatoes, scrubbed

1 medium yellow onion, peeled and diced small

1 red bell pepper, seeded and diced small

1 jalapeño pepper, seeded and minced

2 cloves garlic, peeled and minced

1 tablespoon cumin seeds, toasted (see page 10) and ground

2 teaspoons ancho chile powder

3 ears corn, kernels removed (about 2 cups)

2 cups cooked black beans (see page 6), or one 15-ounce can, drained and rinsed

1 teaspoon salt, or to taste

½ cup chopped cilantro

¼ cup nutritional yeast, optional

One 12-ounce package extra firm silken tofu, drained

½ cup chopped green onion (white and green parts)

1. Preheat the oven to 350°F.
2. Pierce each potato with a fork a few times so that it will release steam during baking. Place the potatoes on a baking sheet and bake for 60 to 75 minutes, or until tender. Let cool until safe to handle.
3. Place the onion and red pepper in a large skillet and sauté over medium heat for 7 to 8 minutes, or until the onion starts to brown. Add water 1 to 2 tablespoons at a time to keep the vegetables from sticking to the pan. Add the jalapeño pepper, garlic, cumin, and chile powder and sauté for another minute. Add the corn, black beans, salt, cilantro, and nutritional yeast (if using) and mix well. Remove from the heat.
4. Puree the silken tofu in blender. Add the pureed tofu to the vegetable mixture in the pan and mix well.
5. Halve each potato lengthwise and scoop out the flesh, leaving a ¼-inch-thick shell. Reserve the flesh for another use. Divide the vegetable filling evenly among the potato halves. Place the filled potatoes on a baking sheet and bake for 30 minutes. Serve garnished with the chopped green onion.

Millet-Stuffed Portobello Mushrooms

WHILE PORTOBELLO MUSHROOMS can be grilled (see page 173) and served alone with brown rice or some other grain for a good meal, they also hold up very well to stuffing and baking. When served on a bed of simply prepared greens, this beautiful dish is perfect for company, or just because.

SERVES 4

> 4 large portobello mushrooms, stemmed
> 2 tablespoons low-sodium soy sauce
> 3 cloves garlic, peeled and minced
> Freshly ground black pepper to taste

FOR THE FILLING:

> 2 cups Vegetable Stock (page 23), or low-sodium vegetable broth
> ⅔ cup millet
> 1 small yellow onion, peeled and diced small
> 1 medium red bell pepper, seeded and diced small
> 1 fennel bulb, trimmed and diced
> 3 cloves garlic, peeled and minced
> 2 sage leaves, minced
> Salt to taste

1. Place the mushrooms, stem side up, in a baking dish and set aside.
2. Combine the soy sauce, garlic, and black pepper in a small bowl to make the marinade. Brush some of the marinade over each mushroom. Set the mushrooms aside while you prepare the filling.

TO MAKE THE FILLING:

3. Bring the vegetable stock to a boil in a medium saucepan. Add the millet and bring the pot back to a boil. Reduce the heat to medium and cook, covered, for 15 minutes, or until the millet is tender.
4. Preheat the oven to 350°F.
5. Place the onion, red pepper, and fennel in a large saucepan and sauté over medium heat for 10 minutes. Add water 1 to 2 tablespoons at a time to keep the vegetables from sticking to the pan. Add the garlic and sage leaves and cook for 2 minutes. Add the millet, mix well, and season with salt and pepper. Remove from the heat.
6. Divide the millet mixture among the 4 mushrooms. Arrange in a baking dish, cover with aluminum foil, and bake for 25 minutes. Remove the foil and bake for another 10 minutes.

Asian Stuffed Mushrooms

TURN THE USUAL stir-fry into a special meal with this recipe. Cilantro is not the norm in pesto, and pesto is not the norm in Asian cooking, but it works—with better than tasty results.

SERVES 4

4 large portobello mushrooms
½ medium yellow onion, peeled and diced small
½ red bell pepper, seeded and diced small
1 head baby bok choy, finely chopped
2 cups cooked brown rice (see page 6)
½ cup Spicy Cilantro Pesto (page 24)
Salt and freshly ground black pepper to taste

1. Preheat the oven to 350°F.
2. Separate the mushroom stems from the caps. Finely chop the stems and set them aside. Place the caps, top side down, in a baking dish and set aside.
3. Heat a large skillet over medium-high heat. Add the chopped mushroom stems, onion, and red pepper and stir-fry for 5 minutes. Add water 1 to 2 tablespoons at a time to keep the vegetables from sticking to the pan. Add the bok choy and cook for 4 minutes. Add the brown rice and cilantro pesto, season with salt and pepper, and mix well. Remove from the heat.
4. Divide the rice mixture among the mushroom caps. Arrange in a baking dish, cover the dish with aluminum foil, and bake for 15 minutes. Uncover and bake for another 10 minutes.

VARIATION

▶ If you'd prefer to stuff these mushrooms Italian-style, omit the yellow onion, red pepper, baby bok choy, and Spicy Cilantro Pesto. Combine the 2 cups of cooked rice with one 14-ounce jar of artichoke hearts, drained and chopped; ½ cup of finely chopped sun-dried tomatoes; ½ cup of Basil Pesto (page 24); and ¼ cup of pine nuts, toasted (see page 10). After filling the mushroom caps, bake, covered, for 20 minutes. Uncover and bake for another 10 minutes. Serve this variation on a bed of wilted spinach or with a green salad.

Stuffed Eggplant

USE ALMOST ANY of the grain pilafs in this book to make this dish (see the section of recipes starting on page 239), or try it with these ingredients. Basmati rice has a mild, nutty flavor that does not need much more than cooking to be a flavorful addition to any recipe.

SERVES 4

2 cups Vegetable Stock (page 23), or low-sodium vegetable broth

1 cup brown basmati rice

1 cinnamon stick

2 medium eggplants, stemmed and halved lengthwise

1 medium yellow onion, peeled and diced small

1 celery stalk, diced small

1 medium red bell pepper, seeded and diced small

2 cloves garlic, peeled and minced

¼ cup finely chopped basil

¼ cup finely chopped cilantro

Salt and freshly ground black pepper to taste

1. Bring the vegetable stock to a boil in a medium saucepan. Add the rice and cinnamon stick and bring the pot back to a boil. Cover and cook over medium heat for 45 minutes, or until tender and the stock is absorbed.

2. Carefully scoop the flesh out of the eggplant halves, leaving a ¼-inch-thick shell. Coarsely chop the pulp and set it aside with the shells.

3. Preheat the oven to 350°F.

4. Place the onion, celery, and red pepper in a large saucepan and sauté over a medium heat for 7 to 8 minutes, or until the vegetables start to brown. Add water 1 to 2 tablespoons at a time to keep the vegetables from sticking to the pan. Add the garlic and eggplant pulp and cook for 5 more minutes, or until the eggplant is tender. Remove from the heat. Add the cooked rice, basil, and cilantro to the eggplant mixture. Season with salt and pepper.

5. Divide the rice mixture evenly among the eggplant shells and place the stuffed eggplants in a baking dish. Cover with aluminum foil and bake for 40 minutes.

Eggplant Rollatini 📷

THIS ITALIAN-STYLE EGGPLANT dish is usually filled with bread crumbs and cheese. This version uses a savory millet and spinach filling—seasoned with fresh basil—and is baked and topped with tomato sauce. It can be served as a side to Baked Ziti (page 251) but can also stand as an entreé alongside a salad or on a bed of pasta.

SERVES 4

3 whole cloves garlic, plus 4 cloves, peeled and minced

2 tablespoons low-sodium soy sauce

¼ cup Vegetable Stock (page 23), or low-sodium vegetable broth

2 large eggplants, stemmed and cut lengthwise into ½-inch slices

1 cup millet

Salt to taste

1 medium yellow onion, peeled and diced small

1 celery stalk, diced small

1 carrot, peeled and grated

6 cups packed chopped spinach

½ cup minced basil

¼ cup nutritional yeast, optional

Freshly ground black pepper to taste

2 cups Tomato Sauce (page 25)

1. Preheat the oven to 350°F.
2. In a small bowl with a fork, or using a mortar and pestle, mash the 3 whole cloves of garlic with the soy sauce.
3. Combine the mashed garlic mixture with the vegetable stock to make a marinade.
4. Place the eggplant slices on a baking sheet and brush with some of the marinade. Bake for 10 minutes. Turn the slices over, brush with more of the marinade, and bake for another 10 to 15 minutes, until the eggplant is tender. Remove the eggplant from the oven and set aside.
5. Bring 3 cups of water to a boil and add the millet and salt. Return to a boil, then reduce the heat to medium and cook, covered, for 20 minutes, or until tender.
6. Place the onion, celery, and carrot in a large saucepan and sauté over medium heat for 7 to 8 minutes. Add water 1 to 2 tablespoons at a time to keep the vegetables from sticking to the pan. Add the remaining minced garlic and cook for 3 minutes. Add the spinach, basil, and nutritional yeast (if using) and season with black pepper. Cook until the spinach is wilted, then remove from the heat, add the cooked millet, and mix well.
7. Spread 1 cup of the tomato sauce in the bottom of a 9 x 13-inch baking dish. Divide the millet mixture among the baked eggplant slices and roll each slice over the millet mixture. Place the eggplant rolls, seam side down, in the prepared baking dish. Cover with the remaining tomato sauce and bake, covered, for 15 minutes.

Delicata Squash Boats

DELICATA SQUASH, THOUGH considered a winter squash, has a lot more in common with summer varieties; it is quicker-cooking than most winter squash and the skin can be eaten when cooked.

SERVES 4

2 delicata squash, halved and seeded
Salt and freshly ground black pepper to taste
1 shallot, peeled and minced
½ red bell pepper, seeded and diced small
6 cups chopped spinach
2 cloves garlic, peeled and minced
1 tablespoon minced sage
2 cups cooked cannellini beans (see page 6), or one 15-ounce can, drained and rinsed
¾ cup whole-grain bread crumbs
3 tablespoons nutritional yeast, optional
3 tablespoons pine nuts, toasted (see page 10)
Zest of 1 lemon

1. Preheat the oven to 350°F. Line a baking sheet with parchment paper.
2. Season the cut sides of the squash with salt and pepper. Place the halves on the prepared baking sheet, cut sides down. Bake until the squash is tender, about 45 minutes.
3. Place the shallot and red pepper in a large saucepan and sauté over medium heat for 2 to 3 minutes. Add water 1 to 2 tablespoons at a time to keep the vegetables from sticking to the pan. Add the spinach, garlic, and sage and cook until the spinach is wilted, 4 to 5 minutes. Add the beans and season with salt and pepper. Cook for another 2 to 3 minutes. Remove from the heat. Add the bread crumbs, nutritional yeast (if using), pine nuts, and lemon zest. Mix well.
4. Divide the bean mixture among the baked squash halves. Place the stuffed squash halves in a baking dish and cover with aluminum foil. Bake for 15 to 20 minutes, or until heated through.

Wild Rice–Stuffed Cabbage Rolls

STUFFED CABBAGE MAY be an Eastern European invention, but luckily it found its way to my dinner table as a kid (although it was years before I realized Mom did not invent it). This version uses a wild rice blend, instead of the traditional rice or barley, but you can use whatever grain you like.

SERVES 6

1 large head savoy cabbage, separated into individual leaves

1 large yellow onion, peeled and diced small

2 carrots, peeled and finely diced

2 celery stalks, diced small

2 cloves garlic, peeled and minced

1 tablespoon minced sage

¼ cup dry sherry

3 cups cooked wild rice blend (see page 6)

Salt and freshly ground black pepper to taste

½ cup Vegetable Stock (page 23), or low-sodium vegetable broth

2 cups Tomato Sauce (page 25)

1. Bring a pot of salted water to a boil. Blanch the cabbage leaves in the boiling water for 5 to 6 minutes. Remove them from the pot and rinse until cool. Set aside.
2. Place the onion, carrots, and celery in a large saucepan and sauté over medium heat for 7 to 8 minutes. Add water 1 to 2 tablespoons at a time to keep the vegetables from sticking to the pan. Add the garlic and sage and cook for 3 minutes. Add the sherry and cook until the liquid is almost evaporated. Remove the pan from the heat, add the wild rice, and season with salt and pepper.
3. Preheat the oven to 350°F.
4. Lay 2 cabbage leaves side by side with a ½-inch overlap. Place ½ cup of the rice filling in the center of the leaves. Fold in the leaves from the sides over the filling, then roll the leaves into a cylinder. Place the roll, seam side down, in a 9 x 13-inch baking dish. Repeat until all the filling is used, reserving any leftover leaves for another use. Add the vegetable stock to the baking dish, cover with aluminum foil, and bake for 10 minutes. Uncover the dish and pour the tomato sauce over the cabbage rolls. Bake for another 15 minutes.

Millet-Stuffed Chard Rolls 📷

MILLET AND CHARD are great alternatives to the usual rice-stuffed cabbage, and the Roasted Red Pepper Sauce (page 25) is perfect when you want something other than tomato sauce.

SERVES 6

12 large Swiss chard leaves, ribs removed

1 large onion, peeled and finely diced

6 cloves garlic, peeled and minced

3 tablespoons minced basil

1 tablespoon thyme

1½ cups millet

5 cups Vegetable Stock (page 23), or low-sodium vegetable broth

½ cup pine nuts, toasted (see page 10)

¼ cup nutritional yeast

Salt and freshly ground black pepper to taste

1 batch Roasted Red Pepper Sauce (page 25)

1. Prepare an ice bath by filling a large bowl with ice and cold water. Bring a pot of water, large enough to hold the chard leaves without bending them, to a boil. Add the chard and blanch the leaves for 20 to 30 seconds until they soften. Submerge the softened leaves in the ice bath to stop their cooking. Set aside.
2. Preheat the oven to 350°F.
3. Place the onion in a large saucepan and sauté over medium heat for 8 minutes. Add water 1 to 2 tablespoons at a time to keep the onion from sticking to the pan. Add the garlic and cook for 2 minutes. Add the basil, thyme, millet, and 4½ cups of vegetable stock and bring to a boil over high heat. Reduce the heat to medium and cook, covered, for 20 minutes, or until the millet is tender. Remove from the heat. Add the pine nuts and nutritional yeast and season with salt and pepper.
4. Place a chard leaf on a flat surface. Spoon some of the millet mixture in the middle of the chard leaf. Fold the large end of the chard over the filling, then fold in the sides and roll up the leaf like a cigar. Place the roll, seam side down, in a 9 x 13-inch baking dish. Repeat with the remaining chard leaves. Pour the remaining ½ cup of vegetable stock into the pan to cover the bottom of the pan. Cover the dish with aluminum foil and bake for 25 minutes, or until the chard leaves have wilted and are tender. Serve topped with the roasted red pepper sauce.

Potato Samosa–Stuffed Chard

TRADITIONAL SAMOSAS ARE deep-fried, vegetable-filled pastries served with coriander chutney. This version uses Swiss chard as the wrapper and is baked, not fried. These can be served as an appetizer, or eaten as a meal served with a salad and any of the pilafs in this book (see the Great Grains chapter starting on page 219).

SERVES 4 TO 8

FOR THE POTATO SAMOSA FILLING:

> 1 medium yellow onion, peeled and diced small
>
> 2 teaspoons black mustard seeds, toasted (see page 10)
>
> 1 teaspoon coriander seeds, toasted and ground
>
> 1 teaspoon garam masala
>
> 1 teaspoon cumin seeds, toasted and ground
>
> 1 jalapeño pepper, seeded and minced
>
> 1 tablespoon grated ginger
>
> ¼ cup finely chopped cilantro
>
> 1 cup green peas
>
> 4 medium Yukon Gold potatoes, peeled, cut into ½-inch dice, boiled, and rinsed until cool
>
> Salt to taste
>
> 8 Swiss chard leaves
>
> Coriander Chutney (page 32)

TO PREPARE THE CHARD:

1. Prepare an ice bath by filling a large bowl with ice and cold water. Bring a pot of water, large enough to hold the chard leaves without bending them, to a boil. Add the chard and blanch the leaves for 20 to 30 seconds, until they soften. Submerge the softened leaves in the ice bath to stop their cooking, then set them aside.

TO MAKE THE POTATO SAMOSA FILLING:

2. Place the onion in a large saucepan and sauté over medium heat for 7 to 8 minutes. Add water 1 to 2 tablespoons at a time to keep the onion from sticking to the pan. Reduce the heat to medium-low and add the mustard seeds, coriander, garam masala, cumin, jalapeño, ginger, and cilantro. Cook for 4 minutes, then remove from the heat. Add the peas and potatoes. Season with salt and mix well.

TO ASSEMBLE THE SAMOSAS:

3. Preheat the oven to 350°F.
4. Place a chard leaf on a flat surface. Spoon some of the potato mixture in the middle of the chard leaf. Fold the large end of the chard over the potato, then fold in the sides and roll up the samosa like a cigar. Place in a baking dish. Repeat with the remaining chard leaves. Pour a little water over the samosas and cover the dish with aluminum foil. Bake for 25 to 30 minutes, or until the chard leaves have wilted and are tender. Serve with Coriander Chutney.

Bean, Corn and Summer Squash Sauté

IN LATE JULY or early August, you might be able to harvest all of the ingredients for this dish from your garden. If not, you'll certainly be able to find them at your farmers' market.

SERVES 4

1 medium red onion, peeled and thinly sliced
4 medium zucchini, cut into ½-inch rounds
4 yellow squash, cut into ½-inch rounds
2 cups corn kernels (from about 3 ears)
2 cups cooked navy beans (see page 6), or one 15-ounce can, drained and rinsed
Zest of 2 lemons
1 cup finely chopped basil
Salt and freshly ground black pepper to taste

Place the onion in a large saucepan and sauté over medium heat for 7 to 8 minutes. Add water 1 to 2 tablespoons at a time to keep the onion from sticking to the pan. Add the zucchini, squash, corn, and beans and cook until the squash is tender, about 8 minutes. Remove from the heat. Stir in the lemon zest and basil and season with salt and pepper.

Fava Bean Ratatouille

FAVA BEANS ARE not traditional in this popular summer stew from France, but the creamy texture of this Mediterranean bean pairs nicely with the texture of the vegetables in this dish.

SERVES 4

1 medium red onion, peeled and thinly sliced
1 red bell pepper, seeded and diced
1 large eggplant, stemmed and cut into ½-inch dice
1 medium zucchini, diced
2 cloves garlic, peeled and finely chopped
2 cups cooked fava beans (see page 6), or one 15-ounce can, drained and rinsed
2 Roma tomatoes, chopped
¼ cup finely chopped basil
Salt and freshly ground black pepper to taste

Place the onion in a large saucepan and sauté over medium heat for 7 to 8 minutes. Add water 1 to 2 tablespoons at a time to keep the onion from sticking to the pan. Add the red pepper and eggplant and cook for 10 minutes. Add the zucchini, garlic, fava beans, and tomatoes and cook for 5 minutes longer. Reduce the heat and cook, uncovered, stirring occasionally, for 15 minutes, or until the vegetables are tender. Remove from the heat. Stir in the basil and season with salt and pepper.

Black Beans and Rice

TOASTING THE CUMIN seeds and oregano really brings out their flavors in this simplest, most filling of dishes.

SERVES 4

1 medium yellow onion, peeled and diced

1 red bell pepper, seeded and diced

2 jalapeño peppers, diced (for less heat, remove the seeds)

5 cloves garlic, peeled and minced

1 teaspoon cumin seeds, toasted (see page 10) and ground

1½ teaspoons dried oregano, toasted

4 cups cooked black beans (see page 6), or two 15-ounce cans, drained and rinsed

Salt and freshly ground black pepper to taste

3 cups cooked brown rice (see page 6)

1 cup chopped cilantro

1 lime, quartered

Place the onion, red pepper, and jalapeño peppers in a large saucepan and sauté over medium heat for 7 to 8 minutes. Add water 1 to 2 tablespoons at a time to keep the vegetables from sticking to the pan. Add the garlic, cumin, and oregano and cook for 3 minutes. Add the black beans and 1 cup of water. Cook for 10 minutes, adding more water if necessary. Season with salt and pepper. Serve over the brown rice and garnish with the cilantro and lime wedges.

Jamaican Black Beans

JAMAICAN FOOD IS a culinary melting pot of Spanish, African, Indian, British, and Chinese influences. This dish is traditionally made with chicken, and although I have tried both seitan and tofu in place of the meat, I prefer it with black beans. The Pineapple Chutney (page 33) is a nice contrast to the earthy beans, and it all sits well on a bed of brown rice.

SERVES 4

> 1 medium yellow onion, peeled and chopped
>
> 1 red bell pepper, seeded and chopped
>
> 4 cloves garlic, peeled and minced
>
> 1 tablespoon curry powder
>
> 1½ teaspoons ground allspice
>
> 1 tablespoon thyme
>
> 2 jalapeño peppers, seeded and minced
>
> 1 teaspoon freshly ground black pepper, or to taste
>
> One 15-ounce can diced tomatoes
>
> 4 cups cooked black beans (see page 6), or two 15-ounce cans, drained and rinsed
>
> Pineapple Chutney (page 33)

Add the onion and red bell pepper to a large saucepan and sauté over medium heat for 10 minutes, or until the onion is tender. Add water 1 to 2 tablespoons at a time to keep the vegetables from sticking to the pan. Stir in the garlic, curry powder, allspice, thyme, jalapeño peppers, and black pepper. Cook for 3 to 4 minutes, then add the tomatoes and black beans and cook, covered, over medium heat for 20 minutes. Serve with the pineapple chutney.

Cuban-Style Black Beans with Cilantro Rice

RECIPE BY JUDY MICKLEWRIGHT

THIS DISH IS inspired by my love for Cuban black beans and rice, a dish that traditionally uses ham hocks to flavor the beans and a significant amount of oil in the rice. These beans are a favorite of mine to keep in the freezer; I separate them into one-cup portions for individual meals, or into several-cup portions for family lunches or dinners. This dish is wonderful with a side of chard, kale, spinach, cabbage, or your favorite vegetable.

SERVES 4

FOR THE BLACK BEANS:

1 pound black beans, soaked overnight (see page 5)

2 tablespoons ground cumin

1 large onion, peeled and diced

2 bay leaves

3 cloves garlic, peeled and minced

3 celery stalks, diced

3 medium carrots, peeled and diced

1 red bell pepper, seeded and diced

2 tablespoons minced oregano

1 cup finely chopped cilantro stems

2 tablespoons apple cider vinegar

½ teaspoon freshly ground white or black pepper

3 tablespoons chopped cilantro leaves

1 medium tomato, chopped (about 1 cup)

Salt to taste

FOR THE CILANTRO RICE:

1 cup brown rice

1 tablespoon low-sodium light brown miso paste

2 tablespoons finely chopped cilantro leaves

TO MAKE THE BLACK BEANS:

1. In a large pot, combine the beans, cumin, onion, bay leaves, garlic, celery, carrots, red pepper, oregano, cilantro stems, and 5 cups of water and bring to a boil. Reduce the heat to a simmer and cook for 90 minutes, or until the beans are tender. Remove one quarter of the beans, mash them in a separate bowl, and return them to the pot. Add the apple cider vinegar, pepper, cilantro leaves, and tomato and stir. Once the beans are fully cooked, season with salt and remove the bay leaves.

TO MAKE THE CILANTRO RICE:

2. Combine the rice, 2 cups of water, and the miso paste in a large saucepan and bring to a boil. Reduce the heat to medium and simmer, covered, for 20 minutes. Reduce the heat to low and simmer for an additional 30 minutes. Fluff the rice and stir in the cilantro.

3. To serve, divide the rice among 4 individual plates and top with the beans.

Hearty Nachos 📷

RECIPE BY JULIEANNA HEVER

THESE NACHOS ARE a meal in themselves. You can also use the versatile "cheese" sauce on potatoes, raw or cooked vegetables, tortillas, and cooked whole grains and legumes.

SERVES 4

FOR THE "CHEESE" SAUCE:

½ cup raw cashews, soaked in warm water for at least 30 minutes, rinsed well

1 tablespoon tahini

1 red bell pepper, roasted (see page 8) and seeded

¼ cup nutritional yeast

1 tablespoon low-sodium soy sauce, or Bragg Liquid Aminos

Zest and juice of ½ lemon

¼ teaspoon cayenne pepper

FOR THE "REFRIED" BEAN DIP:

One 15-ounce can pinto beans, drained and rinsed

1 cup Fresh Tomato Salsa (page 26)

1½ teaspoons chili powder

FOR THE NACHOS:

½ cup finely chopped cilantro, parsley, or lettuce

1 avocado, halved, pitted, peeled, and sliced, optional

½ cup Fresh Tomato Salsa

½ cup diced fresh tomatoes

Baked corn tortillas, cut into chips (see tip, page 207)

TO MAKE THE "CHEESE" SAUCE:

1. In a blender, combine the soaked cashews, tahini, roasted red pepper, nutritional yeast, soy sauce, lemon zest and juice, cayenne pepper, and ¼ cup of water. Blend on high until smooth. Set aside.

TO MAKE THE "REFRIED" BEAN DIP:

2. Add the beans, salsa, and chili powder in the bowl of a food processor. Puree until smooth, adding water, as needed, to achieve a smooth consistency. Place the pureed beans in a medium saucepan and warm over low heat until heated through. Keep warm until ready to serve.

TO ASSEMBLE THE NACHOS:

3. Spread the bean dip evenly onto the bottom of a medium serving bowl or baking dish. Smooth the surface and sprinkle the cilantro over the beans. Pour the "cheese" sauce on top of the cilantro. Garnish with sliced avocado (if using), salsa, and diced fresh tomatoes and serve with the baked corn chips.

"Refried" Beans and Tomatoey Rice

RECIPE BY JUDY MICKLEWRIGHT

THIS IS MY favorite comfort-food dish, I make this when my daughter wants something crunchy for dinner (she loves crunchy food). Every two weeks or so, we have Tostada/Taco Night with crunchy baked tostadas or taco shells (see tip, page 207). I usually make a batch of guacamole (for an interesting twist, try the Not-So-Fat Guacamole, page 27) or slice up an avocado to go with it. I also serve some sautéed cabbage or beet greens. This is another great dish to prepare extra portions of and store in the freezer.

SERVES 8

FOR THE "REFRIED" BEANS:

1 pound pinto beans, soaked overnight (see page 5)

1 large onion, peeled and diced

1 cup finely chopped cilantro stems

3 cloves garlic, peeled and minced

1 bay leaf

2 tablespoons ground cumin

2 tablespoons oregano

Pinch chili powder

¼ cup chopped cilantro leaves

Salt and freshly ground black pepper to taste

FOR THE TOMATOEY RICE:

1 cup brown rice

1 tablespoon low-sodium light brown miso

½ medium onion, peeled and diced

1 teaspoon ground cumin

1 tablespoon oregano

1 teaspoon garlic powder

1 medium bell pepper, seeded and diced (about ½ cup)

3 cups Tomato Sauce (page 25)

Salt and freshly ground black pepper to taste

Baked corn tortillas, for serving, optional (see tip)

TO MAKE THE "REFRIED" BEANS:

1. In a large pot, combine the beans, 4 cups of water, the onion, cilantro stems, garlic, bay leaf, cumin, oregano, and chili powder and bring to a boil. Reduce the heat to low and simmer for 1½ hours. Add more water, as needed, to keep the beans from drying out. Remove one quarter of the beans, mash them in a separate bowl, and return them to the pot. Add the cilantro leaves and season with salt and pepper.

TO MAKE THE TOMATOEY RICE:

2. In a large pot, combine the rice, miso, onion, cumin, oregano, garlic powder, and 2 cups of water and bring to a boil. Reduce the heat to medium and simmer for 20 minutes. Reduce the heat to low and cook for another 10 minutes. Add the bell pepper

and cook for 5 more minutes. Add the tomato sauce and cook for 5 more minutes. Season with salt and pepper.

TIP

▶ If you would like to make tostadas, bake corn tortillas without oil in the oven for around 10 minutes at 350°F. Cast-iron pans distribute heat well and make nice crunchy tostadas. To make baked taco shells, you will need a taco shell rack. Oven temperatures vary, so keep an eye on the first batch to determine the time necessary for your crunchy tortillas. Top the tortillas with the rice and beans and serve hot.

Citrusy Black Bean Taquitos

THE ORANGE ZEST and juice in this recipe brightens the dish and elevates the ordinary black bean to new heights. Serve this with brown rice or cooked quinoa and a salad.

SERVES 4

> 1 large yellow onion, peeled and diced small
>
> 4 cloves garlic, peeled and minced
>
> 2 teaspoons cumin seeds, toasted (see page 10) and ground
>
> 2 chiles in adobo sauce, minced, or 2 teaspoons ancho chile powder
>
> Zest and juice of 2 oranges
>
> 4 cups cooked black beans (see page 6), or two 15-ounce cans, drained and rinsed
>
> Salt to taste
>
> 20 to 24 corn tortillas
>
> 1 batch Tofu Sour Cream (page 28)
>
> 1 batch Not-So-Fat Guacamole (page 27)
>
> 2 cups Fresh Tomato Salsa (page 26)

1. Place the onion in a large saucepan and sauté over medium heat for 8 to 10 minutes. Add water 1 to 2 tablespoons at a time to keep the onion from sticking to the pan. Add the garlic and cook for another minute. Add the cumin, chiles, orange zest and juice, and black beans. Season with salt. Puree the mixture in the bowl of a food processor until smooth but a little chunky.
2. Place the tortillas, a few at a time, in a nonstick skillet over medium-low heat. Heat, turning frequently, until the tortillas soften, 3 to 4 minutes. Wrap the tortillas in a kitchen towel to keep warm and repeat with the remaining tortillas.
3. Spread 3 to 4 tablespoons of the black bean mixture over half of each tortilla, roll it up, starting with the bean-filled half, and set it seam side down on a serving dish. Repeat with the remaining tortillas. Before serving, if desired, warm the taquitos in a 200°F oven for 10 to 15 minutes. (Make sure your serving dish is oven-safe.)
4. Serve with tofu sour cream, guacamole, and salsa.

Texas Caviar

THIS POPULAR APPETIZER also makes a filling meal when served over mixed greens or fresh spinach.

SERVES 4

2½ cups cooked black-eyed peas (see page 5)

3 ears corn, kernels removed (about 2 cups)

1 medium ripe tomato, diced

½ medium red onion, peeled and diced small

½ red bell pepper, seeded and diced small

1 jalapeño pepper, seeded and minced

½ cup finely chopped cilantro

¼ cup plus 2 tablespoons balsamic vinegar

3 cloves garlic, peeled and minced

1 teaspoon cumin seeds, toasted (see page 10) and ground

Salt to taste

Mix all ingredients in a large bowl and refrigerate until well chilled, about 1 hour.

Lucky Black-Eyed Pea Stew

RECIPE BY DARSHANA THACKER

THIS IS A hearty and delicious dish accented with beets and carrots. Serve with brown rice and a side of vegetables.

SERVES 4, OR 6 AS A SIDE

½ cup black-eyed peas, soaked (see page 5)

1 large carrot, peeled and cut into ½-inch pieces (about ¾ cup)

1 large beet, peeled and cut into ½-inch pieces (about ¾ cup)

¼ cup finely chopped parsley

¼ teaspoon cumin seeds, toasted and ground (see page 10)

¼ teaspoon turmeric

¼ teaspoon cayenne pepper

⅛ teaspoon asafetida

¼ teaspoon salt, or to taste

½ teaspoon fresh lime juice

Combine the black-eyed peas in a pot with 3 cups of water and cook over medium heat for 20 to 25 minutes. Add the carrot and beet and cook for another 10 minutes. Add more water, as needed, if the stew gets too thick. Add the parsley, cumin, turmeric, cayenne pepper, and asafetida and cook for another 5 to 7 minutes. Season with salt. Remove the pot from the heat and add the lime juice.

Koshari (Lentils with Rice and Macaroni)

THIS OIL-FREE, WHOLE-GRAIN version of a popular Egyptian street food is worth using the various pans needed to make it. Although it's best to cook the individual elements separately to retain their separate flavors, if you don't feel like doing quite so many dishes there is a shortcut: Cook the lentils and rice together in the same pot for the first 35 minutes, then add the macaroni during the last 10 minutes of cooking—just make sure to add enough water to accommodate everything.

SERVES 6

1 cup green lentils, rinsed

Salt to taste

1 cup medium-grain brown rice

1 large onion, peeled and minced

4 cloves garlic, peeled and minced

1 teaspoon ground cumin

1 teaspoon ground coriander

½ teaspoon ground allspice

½ teaspoon crushed red pepper flakes

2 tablespoons tomato paste

3 large tomatoes, diced small

1 cup whole-grain elbow macaroni, cooked according to package directions, drained, and kept warm

1 tablespoon brown rice vinegar

1. Add the lentils to a medium saucepan with 3 cups of water. Bring the pot to a boil over high heat, reduce the heat to medium, and cook, covered, for 40 to 45 minutes, or until the lentils are tender but not mushy. Drain any excess water from the lentils, season with salt, and set aside.
2. Add the brown rice and 2 cups of water to a separate medium saucepan. Cover the pan with a tight-fitting lid and bring it to a boil over high heat. Reduce the heat to medium and cook for 45 minutes.
3. Heat a large skillet over high heat. Place the onion in the skillet and sauté over medium heat for 15 minutes, or until it is well browned. Add water 1 to 2 tablespoons at a time to keep the onion from sticking to the pan (see tip). Add the garlic and cook for 3 to 4 minutes more. Add the cumin, coriander, allspice, crushed red pepper flakes, and tomato paste and cook for 3 minutes longer. Add the fresh tomatoes and cook over medium heat for 15 minutes, or until the tomatoes start to break down. Season with salt.
4. To serve, combine the lentils, rice, tomato mixture, cooked macaroni, and brown rice vinegar in a large bowl.

TIP

▶ To caramelize onions without oil, use as little water as possible when cooking them; the browner they get, the more flavor they give the dish.

Mujadara (Lentils with Rice and Caramelized Onions)

I USED TO own a vegan bakery in a public market. The stall next to mine was a Middle Eastern restaurant that made homemade falafel and the best mujadara I've ever had. Like their version, my recipe uses cinnamon and allspice. Other variations on this traditional dish use other spices, such as cumin, but the most important element is always the caramelized onions. The browner the onions, the more intense the flavor. Caramelizing onions without oil requires some attention—so no walking off for any length of time. I like cooking the brown rice separately to ensure that it does not make the dish gummy if it is accidentally overcooked.

SERVES 4

> 1½ cups green lentils, rinsed
> ¾ teaspoon ground cinnamon
> ½ teaspoon ground allspice
> ¾ cup brown basmati rice
> 3 large yellow onions, peeled and diced
> Salt and freshly ground black pepper to taste

1. Add the lentils to a large pot with 5 cups of water and bring to a boil over high heat. Reduce the heat to medium and simmer for 30 minutes. Add the cinnamon and allspice and cook for another 15 to 20 minutes, until the lentils are tender.
2. In a separate medium saucepan, bring 1½ cups of water to a boil. Add the rice and bring to a boil over high heat. Reduce the heat to medium and cook the rice, covered, for 45 minutes, or until tender.
3. Heat a large skillet over a high heat. Add the onions to the skillet and cook, stirring frequently, for 10 minutes. Add water 1 to 2 tablespoons at a time to keep the onions from sticking to the pan (see tip, page 210). Reduce the heat to medium-low and continue cooking until they are browned, about 10 minutes. Add the lentils and rice to the onions and mix well. Season with salt and pepper.

Red Lentil Dal

QUICK-COOKING RED LENTILS are my favorite legume. They have plenty of flavor without needing much added to them, and they cook in less than 30 minutes. Serve this dish over brown rice with a salad.

SERVES 4

1 large yellow onion, peeled and diced

2 cloves garlic, peeled and minced

1 bay leaf

1 tablespoon grated ginger

1 teaspoon turmeric

1 tablespoon cumin seeds, toasted (see page 10) and ground

1 tablespoon coriander seeds, toasted and ground

½ teaspoon crushed red pepper flakes

2 cup red lentils, rinsed

Salt to taste

Zest of 1 lemon

Place the onion in a large saucepan and sauté over medium heat for 10 minutes. Add water 1 to 2 tablespoons at a time to keep the onion from sticking to the pan. Add the garlic, bay leaf, ginger, turmeric, cumin, coriander, and crushed red pepper flakes and cook for another minute. Add the lentils and 4 cups of water and bring the pot to a boil over high heat. Reduce the heat to medium and cook, covered, for 20 to 25 minutes, or until the lentils are tender and have started to break down. Remove from the heat. Season with salt and add the lemon zest.

Chana Saag 📷

SAAG PANEER, AN Indian dish made with spiced spinach and homemade cheese, was always one of my favorite Indian dishes. It is full of flavor and perfectly spiced. Chana Saag (Chickpeas and Spinach) comes in as a close second, but it is a much healthier option since it doesn't include cheese. Serve this delicious dish with brown basmati rice or your favorite cooked grain.

SERVES 4

> **1 medium yellow onion, peeled and diced small**
>
> **1 jalapeño pepper, minced (for less heat, remove the seeds)**
>
> **3 cloves garlic, peeled and minced**
>
> **1 tablespoon grated ginger**
>
> **2 teaspoons ground cumin**
>
> **1 teaspoon ground coriander**
>
> **1 teaspoon turmeric**
>
> **1 teaspoon fenugreek**
>
> **1 teaspoon crushed red pepper flakes, or to taste**
>
> **1 large tomato, finely chopped**
>
> **1 cup unsweetened plain almond milk**
>
> **2 pounds fresh spinach, chopped (about 12 cups)**
>
> **2 cups cooked chickpeas (see page 6), or one 15-ounce can, drained and rinsed**
>
> **Salt to taste**

Place the onion in a large saucepan and sauté over medium-high heat for 8 to 10 minutes, or until it is browned. Add water 1 to 2 tablespoons at a time to keep the onion from sticking to the pan. Reduce the heat to medium-low and add the jalapeño pepper, garlic, ginger, cumin, coriander, turmeric, fenugreek, and crushed red pepper flakes. Cook, stirring often, for 4 minutes, adding water only as needed. Add the tomato and cook for another 5 minutes, then add the almond milk, spinach, and chickpeas. Cover the pot and reduce the heat to medium-low. Cook until the spinach is wilted, about 10 minutes. Season with salt.

Curried Chickpeas and Rice

RECIPE BY DARSHANA THACKER

SERVE THIS SIMPLE, yet flavorful, dish with a mild soup or stew, or a salad.

SERVES 4

1 cup brown basmati rice
¼ cup finely chopped green scallions
¼ teaspoons cumin seeds, toasted (see page 10)
¼ teaspoons curry powder
½ teaspoons salt, or to taste
1½ cups cooked chickpeas (see page 6)
½ tablespoon fresh lime juice

1. Rinse the rice and add it to a pot with 2½ cups of water. Bring to a boil over high heat and cook, uncovered, for 20 minutes. Reduce the heat to medium and simmer the rice, covered, for 10 minutes.
2. Add the scallions to a medium saucepan with 2 tablespoons of water and cook until soft. Add the cumin seeds, curry powder, salt, and chickpeas and cook for a minute. Add the cooked rice, cook for another minute, and remove the pan from the heat. Add the lime juice and serve hot.

NOTE ▶ Caramelized onions, chopped fresh tomatoes, and fresh herbs such as mint and cilantro make good add-ins to this dish.

North African Chickpeas and Vegetables

CHERMOULA IS A thick sauce used in North African cooking, often to marinate fish for grilling, but it tastes great with vegetable dishes too. Serve this hearty dish over couscous or brown rice. The sauce, though it has a long list of ingredients, takes only a few minutes to make and tastes great on grilled cauliflower or eggplant, too.

SERVES 4

FOR THE CHERMOULA SAUCE:

1 large tomato, chopped

½ cup kalamata olives, pitted

1 cup chopped cilantro

6 cloves garlic, peeled and minced

Zest of 1 lemon and juice of 2 lemons

1 tablespoon sweet paprika

2 teaspoons ground coriander

2 teaspoons ground cumin

¼ teaspoon cayenne pepper, or to taste

Salt to taste

FOR THE VEGETABLES:

1 medium yellow onion, peeled and cut into ½-inch rings

1 medium red bell pepper, seeded and cut into ½-inch strips

8 ounces button mushrooms, sliced

1 medium zucchini, halved lengthwise and cut into ½-inch slices

1 medium yellow squash, halved lengthwise and cut into ½-inch slices

2 cups cooked chickpeas (see page 6), or one 15-ounce can, drained and rinsed

Salt and freshly ground black pepper to taste

TO MAKE THE CHERMOULA SAUCE:

1. Combine the tomato, olives, cilantro, garlic, lemon zest and juice, paprika, coriander, cumin, cayenne pepper, and salt in a blender and process until smooth and creamy. Set aside.

TO MAKE THE VEGETABLES:

2. Place the onion, red pepper, and mushrooms in a large saucepan and sauté over medium-high heat for 8 to 10 minutes. Add water 1 to 2 tablespoons at a time to keep the vegetables from sticking to the pan. Add the zucchini, yellow squash, and chickpeas and cook for 10 minutes. Add the chermoula sauce and cook for 5 minutes longer. Season with salt and pepper.

Chickpea Caponata

CAPONATA IS USUALLY served chilled as an appetizer, but it's just as good eaten warm as an entrée when served over brown rice. The added chickpeas make it an even heartier meal.

SERVES 4

1 medium yellow onion, peeled and diced

2 celery stalks, chopped

1 medium eggplant, stemmed and diced

2 ripe Roma tomatoes, diced

2 cups cooked chickpeas (see page 6), or one 15-ounce can, drained and rinsed

½ cup kalamata olives, pitted and coarsely chopped

3 tablespoons capers

3 tablespoons red wine vinegar

¼ cup golden raisins

¼ cup pine nuts, toasted (see page 10), optional

½ cup chopped basil

Salt and freshly ground black pepper to taste

Place the onion and celery in a large saucepan and sauté over medium heat for 10 minutes. Add water 1 to 2 tablespoons at a time to keep the vegetables from sticking to the pan. Add the eggplant, tomatoes, and chickpeas and cook, covered, for 15 minutes, or until the vegetables are tender. Stir in the olives, capers, red wine vinegar, raisins, and pine nuts (if using) and cook for 5 minutes more. Remove from the heat and add the basil. Season with salt and pepper.

Spicy Chickpeas and Fennel

THE INSPIRATION FOR this dish comes from a pasta dish made from a spicy sausage seasoned with fennel, oregano, and crushed red pepper flakes. It has a little kick and the pronounced aroma of herbs and spices. Serve this over brown rice or Basic Polenta (page 229) with a salad.

SERVES 4

- **1 large yellow onion, peeled and chopped**
- **1 large fennel bulb, trimmed and thinly sliced**
- **4 cloves garlic, peeled and minced**
- **1 tablespoon minced oregano**
- **1½ teaspoons ground fennel seeds**
- **1 teaspoon crushed red pepper flakes**
- **One 28-ounce can diced tomatoes**
- **4 cups cooked chickpeas (see page 6), or two 15-ounce cans, drained and rinsed**
- **Chopped flat-leaf Italian parsley**

Place the onion and fennel in a large saucepan, and sauté over medium heat for 10 minutes, or until the vegetables are tender. Add water 1 to 2 tablespoons at a time to keep the vegetables from sticking to the pan. Add the garlic, oregano, fennel seeds, and crushed red pepper flakes and cook for 3 minutes. Add the tomatoes and chickpeas and bring the pan to a boil over high heat. Reduce the heat to medium and cook, covered, for 20 minutes. Serve garnished with the parsley.

White Beans and Escarole with Parsnips

PARSNIPS ARE NOT the usual in this popular Italian dish, but the sweet and pungent root vegetable goes well with the mildly bitter greens. Serve this as is for a light meal, or over brown basmati rice for something more filling. Any beans and almost any green leafy vegetable will work for this dish. If you don't like parsnips, use carrots, or simply leave them out of the dish.

SERVES 4

1 medium yellow onion, peeled and diced

2 large parsnips, peeled and diced

4 cloves garlic, peeled and minced

1 large head escarole, soaked in cool water, rinsed well to remove any dirt, and chopped

4 cups cooked cannellini beans (see page 6), or two 15-ounce cans, drained and rinsed

Salt and freshly ground black pepper to taste

Place the onion in a large skillet and sauté over medium heat for 5 minutes. Add water 1 to 2 tablespoons at a time to keep the onion from sticking to the pan. Add the parsnips and garlic and cook for 4 minutes. Add the escarole and cook until tender, about 15 minutes. Add the beans, season with salt and pepper, and cook for 5 minutes longer.

TIP

▶ This dish can also be made in a slow cooker. Combine the onion, parsnips, garlic, beans, and about 1½ cups of water. Cook on low for 8 hours, or until the vegetables are tender. Add the escarole during the last 20 minutes of cooking. Season with salt and pepper.

Rice Dishes

Pineapple "Fried" Rice

SWEET AND TANGY pineapple brightens this fried rice dish, and serrano chile brings the heat. Keep a container of cooked brown rice on hand in the refrigerator to use in stir-fries and wraps, and to complement bean dishes throughout the week.

SERVES 4

> 1 medium yellow onion, peeled and thinly sliced
>
> 1 serrano chile, sliced into thin rings (for less heat, remove the seeds)
>
> 4 cloves garlic, peeled and minced
>
> ½ cup Chinese Brown Sauce (page 35)
>
> 4 cups cooked brown rice (see page 6), fully cooled
>
> Two 8-ounce cans pineapple chunks, drained (about 1½ cups)
>
> ½ cup cooked peas, thawed if frozen
>
> ½ cup cashews, toasted (see page 10)
>
> ½ cup chopped cilantro

Heat a large skillet over high heat. Add the onion and chile and stir-fry for 4 to 5 minutes. Add water 1 to 2 tablespoons at a time to keep the vegetables from sticking to the pan. Add the garlic and cook for 30 seconds, stirring constantly. Add the Chinese brown sauce and cook for 30 seconds. Add the rice, pineapple, peas, cashews, and cilantro and cook until heated through.

GREAT GRAINS

Red Curry "Fried" Rice

THAI RED CURRY paste is like having instant stir-fry sauce in a jar, adding just enough flavor without a lot of effort. Toast the almonds carefully—they go from toasted to burnt very quickly.

SERVES 2

½ medium yellow onion, peeled and cut into ½-inch strips

2 large leeks (white and light green parts), thinly sliced and rinsed

2 cups shiitake mushrooms, trimmed and thinly sliced

2 medium carrots, peeled and cut into matchsticks

4 teaspoons Thai red curry paste

¼ cup slivered almonds, toasted (see page 10), optional

4 green onions (white and green parts), chopped

2 cups cooked brown rice (see page 6), fully cooled

Salt and freshly ground black pepper to taste

Heat a large skillet over high heat. Add the onion, leeks, mushrooms, and carrots and cook, stirring frequently, for 5 to 6 minutes. Add water 1 to 2 tablespoons at a time to keep the vegetables from sticking to the pan. Stir in the curry paste and cook for another 30 seconds. Add the almonds (if using), green onions, and rice and cook until heated through. Season with salt and pepper.

Stir-Fried Rice with Asparagus and Red Pepper

THE LEMON AND jalapeño pepper add a little zing to this easy stir-fry. If you want a little less heat, remove the seeds and membrane from the jalapeño.

SERVES 2

½ pound asparagus, trimmed and cut into 1-inch pieces

½ medium yellow onion, peeled and thinly sliced

½ medium red bell pepper, seeded and julienned

¼ cup Chinese Brown Sauce (page 35)

Zest and juice of 1 lemon

3 tablespoons minced jalapeño pepper (for less heat, remove the seeds)

3 cups cooked brown rice (see page 6), fully cooled

Heat a large skillet over high heat. Add the asparagus, onion, and red pepper and cook for 4 to 5 minutes, stirring frequently. Add water 1 to 2 tablespoons at a time to keep the vegetables from sticking to the pan. Add the Chinese brown sauce, lemon zest and juice, and jalapeño pepper and cook for another minute. Add the brown rice and cook until heated through.

Stir-Fried Bok Choy and Rice in Garlic Sauce

QUICK-COOKING BABY BOK choy adds freshness to any dish in which it is used. Use the leaves as well as the stalks in this recipe. Sherry is a popular addition to many Chinese stir-fry dishes, but buy the real thing, not the cooking sherry found in most Asian sections of the supermarket, as it has much more salt than real sherry.

SERVES 2

½ medium yellow onion, peeled and diced
½ medium red bell pepper, seeded and diced
1 bunch baby bok choy, trimmed and chopped
3 cloves garlic, peeled and minced, or to taste
¼ cup Chinese Brown Sauce (page 35), or to taste
2 tablespoons dry sherry, optional
½ teaspoon crushed red pepper flakes
2 cups cooked brown rice (see page 6), fully cooled
4 green onions (white and green parts), thinly sliced

Heat a large skillet over high heat. Add the onion and red pepper and cook for 4 minutes. Add water 1 to 2 tablespoons at a time to keep the vegetables from sticking to the pan. Add the baby bok choy and cook for 3 minutes. Add the garlic, Chinese Brown Sauce, sherry (if using), crushed red pepper flakes, and brown rice. Cook until heated through, then stir in the green onions.

Sweet-and-Sour "Meatball" Stir-Fry

SAVORY "MEATBALLS" AND stir-fried vegetables pair excellently in Pineapple Sweet-and-Sour Sauce (page 33). The "meatballs" do not keep well in the sauce, though, so keep them separate until ready to serve.

SERVES 4

1 medium yellow onion, peeled and diced
1 medium red bell pepper, seeded and diced
1 medium head broccoli, cut into florets
One 14-ounce can pineapple chunks, drained
1 batch Pineapple Sweet-and-Sour Sauce (page 33)
4 cups cooked brown rice (see page 6)
1 batch "Meatballs" (page 159)
3 green onions (white and green parts), thinly sliced

1. Heat a large skillet over high heat. Add the onion and red pepper and stir-fry for 3 minutes. Add water 1 to 2 tablespoons at a time to keep the vegetables from sticking to the pan. Add the broccoli and cook until tender, about 5 minutes. Add the pineapple and sweet-and-sour sauce and cook until heated through.
2. To serve, divide the brown rice among 4 individual plates and top with the vegetable mixture and the "meatballs." Garnish with the green onions.

Eggplant and Chickpea Rice Pilaf

EGGPLANT MAY APPEAR most often as Eggplant Parmesan in the United States, but it is made into thousands of different recipes around the world, from baba ghanoush in the Middle East to punjabi eggplant in northern India, and in pilaf dishes like this one.

SERVES 4

2 cups Vegetable Stock (page 23), or low-sodium vegetable broth

1 cup brown basmati rice

1 large yellow onion, peeled and diced small

6 cloves garlic, peeled and minced

2 jalapeño peppers, seeded and minced

1 tablespoon cumin seeds, toasted (see page 10) and ground

1 tablespoon ground coriander

1 teaspoon turmeric

1 large eggplant, stemmed and cut into ½-inch cubes

2 cups cooked chickpeas (see page 6), or one 15-ounce can, drained and rinsed

¼ cup finely chopped mint

½ cup finely chopped basil

Salt to taste

½ cup finely chopped cilantro

1. Bring the vegetable stock to a boil in a medium saucepan. Add the rice and bring the mixture back to a boil over high heat. Reduce the heat to medium and cook, covered, until the rice is tender, about 45 minutes.
2. Place the onion in a large saucepan and sauté over medium heat for 7 to 8 minutes. Add water 1 to 2 tablespoons at a time to keep the onion from sticking to the pan. Add the garlic, jalapeño peppers, cumin, coriander, turmeric, and eggplant and cook until the eggplant is tender, about 12 minutes. Add the cooked rice, chickpeas, mint, and basil. Season with salt and serve garnished with the cilantro.

Sweet Potato and Cauliflower Rice Pilaf

MADE WITH COUSCOUS, this dish would be more of a traditional North African dish, but brown rice makes it gluten-free, and basmati rice makes the dish even more delicious.

SERVES 4

3 to 3½ cups Vegetable Stock (page 23), or low-sodium vegetable broth

1½ cups brown basmati rice

1 large cinnamon stick

2 whole cloves

2 cardamom pods

1 medium yellow onion, peeled and cut into ½-inch dice

1 medium carrot, peeled and cut into ½-inch dice

1 medium sweet potato, peeled and cut into ½-inch dice

½ small head cauliflower, cut into florets

2 cloves garlic, peeled and minced

1 cup peas, thawed if frozen

½ cup chopped cilantro

1 large pinch saffron, soaked in 3 tablespoons hot water

Salt to taste

1. Bring 3 cups of the vegetable stock to a boil and add the rice, cinnamon stick, cloves, and cardamom pods. Bring the mixture back to a boil over high heat, then reduce the heat to medium and cook, covered, until the rice is tender, about 45 minutes. Check the rice for tenderness and add more stock, if needed, and cook for another 10 minutes if necessary. Remove the cinnamon stick, cloves, and cardamom pods before serving.

2. Place the onion in a large saucepan and sauté over medium-high heat for 7 to 8 minutes, or until the onion is tender and starting to brown. Add water 1 to 2 tablespoons at a time to keep the onion from sticking to the pan. Add the carrot and sweet potato and cook for 10 minutes. Add the cauliflower and garlic and cook 6 to 7 minutes longer, or until the cauliflower is tender. Add the peas, cilantro, and saffron and its soaking liquid and season with salt. Add the cooked rice and mix well.

Green Chile Rice with Black Beans

BLACK BEANS ARE not usually added to this popular Mexican rice dish, but their addition makes it into a one-pot meal. Use whatever beans you have on hand, or leave them out if you want to serve this as a side dish.

SERVES 4

1 poblano chile pepper, seeded and diced small

One 4-ounce can mild green chiles

1 cup coarsely chopped cilantro

½ cup spinach

4 cups Vegetable Stock (page 23), or low-sodium vegetable broth

1½ cups medium-grain brown rice

1 medium yellow onion, peeled and diced small

1 teaspoon ground cumin

1 jalapeño pepper, seeded and minced

2 cups cooked black beans (see page 6), or one 15-ounce can, drained and rinsed

Zest of 1 lime

Salt to taste

1. Add the poblano pepper, green chiles, cilantro, and spinach to a blender and puree. Add some of the vegetable stock, as needed, to achieve a smooth consistency. Add the mixture to a medium saucepan with the remaining vegetable stock. Add the brown rice and bring to a boil over high heat. Reduce the heat to medium and cook, covered, until the rice is tender, 45 to 50 minutes.

2. Place the onion in a large saucepan and sauté over medium heat for 7 to 8 minutes. Add water 1 to 2 tablespoons at a time to keep the onion from sticking to the pan. Add the cumin, jalapeño pepper, and black beans and cook for 5 minutes longer. Fold in the cooked rice and lime zest. Season with salt.

Vegetable Biryani

BIRYANI IS A rice dish that originated in what is now Iran and was popularized in Indian restaurants across the United States. This healthy version uses brown basmati rice and skips the oil. The ingredient list is long, but the dish well worth the effort. Try it with Coriander Chutney (page 32) and whole-grain flatbread.

SERVES 4 TO 6

FOR THE RICE:

> **2 cups brown basmati rice**
>
> **2 teaspoons turmeric**
>
> **1 teaspoon ground cumin**
>
> **1 teaspoon ground coriander**
>
> **½ teaspoon ground cardamom**
>
> **½ teaspoon ground cinnamon**
>
> **Salt to taste**

FOR THE VEGETABLES:

> **1 medium yellow onion, peeled and diced**
>
> **2 stalks broccoli, cut into florets**
>
> **1 small head cauliflower, cut into florets**
>
> **2 medium carrots, peeled and thinly sliced**
>
> **6 cloves garlic, peeled and minced**
>
> **2 teaspoons ground coriander**
>
> **1 teaspoon whole cumin seeds, toasted (see page 10) and ground**
>
> **2 tablespoons grated ginger**
>
> **½ cup golden raisins**
>
> **¼ cup sliced almonds, toasted**
>
> **Salt to taste**

TO MAKE THE RICE:

1. Bring 4 cups of water to a boil in a medium saucepan. Add the rice and bring the pot back to a boil over high heat. Reduce the heat to medium and cook the rice, covered, for 40 minutes. Stir in the turmeric, cumin, coriander, cardamom, and cinnamon, season with salt, and cook for another 5 minutes, or until the rice is tender.

TO MAKE THE VEGETABLES:

2. Place the onion in a large saucepan and sauté over medium heat for 8 minutes. Add water 1 to 2 tablespoons at a time to keep the onion from sticking to the pan. Add the broccoli, cauliflower, and carrots to the pan and cook until the vegetables are tender, 8 to 10 minutes. Add the garlic, coriander, cumin, and ginger, mix well, and cook for another 5 minutes. Add the cooked rice, raisins, and almonds. Season with additional salt and mix well.

Wild Rice, Cabbage and Chickpea Pilaf

THIS RECIPE CAME about like a lot of my recipes: I had leftover ingredients in the fridge that needed to be used, and they all ended up in the same pan. When a dish succeeds with leftovers, it generally becomes even better when prepared with fresh ingredients.

SERVES 4

½ cup wild rice
1 medium onion, peeled and diced small
1 medium carrot, peeled and grated
1 small red bell pepper, seeded and diced small
3 cloves garlic, peeled and minced
1 tablespoon grated ginger
1½ cups chopped green cabbage
1 cup cooked chickpeas (see page 6)
1 bunch green onions (white and green parts), thinly sliced
3 tablespoons chopped cilantro
Salt and freshly ground black pepper to taste

1. Bring 2 cups of water to a boil in a large saucepan. Add the wild rice and bring the water back to a boil over high heat. Reduce the heat to medium and cook, covered, for 55 to 60 minutes. Drain off any excess water and set aside.
2. Heat a large skillet over a medium heat. Add the onion, carrot, and red pepper and sauté the vegetables for 10 minutes. Add water 1 to 2 tablespoons at a time to keep the vegetables from sticking to the pan. Add the garlic and ginger and cook for another minute. Add the cabbage and cook for 10 to 12 minutes, or until the cabbage is tender. Add the chickpeas, green onions, and cilantro. Season with salt and pepper and cook for another minute to heat the chickpeas. Remove from the heat, add the cooked wild rice, and mix well.

Ethiopian Wild Rice Pilaf

BERBERE IS A spice blend used in Ethiopian cooking, and it can be found in gourmet spice shops or online (or you can make your own—see page 125). It is an unusual blend of spices such as cardamom, ginger, nutmeg, cloves, and fenugreek, and it resembles the Indian spice garam masala. It is worth the effort to find (or make) and have on hand to make ordinary dishes special.

SERVES 4

2 medium leeks (white and light green parts), diced and rinsed

2 cloves garlic, peeled and minced

¾ teaspoon Berbere Spice Blend (page 125), or to taste

4 cups cooked wild rice blend (see page 6)

2 cups cooked adzuki beans (see page 6), or one 15-ounce can, drained and rinsed

Zest of 1 orange

Salt and freshly ground black pepper to taste

4 green onions (white and green parts), thinly sliced

Place the leeks in a large saucepan and sauté over medium heat for 10 minutes. Add water 1 to 2 tablespoons at a time to keep the leeks from sticking to the pan. Add the garlic and cook for 2 minutes. Add the berbere and cook for 30 seconds. Stir in the wild rice, beans, and orange zest and season with salt and pepper. Cook until the mixture is heated through. Garnish with the green onions.

Corn, Polenta and Millet Dishes

Whole-Grain Corn Muffins

RECIPE BY JULIEANNA HEVER

THE PERFECT ADDITION to a piping hot bowl of chili, soup, or stew is a lightly sweetened, warm corn muffin (or two). Or you can enjoy them for breakfast all on their own.

MAKES 12 MUFFINS

1½ tablespoons ground flaxseed

1 cup unsweetened plain almond milk

½ cup unsweetened applesauce

½ cup 100% pure maple syrup

1 cup cornmeal

1 cup oat flour

1 teaspoon baking soda

1 teaspoon baking powder

½ teaspoon salt

1 cup corn kernels (from about 2 ears)

1. Preheat the oven to 375°F. Line a 12-cup muffin pan with paper muffin liners or have ready a 12-cup silicone muffin pan.
2. In a small bowl, combine the flaxseeds with the almond milk and set aside, to allow it to gel, for 5 minutes.
3. In a large mixing bowl, stir the applesauce and maple syrup together. Add the flaxseed–almond milk mixture. Sift in the cornmeal, oat flour, baking soda, baking powder, and salt. Stir until well combined, but avoid overmixing. Fold in the corn kernels.
4. Spoon out equal portions of batter into the muffin cups. Bake for 20 minutes, or until a toothpick inserted into the center comes out clean. Serve warm.

Basic Polenta

ALSO KNOWN AS mush, or gruel, this grain dish was once considered peasant food, but it has enjoyed a popular resurgence in today's culinary world. It can be served soft and creamy, or allowed to set and be cut and used in any number of dishes.

SERVES 4 TO 6

1½ cups coarse cornmeal
¾ teaspoon salt, or to taste

Bring 5 cups of water to a boil in a large saucepan. Whisk in the cornmeal, a little at a time. Cook, stirring often, until the mixture is thick and creamy, about 30 minutes. Season with salt and serve, or pour the polenta into a pan and refrigerate until set, about 1 hour.

Creamy Polenta with Wild Mushrooms

POLENTA, MADE FROM cornmeal, is as versatile as any grain dish. Make it creamy, as in this dish, or let it set, become firm, then slice and bake it for a firmer texture. Here the polenta serves as the perfect base for a savory mushroom mixture.

SERVES 4 TO 6

1 shallot, peeled and minced
2 cloves garlic, peeled and minced
1 ounce porcini mushrooms, soaked for 30 minutes in 1 cup of water that has just been boiled, and coarsely chopped
1 pound wild mushrooms (such as cremini, chanterelle, or shiitake), thinly sliced
Salt and freshly ground black pepper to taste
1 batch Basic Polenta (above), kept warm
Chopped parsley

1. Place the shallot and garlic in a large saucepan and sauté over a medium-low heat for 5 minutes. Add water 1 to 2 tablespoons at a time to keep the vegetables from sticking to the pan. Add the porcini mushrooms and their soaking liquid and the wild mushrooms. Cook until the mushrooms are tender, about 10 minutes. Season with salt and pepper.
2. To serve, divide the polenta among 4 individual plates. Top with some of the mushrooms and garnish with parsley.

Polenta Triangles with Creamy Sun-Dried Tomato Sauce

TO KEEP THIS dish healthy, look for sun-dried tomatoes that are not packed in oil.

SERVES 6

> 1 batch Basic Polenta (page 229), poured into a nonstick loaf pan and refrigerated until set, about 2 to 3 hours
> 2 shallots, peeled and minced
> 2 cloves garlic, peeled and minced
> 1 cup sun-dried tomatoes, soaked in 2 cups warm water for 30 minutes, drained, and chopped
> 1 teaspoon minced thyme
> 1 batch No-Cheese Sauce (page 29)
> ½ cup minced basil
> Salt and freshly ground black pepper to taste
> Chopped parsley

1. Preheat the oven to 350°F.
2. Slice the polenta into 6 rectangles, then cut each piece in half on the diagonal to form triangles. Place the triangles on a nonstick baking sheet and bake for 15 minutes, or until heated through.
3. Meanwhile, place the shallots in a large saucepan and sauté over medium heat for 5 minutes. Add water 1 to 2 tablespoons at a time to keep the shallots from sticking to the pan. Add the garlic and cook for 2 minutes. Add the sun-dried tomatoes, thyme, and No-Cheese Sauce and cook for 10 minutes over medium-low heat, stirring frequently. Add the basil and season with salt and pepper.
4. To serve, place 2 polenta triangles in the center of each plate. Spoon some of the sauce over the polenta. Garnish with the chopped parsley.

Polenta Triangles with Mushroom Olive Sauce

THE MUSHROOM OLIVE sauce in this dish can be served over pasta or any grain, but serving it with polenta triangles makes for a nice presentation.

SERVES 6

1 batch Basic Polenta (page 229), poured into a nonstick loaf pan and refrigerated until set, about 2 to 3 hours

½ medium yellow onion, peeled and diced small

1 pound cremini or button mushrooms, thinly sliced

3 cloves garlic, peeled and minced

1 tablespoon minced thyme

½ teaspoon ground nutmeg

1 cup dry white wine

Zest and juice of 1 lemon

½ cup kalamata olives, pitted and chopped

1 batch No-Cheese Sauce (page 29)

Salt and freshly ground black pepper to taste

Chopped parsley

1. Preheat the oven to 350°F.
2. Slice the polenta into 6 rectangles and cut each piece in half on the diagonal to form triangles. Place on a nonstick baking sheet and bake for 15 minutes, or until heated through.
3. Place the onion and mushrooms in a large saucepan and sauté over medium heat for 7 to 8 minutes. Add water 1 to 2 tablespoons at a time to keep the vegetables from sticking to the pan. Add the garlic, thyme, and nutmeg and cook for 2 minutes. Add the wine and cook, at a simmer, until the liquid is reduced by half. Add the lemon zest and juice, olives, and No-Cheese Sauce and simmer for 5 minutes. Season with salt and pepper.
4. To serve, place 2 polenta triangles in the center of each plate and spoon some of the sauce over the polenta. Garnish with the parsley.

Polenta Pizza with Tomatoes and Basil

MAKE A NON-TRADITIONAL "pizza" with polenta instead of dough, and a few people may wonder if you have lost your mind. But if you're after a low-fat, super-healthy alternative to regular pizza, you have to try this dish. The polenta will soften as it bakes, so you may need to eat this with a fork.

MAKES TWO 9-INCH PIZZAS

1 batch Basic Polenta (page 229), kept warm
3 large tomatoes, thinly sliced
Salt and freshly ground black pepper to taste
¼ cup nutritional yeast, optional
2 cups finely chopped basil

1. Divide the polenta between two 9-inch round nonstick baking pans and refrigerate until set, about 1 hour.
2. Preheat the oven to 425°F.
3. Arrange the tomato slices over the polenta and season with salt and pepper. Sprinkle the nutritional yeast over the polenta, if desired, and bake for 10 to 12 minutes. Remove from the oven, top with the basil, and let sit for 10 minutes before serving.

Polenta Pizza with Pesto, Caramelized Onions and Potatoes

ARTISAN PIZZA HAS become the rage in the United States and sometimes even boasts a whole-grain crust, but my guess is that high-fat pepperoni pizza is still number one in pizza sales, unfortunately. You can make this dish with a traditional crust but this healthy, plant-based version really is a nice change. The pesto and caramelized onions add a ton of flavor to the dish. Try this with arugula pesto for even more of a change.

MAKES TWO 9-INCH PIZZAS

1 batch Basic Polenta (page 229), kept warm

2 large Yukon Gold potatoes, thinly sliced

2 medium yellow onions, peeled and diced

1 cup Basil Pesto (page 24)

¼ cup nutritional yeast, optional

Salt and freshly ground black pepper to taste

1. Divide the polenta between two 9-inch round nonstick baking pans, and refrigerate until set, about 1 hour.
2. Steam the potatoes in a double boiler or steamer basket over medium heat until tender. Set aside and let cool.
3. Place the onions in a medium saucepan and sauté over medium heat for 15 minutes, or until well browned. Add water 1 to 2 tablespoons at a time to keep the onions from sticking to the pan. Remove from the heat and set aside.
4. Preheat the oven to 425°F.
5. Divide the pesto in half and spread over each of the two pans of polenta. Arrange the potatoes over the pesto, top with the caramelized onions, and sprinkle with the nutritional yeast, if desired. Season with salt and pepper. Bake for 10 to 12 minutes. Let sit for 10 minutes before serving.

Millet-Topped Tostadas

TOSTADA LITERALLY MEANS "toasted" in Spanish, and the name is used to refer to any number of dishes made using a tortilla that has been deep fried or toasted until crispy and topped with beans, vegetables, meat, or stews. Spiced millet is not normally included, but it makes the dish healthy and hearty.

SERVES 6

1½ cups Vegetable Stock (page 23), or low-sodium vegetable broth

½ cup millet

1 small yellow onion, peeled and diced small

1 poblano pepper, seeded and minced

4 cloves garlic, peeled and minced

1½ teaspoons ground cumin

1½ teaspoons chopped fresh oregano

½ teaspoon freshly ground black pepper, or to taste

2 tablespoons mellow white miso, dissolved in ¼ cup hot water

¼ cup tomato puree

2 tablespoons nutritional yeast, optional

Salt to taste

6 corn tortillas

1 batch "Refried" Beans (page 206), warmed

4 cups shredded romaine lettuce

1 cup Fresh Tomato Salsa (page 26)

Chopped cilantro

1. Preheat the oven to 350°F.
2. Add the vegetable stock to a medium saucepan and bring to a boil over high heat. Add the millet and bring the mixture back to a boil. Reduce the heat to medium and cook, covered, for 20 minutes, or until the millet is tender.
3. Place the onion and poblano pepper in a large saucepan and sauté over medium heat for 7 to 8 minutes. Add water 1 to 2 tablespoons at a time to keep the vegetables from sticking to the pan. Add the garlic, cumin, oregano, and black pepper and cook for another minute. Add the miso, tomato puree, and nutritional yeast (if using) and mix well. Add the millet to the onion mixture, season with salt, and mix well. Spoon the millet mixture onto a nonstick rimmed baking sheet and bake for 15 minutes.
4. Remove the millet from the oven and, using a spatula, break apart the mixture.
5. Spread the corn tortillas on a baking sheet and bake until crispy, about 10 minutes.
6. To assemble the tostadas, place a tortilla on each of 6 individual plates. Divide the refried beans among the tortillas and spread them evenly. Top the beans with some of the millet mixture, followed by the romaine lettuce and salsa. Serve garnished with the cilantro.

Cabbage and Millet Pilaf

THIS DISH MAKES great use of fresh herbs. You can substitute dried if necessary, but the freshness of the herbs really makes a huge difference in flavor.

SERVES 4

2¼ cups Vegetable Stock (page 23), or low-sodium vegetable broth

¾ cup millet

1 medium leek (white and light green parts), diced and rinsed

1 medium carrot, peeled and diced

1 celery stalk, diced

2 cloves garlic, peeled and minced

1 teaspoon minced thyme

1 tablespoon minced dill

3 cups chopped cabbage

Salt and freshly ground black pepper to taste

1. In a medium saucepan, bring the vegetable stock to a boil over high heat. Add the millet and bring the pot back to a boil over high heat. Reduce the heat to medium and cook, covered, for 20 minutes, or until the millet is tender and all the vegetable stock is absorbed.

2. Place the leek, carrot, and celery in a large saucepan and sauté over medium heat for 7 to 8 minutes. Add water 1 to 2 tablespoons at a time to keep the vegetables from sticking to the pan. Add the garlic, thyme, dill, and cabbage and cook, stirring frequently, over medium heat until the cabbage is tender, about 10 minutes. Add the cooked millet and cook for another 5 minutes, stirring frequently. Season with salt and pepper.

Millet Loaf

UNLIKE MOST VEGETARIAN "meat loaves" that use beans, grains, or processed soy foods for the filling and taste nothing like Mom's, millet makes a great loaf, since it takes on the flavor of whatever spices you cook with it. Make sure to put the mixture into the baking dish as soon as you finish incorporating the spices—millet loses its binding power as it cools. (If that happens, just add Barbecue Sauce [page 36] and make Sloppy Joes.) Sliced leftovers make great sandwiches—I like mine simple, on whole-grain bread with Dijon mustard.

SERVES 6

> 2½ cups Vegetable Stock (page 23), or low-sodium vegetable broth or water
> ¾ cup millet
> 1 large yellow onion, peeled and diced small
> 4 cloves garlic, peeled and minced
> 1 tablespoon sage
> 1 tablespoon thyme
> ⅛ teaspoon ground nutmeg
> ½ teaspoon freshly ground black pepper
> 2 tablespoons mellow white miso, dissolved in ¼ cup hot water
> ¼ cup nutritional yeast, optional
> ¼ to ¾ cup Tomato Sauce (page 25)
> Salt to taste
> ½ cup ketchup, optional

1. Preheat the oven to 350°F.
2. Place the vegetable stock in a medium saucepan and bring to a boil over high heat. Add the millet and bring the mixture back to a boil. Reduce the heat to medium and cook, covered, for 20 minutes, or until the millet is tender.
3. Place the onion in a large saucepan and sauté over medium heat for 7 to 8 minutes. Add water 1 to 2 tablespoons at a time to keep the onion from sticking to the pan. Add the garlic, sage, thyme, nutmeg, and black pepper and cook for another minute. Add the miso, nutritional yeast (if using), and ¼ cup of the tomato sauce and mix well. Add the millet, season with salt, and mix well.
4. Immediately spoon the mixture into a nonstick loaf pan and press it firmly into the pan. Top with another ½ cup of tomato sauce or ketchup and bake for 30 minutes.
5. Remove from the oven and let sit for 10 minutes before slicing.

VARIATIONS

▶ Millet Loaf can be readily transformed into Barbecue Millet Balls. Prepare 1 batch of Millet Loaf. Instead of spooning the millet mixture into a loaf pan, use a small ice-cream scoop or a scant ¼-cup measure to form the mixture into balls. Place them on a nonstick baking sheet or a baking sheet lined with parchment paper. Bake for 15 minutes in a 350°F preheated oven. To serve, divide the millet balls among 6 plates and spoon 3 cups of heated Barbecue Sauce (page 36) over them. They do not sit well in the sauce for any length of time, so pour the sauce over them just before serving. Serve these with a salad and a cooked grain of your choice.

▶ The Barbecue Millet Balls can also be made into Swedish "Meatballs," probably the best-known Scandinavian dish. Prepare the millet balls as in the variation above, through baking. While the millet balls bake, place 2 batches of No-Cheese Sauce (page 29) in a small saucepan and add 1 teaspoon of ground nutmeg. Cook the sauce over low heat until heated through, about 5 minutes. To serve, divide the millet balls among 6 plates and spoon the sauce over them (again, the millet balls do not sit well in sauce for any length of time, so add the sauce no more than 5 minutes before serving). Serve these over pasta, with brown rice, or as an appetizer at your next potluck.

Curried Millet Cakes with Red Pepper Coriander Sauce 📷

SERVE THIS DELICIOUS dish with Coriander Chutney (page 32) and brown basmati rice.

SERVES 6

> 3 cups Vegetable Stock (page 23), or low-sodium vegetable broth
> 1 cup millet
> 1 large yellow onion, peeled and diced small
> 4 cloves garlic, peeled and minced
> 1 tablespoon curry powder
> ½ teaspoon crushed red pepper flakes
> 2 tablespoons mellow white miso, dissolved in ¼ cup hot water
> 2 tablespoons tomato puree
> ¼ cup nutritional yeast, optional
> Salt to taste
> 1 batch Red Pepper Coriander Sauce (below), warmed

1. Preheat the oven to 350°F.
2. Place the vegetable stock in a medium saucepan and bring to a boil over high heat. Add the millet and bring the mixture back to a boil. Reduce the heat to medium and cook, covered, for 20 minutes, or until the millet is tender.
3. Place the onion in a large saucepan and sauté over medium heat for 7 to 8 minutes. Add water 1 to 2 tablespoons at a time to keep the onion from sticking to the pan. Add the garlic, curry powder, and crushed red pepper flakes and cook for another minute. Add the miso, tomato puree, and nutritional yeast (if using) and mix well. Add the millet, season with salt, and mix well.
4. Line a baking sheet with parchment paper. Using an-ice cream scoop or a ⅓-cup measure, shape the millet mixture into 12 round cakes. Place the cakes on the prepared baking sheet and bake for 15 minutes.
5. To serve, spoon some of the warm Red Pepper Coriander Sauce onto a plate and top with two of the millet cakes.

Red Pepper Coriander Sauce

> One 12-ounce package extra firm silken tofu, drained
> 2 large red bell peppers, roasted (see page 8) and seeded
> 3 cloves garlic, peeled and chopped
> ¼ cup chopped cilantro
> 1 teaspoon salt, or to taste
> ½ teaspoon crushed red pepper flakes
> Zest and juice of 1 lime

Combine all ingredients in the bowl of a food processor and puree until smooth and creamy. Warm in a saucepan before using. Refrigerate any unused sauce in an airtight container.

Quinoa and Other Grain Dishes

Quinoa Pilaf with Apricots, Pistachios and Mint

PILAFS ARE TRADITIONALLY rice or bulgur dishes made with the grain toasted in fat before any other liquid and spices are added. I leave out the fat but use other ways of adding flavor to the dish. With quick-cooking quinoa you can have a meal ready in less than 30 minutes. Eat this dish with a salad for a delicious light meal, or in a lettuce wrap with Hummus (page 139). The mint and orange add brightness to the dish, but you could also use cilantro and lime for a nice change.

SERVES 4

> 2 shallots, peeled and diced small
> 1 medium red bell pepper, seeded and diced small
> 4 cups cooked quinoa (see page 6), made with 4 cups Vegetable Stock (page 23) or low-sodium vegetable broth
> ¾ cup dried unsulfured apricots, chopped (see page 9 for more on sulfites and sulfur dioxide)
> Zest and juice of 1 orange
> 3 tablespoons chopped mint
> ½ teaspoon crushed red pepper flakes
> Salt to taste
> ¼ cup pistachios, toasted (see page 10)

Place the shallots and red pepper in a medium saucepan and sauté over medium heat for 10 minutes. Add water 1 to 2 tablespoons at a time to keep the vegetables from sticking to the pan. Add the quinoa, apricots, orange zest and juice, mint, and crushed red pepper flakes and cook until heated through, about 5 minutes. Season with salt and garnish with the pistachios.

Orange Quinoa with Black Beans

FRESH GINGER AND orange brighten the earthy black bean and the mild, nutty quinoa.

SERVES 4

1½ cups quinoa, rinsed and drained

1½ teaspoons cumin seeds, toasted (see page 10) and ground

2 cups cooked black beans (see page 6), or one 15-ounce can, drained and rinsed

1½ teaspoons grated ginger

2 tablespoons balsamic vinegar

Zest and juice of 1 orange (about ¼ cup juice)

4 green onions (white and green parts), thinly sliced

Salt and freshly ground black pepper to taste

1. Add 3 cups of water to a medium pot with a tight-fitting lid and bring to a boil over high heat. Add the quinoa and return the pot to a boil over high heat. Reduce the heat to medium-low and cook the quinoa, covered, for 15 to 20 minutes, or until tender.
2. Place the quinoa in a large bowl and add the cumin, black beans, ginger, vinegar, orange zest and juice, and green onions. Mix well and season with salt and pepper.

Spinach, Mushroom and Quinoa Pilaf

LEEKS AND MUSHROOMS add an earthiness to this dish. Porcini mushrooms are expensive, but a little goes a long way in adding flavor to your favorite mushroom recipe.

SERVES 4

⅓ ounce porcini mushrooms, soaked for 30 minutes in 1 cup of water that has just been boiled, and roughly chopped

2 large leeks (white and light green parts), diced and rinsed

8 ounces cremini mushrooms, thinly sliced

3 cloves garlic, peeled and minced

1 tablespoon thyme

2 cups Vegetable Stock (page 23), or low-sodium vegetable broth, plus more as needed

1½ cups quinoa

6 cups baby spinach, chopped

Salt and freshly ground black pepper to taste

¼ cup pine nuts, toasted (see page 10), optional

1. Drain the porcini mushrooms, reserving the liquid. Finely chop the mushrooms and set aside.
2. Place the leeks and cremini mushrooms in a large saucepan and sauté over medium heat for 10 minutes. Add water 1 to 2 tablespoons at a time to keep the vegetables from sticking to the pan. Add the garlic and thyme and cook for 30 seconds.
3. Combine the porcini mushroom soaking liquid and vegetable stock. Add more vegetable stock as needed to make 3 cups. Add the liquid, quinoa, and chopped porcini mushrooms to the pan with the sautéed mushrooms and bring the pan to a boil over high heat. Reduce the heat to medium and cook the quinoa, covered, for 15 minutes, or until it is tender. Stir in the spinach and cook for another 5 minutes, or until the spinach is wilted. Season with salt and pepper and garnish with the pine nuts, if desired.

Bulgur Pilaf with Chickpeas and Summer Squash

FRESH HERBS LIKE basil and thyme are easy to grow, making them an inexpensive addition to the garden pantry. As a bonus, thyme is a perennial, so you plant it once and it comes back to visit you year after year.

SERVES 4

- **1 medium yellow onion, peeled and diced**
- **1 clove garlic, peeled and minced**
- **1 teaspoon minced thyme**
- **1 medium zucchini, halved lengthwise and cut into ½-inch slices**
- **1 medium yellow squash, halved lengthwise and cut into ½-inch slices**
- **2 cups cooked chickpeas (see page 6), or one 15-ounce can, drained and rinsed**
- **2 cups bulgur, cooked (see page 6), made with 4 cups Vegetable Stock (page 23) or low-sodium vegetable broth**
- **¼ cup minced basil**
- **Salt and freshly ground black pepper to taste**

Place the onion in a large saucepan and sauté over medium heat for 10 minutes. Add water 1 to 2 tablespoons at a time to keep the onion from sticking to the pan. Add the garlic and thyme and cook for 3 minutes more. Stir in the zucchini, yellow squash, and chickpeas and cook for 10 minutes, or until the vegetables are tender. Stir in the cooked bulgur and cook for another 5 minutes, then add the basil, season with salt and pepper, and cook for another minute.

Bulgur Chickpea Pilaf

I MAKE THIS dish a lot because I always have these ingredients in my pantry, they come together easily, and they taste great together. Sometimes I make it with quinoa for gluten-free friends, and for a Southwest version, I make it with 2 teaspoons of cumin, lime zest and juice instead of lemon, and a garnish of ½ cup of finely chopped cilantro (in addition to the green onions).

SERVES 4

1 medium yellow onion, peeled and diced small

3 cloves garlic, peeled and minced

1½ tablespoons grated ginger

1½ cups bulgur

3 cups Vegetable Stock (page 23), or low-sodium vegetable broth

2 cups cooked chickpeas (see page 6), or one 15-ounce can, drained and rinsed

1 Roma tomato, chopped

Zest and juice of 1 lemon

Salt and freshly ground black pepper to taste

4 green onions (white and green parts), thinly sliced

1. Place the onion in a large saucepan and sauté over medium heat for 10 minutes. Add water 1 to 2 tablespoons at a time to keep the onion from sticking to the pan. Stir in the garlic and ginger and cook for 30 seconds. Add the bulgur and vegetable stock and bring to a boil over high heat. Reduce the heat to medium and cook, covered, until the bulgur is tender, about 15 minutes.
2. Stir in the chickpeas, tomato, and lemon zest and juice and cook for another 5 minutes. Season with salt and pepper and serve garnished with the green onions.

Bulgur Pilaf with Walnuts and Dried Fruit

THIS IS A sweet and savory pilaf with a hint of cinnamon.

SERVES 4

> **1 medium yellow onion, peeled and diced**
>
> **2 cloves garlic, peeled and minced**
>
> **2 cups bulgur**
>
> **½ cup golden raisins**
>
> **½ cup dried unsulfured apricots, chopped (see page 9 for more on sulfites and sulfur dioxide)**
>
> **1 cinnamon stick**
>
> **2 teaspoons ground coriander**
>
> **3½ cups Vegetable Stock (page 23), or low-sodium vegetable broth**
>
> **2 green onions (white and green parts), thinly sliced**
>
> **Salt and freshly ground black pepper to taste**
>
> **½ cup walnuts, toasted (see page 10) and coarsely chopped**

Place the onion in a large saucepan and sauté over a medium-high heat until golden, about 7 to 8 minutes. Add water 1 to 2 tablespoons at a time to keep the onion from sticking to the pan. Add the garlic and cook for 1 minute. Add the bulgur, raisins, apricots, cinnamon stick, and coriander. Add the stock and bring to a boil over high heat. Reduce the heat to medium and cook, covered, until the bulgur is tender, about 15 minutes. Remove from the heat, pick out the cinnamon stick, and stir in the green onions. Season with salt and pepper and serve garnished with the chopped walnuts.

Barley and White Bean Pilaf

A HINT OF orange and fresh dill make unusual flavoring partners in this hearty pilaf with delicious results.

SERVES 4

> **1 medium yellow onion, peeled and finely diced**
>
> **1 celery stalk, finely diced**
>
> **1 medium carrot, peeled and finely diced**
>
> **1½ cups pearled barley**
>
> **2-inch piece orange peel**
>
> **1 cinnamon stick**
>
> **3 cups Vegetable Stock (page 23), or low-sodium vegetable broth**
>
> **2 cups cooked navy or other white beans (see page 6), or one 15-ounce can, drained and rinsed**
>
> **¼ cup finely chopped dill**

Place the onion, celery, and carrot in a large saucepan and sauté over medium heat for 7 to 8 minutes. Add water 1 to 2 tablespoons at a time to keep the vegetables from sticking to the pan. Add the barley, orange peel, cinnamon stick, and vegetable stock and bring the pan to a boil over high heat. Reduce the heat to medium and cook for 35 minutes. Add the beans and cook for another 10 minutes, until the barley is tender. Remove from the heat and stir in the dill.

Barley and Sweet Potato Pilaf 📷

BARLEY IS UNUSUAL in pilafs, but it works well when you want a change from rice. Tarragon has a flavor similar to fennel but milder. Serve this on a bed of spinach for a filling meal.

SERVES 4

1 medium onion, peeled and chopped

2 cloves garlic, peeled and minced

3½ cups Vegetable Stock (page 23), or low-sodium vegetable broth

1½ cups pearled barley

1 large sweet potato (about ¾ pound), peeled and diced small

¼ cup minced tarragon

Zest and juice of 1 lemon

Salt and freshly ground black pepper to taste

Place the onion in a large saucepan and sauté over medium heat for 6 minutes. Add water 1 to 2 tablespoons at a time to keep the onion from sticking to the pan. Add the garlic and cook 3 minutes more. Add the vegetable stock and barley and bring the pot to a boil over high heat. Reduce the heat to medium and cook, covered, for 30 minutes. Add the sweet potato and cook for 15 minutes longer, or until the potato and barley are tender. Remove from the heat, stir in the tarragon and lemon zest and juice, and season with salt and pepper.

Mushroom Barley Risotto

RISOTTO MADE FROM barley is a heartier version of the traditional one, made from Arborio rice, and it's higher in fiber, an added bonus.

SERVES 3 TO 4

> **1 ounce dried porcini mushrooms, soaked for 30 minutes in 1 cup of water that has just been boiled**
> **3 large shallots, peeled and finely diced**
> **8 ounces cremini mushrooms, sliced**
> **2 sage leaves, minced**
> **3 cloves garlic, peeled and minced**
> **1½ cups pearled barley**
> **½ cup dry white wine**
> **3 to 4 cups Vegetable Stock (page 23), or low-sodium vegetable broth**
> **¼ cup nutritional yeast, optional**
> **Salt and freshly ground black pepper to taste**

1. Drain the porcini mushrooms, reserving the liquid. Finely chop the mushrooms and set aside.
2. Place the shallots in a 2-quart saucepan and sauté over medium heat for 4 to 5 minutes. Add water 1 to 2 tablespoons at a time to keep the shallots from sticking to the pan. Add the cremini mushrooms and cook for another 5 minutes. Let the mushrooms brown by adding as little water as possible, while still making sure they don't stick to the pan. Add the sage, garlic, barley, and white wine and cook for 1 minute. Add 2 cups of the vegetable stock and the reserved porcini soaking liquid and bring the mixture to a boil over high heat. Reduce the heat to medium and cook, covered, for 25 minutes. Add more broth if necessary and cook for another 15 to 20 minutes. Stir in the chopped porcini mushrooms and nutritional yeast (if using). Season with salt and pepper and serve immediately.

Kasha Varnishkes
(Buckwheat Groats with Bow-Tie Pasta)

THIS EASTERN EUROPEAN dish is traditionally made with farfalle (bow-tie pasta), buckwheat groats, and caramelized onions. Buckwheat, in spite of its name, is gluten-free and has a nutty flavor, set off nicely in this dish by the sweetness of the caramelized onions. The fresh dill is not the usual flavoring, but it adds a layer of freshness. If you are making this dish gluten-free, use your favorite gluten-free pasta in place of the whole-grain farfalle.

SERVES 4

2 cups Vegetable Stock (page 23), or low-sodium vegetable broth

1 cup buckwheat groats

1 large yellow onion, peeled and diced small

8 ounces button mushrooms, sliced

½ pound whole-grain farfalle, cooked according to package directions, drained, and kept warm

2 tablespoons finely chopped dill

Salt and freshly ground black pepper to taste

1. Place the vegetable stock in a medium saucepan and bring to a boil over high heat. Add the buckwheat groats and bring the pot back to a boil over high heat. Reduce the heat to medium and cook, uncovered, until the groats are tender, about 12 to 15 minutes.

2. Place the onion in a large saucepan and sauté over medium heat until well browned, about 15 minutes. Add water 1 to 2 tablespoons at a time to keep the onion from sticking, but use as little water as possible. Add the mushrooms and cook for another 5 minutes. Remove from the heat. Add the cooked pasta, buckwheat groats, and dill. Season with salt and pepper.

Summer Vegetable Pesto Bake

THE LATE SUMMER garden is always full of tomatoes, squash, and basil, and gardeners everywhere are always looking for new ways to use these summer staples. Here's another recipe to add to that list of summer's best meals. Try an arugula pesto for a sharper flavor.

SERVES 8

2 large yellow onions, peeled and sliced into thin rings

2 large Yukon Gold potatoes, cut into ½-inch rounds

Salt and freshly ground black pepper to taste

2 large zucchini, cut into ½-inch slices

1 batch Basil Pesto (page 24)

2 large yellow squash, cut into ½-inch rounds

2 large tomatoes, cut into ¾-inch rounds

1. Preheat the oven to 350°F.
2. Place the onions in a saucepan or large skillet and sauté over medium heat for 10 minutes, or until the onions are browned. Add water 1 to 2 tablespoons at a time, as needed to keep the onions from sticking to the pan. Set aside.
3. Place the potatoes in a double boiler or steamer basket and steam for 8 to 10 minutes, or until al dente. Season with salt and black pepper and set aside.
4. Place a layer of zucchini in the bottom of a 9 x 13-inch nonstick pan. Season with salt and pepper, and dollop with small spoonfuls of the basil pesto. Add a layer of yellow squash, season with salt and pepper, and dollop with small spoonfuls of the basil pesto. Add a layer of the steamed potatoes, and dollop with small spoonfuls of the basil pesto. Repeat until the zucchini, yellow squash, and potatoes are used up. Top with the tomato slices, and then the caramelized onions. Season again with salt and pepper.
5. Bake the casserole for 30 minutes. Let sit for 10 minutes before serving.

CASSEROLES

Broccoli Rice Casserole

THIS DISH WILL get even the most finicky kid in the house to eat vegetables—it's delicious.

SERVES 6

> 3 cups Vegetable Stock (page 23), or low-sodium vegetable broth
> 1½ cups brown rice
> 3 cups broccoli florets (from about 2 medium bunches)
> 1 batch No-Cheese Sauce (page 29)
> Freshly ground black pepper to taste
> Paprika to taste

1. Add the vegetable stock to a medium saucepan and bring it to a boil over high heat. Add the brown rice, cover, and bring it back to a boil over high heat. Reduce the heat to medium and cook, covered, for 45 minutes, or until the rice is tender.
2. Place the broccoli florets in a double boiler or steamer basket and steam for 5 minutes, or until crisp-tender. Rinse until cool and set aside.
3. Preheat the oven to 350°F.
4. Add the rice to a bowl with the No-Cheese Sauce and steamed broccoli and mix well. Spread the rice mixture in the bottom of a 9 x 13-inch baking dish and sprinkle the casserole with black pepper and paprika.
5. Bake the casserole for 35 to 40 minutes, or until bubbly.

Baked Ziti

THIS EASY BAKED pasta dish is comfort food at its best. Here it gets a healthy makeover with whole-grain pasta and my low-fat, no-fuss No-Cheese Sauce—yum!

SERVES 6

1 large yellow onion, peeled and diced
4 cloves garlic, peeled and minced
2 tablespoons chopped oregano
One 28-ounce can diced tomatoes
Salt and freshly ground black pepper to taste
1 pound whole-grain ziti
1 batch No-Cheese Sauce (page 29)

1. Bring a large pot of salted water to a boil.
2. Preheat the oven to 375°F.
3. Place the onion in a large saucepan and sauté over medium-high heat for 7 to 8 minutes, or until the onion starts to brown. Add water 1 to 2 tablespoons at a time to keep the onion from sticking to the pan. Add the garlic and oregano and cook for another minute. Add the tomatoes, season with salt and pepper, and cook over medium heat for 5 minutes.
4. Cook the pasta in the boiling water until it is not quite al dente (it will finish cooking in the oven). Drain the noodles and add them to the tomato mixture. Mix well and pour into a 9 x 13-inch baking dish. Top with the No-Cheese Sauce and bake, uncovered, for 25 to 30 minutes, or until bubbly.

VARIATION
▶ Sauté 1 pound of sliced mushrooms with the onion.

Mac and "Cheese"

I'VE NEVER BEEN much of a fan of plant-based macaroni and "cheese" dishes. Either they have an overwhelming flavor of nutritional yeast or, if they use a cashew sauce, they are very high in fat. This version is a balance of all of those versions that came before it—great flavor, not so much fat, and a crispy top even without the usual bread crumbs. The smoked paprika gives the sauce the flavor of smoked gouda, but you could leave it out and use dill or any other fresh herbs to your taste.

SERVES 4

> 12 ounces whole-grain elbow macaroni, cooked according to package directions, drained, and kept warm
>
> 1 batch No-Cheese Sauce (page 29)
>
> 1½ teaspoons smoked paprika, or to taste
>
> ¼ teaspoon cayenne pepper, optional

1. Preheat the oven to 350°F.
2. Place the cooked pasta in a large bowl. Add the No-Cheese Sauce, paprika, and cayenne pepper (if using) and mix well.
3. Spoon the mixture into a 9 x 13-inch baking dish and bake for 30 minutes, or until bubbly.

Southwestern Mac and "Cheese" 📷

MACARONI AND "CHEESE" gets a kick with corn, peppers, black beans, and spices.

SERVES 4

> 1 medium yellow onion, peeled and diced
>
> 1 medium red bell pepper, seeded and diced
>
> 2 cups corn kernels (from about 3 ears)
>
> 1 jalapeño pepper, seeded and minced
>
> 2 teaspoons ground cumin
>
> 2 teaspoons ancho chile powder
>
> Salt to taste
>
> 1 batch No-Cheese Sauce (page 29)
>
> 2 cups cooked black beans (see page 6), or one 15-ounce can, drained and rinsed
>
> ½ pound whole-grain elbow macaroni, cooked according to package directions, drained, and kept warm

1. Preheat the oven to 350°F.
2. Place the onion and red pepper in a large saucepan and sauté over medium heat for 10 minutes. Add water 1 to 2 tablespoons at a time to keep the vegetables from sticking to the pan. Add the corn, jalapeño pepper, cumin, and chile powder and cook for 30 seconds. Remove from the heat and season with salt. Stir in the No-Cheese Sauce, beans, and cooked macaroni.
3. Spoon the mixture into a 9 x 13-inch baking dish and bake for 30 minutes, or until bubbly.

Cauliflower and White Bean Bake

IN THIS DISH, cauliflower and beans are baked in a tangy sauce—with a kick! Use any white bean you like in place of the navy beans.

SERVES 6

1 medium head cauliflower, cut into florets, steamed for 4 minutes, and rinsed until cool

One 6-ounce can diced mild green chiles, drained

Zest of 1 lime and juice of 2 limes

4 cups cooked navy beans (see page 6), or two 15-ounce cans, drained and rinsed

1 batch No-Cheese Sauce (page 29)

2 tablespoons ancho chile powder

2 teaspoons crushed red pepper flakes

1. Preheat the oven to 375°F.
2. Combine the cauliflower, diced chiles, lime zest and juice, and beans in a large bowl. Spoon the mixture into the bottom of a 9 x 13-inch baking dish. Set aside.
3. Combine the No-Cheese Sauce with the ancho chile powder and crushed red pepper flakes. Pour the sauce over the cauliflower mixture and bake for 30 minutes, or until bubbly.

Mexican-Style Bean and Rice Casserole

HERE, THE CLASSIC beans and rice combination gets a kick with ancho chile powder and cumin, the No-Cheese Sauce (page 29) adds a creamy texture, and the health benefits are bumped up with zucchini, black beans, and corn.

SERVES 4

1 large yellow onion, peeled and diced

1 red bell pepper, seeded and diced

3 cloves garlic, peeled and minced

1 tablespoon cumin seeds, toasted (see page 10) and ground

2 teaspoons ancho chile powder

2 cups cooked brown rice (see page 6)

2 medium zucchini, cut into ½-inch dice

2 cups cooked black beans (see page 6), or one 15-ounce can, drained and rinsed

3 ears corn, kernels removed (about 2 cups)

1 batch No-Cheese Sauce (page 29)

Chopped cilantro

1. Preheat the oven to 350°F.
2. Place the onion and red pepper in a large saucepan and sauté over medium heat for 7 to 8 minutes, or until the onion starts to brown. Add water 1 to 2 tablespoons at a time to keep the vegetables from sticking to the pan. Add the garlic and cook for 4 minutes. Add the cumin and chile powder and cook for another 30 seconds. Remove from the heat. Add the cooked rice, zucchini, black beans, corn, and No-Cheese Sauce and mix well.
3. Spoon the mixture into an 8 x 8-inch baking dish. Bake for 25 minutes, or until bubbly. Serve garnished with the cilantro.

VARIATION

▶ To turn this recipe into enchiladas, wrap 12 corn tortillas in aluminum foil and heat in a preheated 350°F oven for 15 minutes, until warmed and softened. Place a tortilla on a flat surface and spread ⅓ cup of the bean and rice filling along the center of the tortilla and roll it up, then set it, seam side down, in a 9 x 13-inch baking dish. Repeat until all of the tortillas are used. (You will have leftover bean and rice filling; reserve for another purpose.) Pour 1 batch of Enchilada Sauce (page 255) over the enchiladas and bake for 20 minutes. Serve garnished with 4 thinly sliced green onions, ½ cup of chopped cilantro, and dollops of Tofu Sour Cream (page 28).

Enchilada Sauce

MAKES 2½ CUPS

½ small yellow onion, peeled and diced small

3 cloves garlic, peeled and minced

¼ cup ancho chile powder, toasted (see page 10)

1 teaspoon ground cumin, toasted

1 cup Tomato Sauce (page 25)

1½ cups Vegetable Stock (page 23), or low-sodium vegetable broth

Salt to taste

Place the onion in a large saucepan and sauté for 5 minutes over medium heat. Add water 1 to 2 tablespoons at a time to keep the onion from sticking to the pan. Add the garlic and toasted spices and cook for another minute. Add the tomato sauce and vegetable stock and cook over medium heat for 10 minutes. Season with salt.

TIP

▶ Toast the ancho chile powder and the cumin together in the same pan to save yourself time and meld the flavors. Be sure to toast until fragrant but not burnt.

Vegetable Enchiladas with Bean Sauce

ANASAZI BEANS CAN be found in gourmet markets, but if you can't find them, use pinto beans instead. You can also make this dish with Salsa Verde (page 26) instead of the bean sauce.

SERVES 4

FOR THE BEAN SAUCE:

> 1 cup anasazi beans, soaked (see page 6)
>
> 1 small onion, peeled and diced
>
> 2 cloves garlic, peeled and minced
>
> 1 jalapeño pepper, seeded and minced
>
> 1 teaspoon cumin seeds, toasted (see page 10) and ground
>
> 1 teaspoon ancho chile powder
>
> Salt to taste
>
> ¾ cup to 1 cup Vegetable Stock (page 23), or low-sodium vegetable broth, as needed

FOR THE VEGETABLE FILLING:

> 1 medium yellow onion, peeled and diced small
>
> 1 red bell pepper, seeded and diced small
>
> 1 medium zucchini, diced small
>
> 2 ears corn, kernels removed (about 1 cup)
>
> 4 cloves garlic, peeled and minced
>
> 1 jalapeño pepper, seeded and minced
>
> 1 teaspoon cumin seeds, toasted and ground
>
> 1 teaspoon oregano
>
> 2 teaspoons ancho chile powder
>
> Salt to taste
>
> 8 to 10 corn tortillas
>
> Chopped cilantro

TO MAKE THE BEAN SAUCE:

1. Add the beans to a large pot with enough water to cover and bring to a boil over high heat. Reduce the heat to medium and simmer the beans until tender, about 2 hours, adding water as necessary to keep immersed. Drain and set aside.
2. Place the onion in a large saucepan and sauté over medium heat until tender, 7 to 8 minutes. Add water 1 to 2 tablespoons at a time to keep the onion from sticking to the pan. Add the beans, garlic, jalapeño pepper, cumin, chile powder, and salt and cook for 5 minutes more. Remove from the heat.
3. Puree the beans until smooth using an immersion blender or a blender, adding as much of the vegetable stock as needed to achieve a creamy consistency.

TO MAKE THE VEGETABLE FILLING:

4. Place the onion and red pepper in a large saucepan and sauté over medium heat until tender, 8 to 10 minutes. Add water 1 to 2 tablespoons at a time to keep the vegetables from sticking to the pan. Add the zucchini, corn, garlic, jalapeño pepper, cumin, oregano, and chile powder and cook for 5 minutes, or until the zucchini is tender. Season with salt.

TO ASSEMBLE THE ENCHILADAS:

5. Preheat the oven to 350°F.
6. Wrap the tortillas in aluminum foil and heat them in the oven for 15 minutes.
7. Place a tortilla on a flat surface and spoon ¼ cup of the vegetable filling in the center of the tortilla. Wrap the tortilla around the filling and place it, seam side down, in a 9 x 13-inch baking dish. Repeat with the remaining tortillas. Pour the bean sauce over the enchiladas and bake for 20 minutes, or until heated through. Serve garnished with the cilantro.

Eggplant Polenta Casserole 📷

CASSEROLES AREN'T THE usual fare in the summer, since they require lots of time around a hot oven, but this dish of creamy polenta on top of a stew of summer's peak produce cries out for the making. Save this dish for a rainy summer day when it's not sweltering outside.

SERVES 6 TO 8

1 large yellow onion, peeled and diced

1 large red bell pepper, seeded and diced

2 large eggplants (about 3 pounds), stemmed and diced

8 cloves garlic, peeled and minced

2 large tomatoes, diced

Salt and freshly ground black pepper to taste

1 cup chopped basil

1 batch Basic Polenta (page 229), kept warm

1. Preheat the oven to 350°F.
2. Place the onion in a large saucepan and sauté over medium heat for 10 minutes. Add water 1 to 2 tablespoons at a time to keep the onion from sticking to the pan. Add the red pepper, eggplant, and garlic. Cook, covered, for 15 minutes, stirring occasionally, adding more water as needed. Stir in the tomatoes, season with salt and pepper, and cook for another 10 minutes.
3. Add the basil and spoon the mixture into a 9 x 13-inch baking dish. Spoon the polenta over the eggplant mixture and bake for 30 minutes.

Tuscan-Style Shepherd's Pie

CREAMY POLENTA STANDS in for mashed potatoes atop this otherwise simple bean dish.

SERVES 4

1 medium yellow onion, peeled and diced

1 medium carrot, peeled and diced

2 celery stalks, diced

4 cloves garlic, peeled and minced

1 teaspoon minced rosemary

1 teaspoon minced thyme

2 large Yukon Gold potatoes, diced

2 cups Vegetable Stock (page 23), or low-sodium vegetable broth

4 cups cooked cannellini beans (see page 6), or two 15-ounce cans, drained and rinsed

Salt and freshly ground black pepper to taste

1 batch Basic Polenta (page 229), kept warm

1. Preheat the oven to 350°F.
2. Place the onion, carrot, and celery in a large saucepan and sauté over medium heat for 5 minutes. Add water 1 to 2 tablespoons at a time to keep the vegetables from sticking to the pan. Stir in the garlic, rosemary, and thyme and cook for 3 minutes. Add the potatoes and vegetable stock and cook until tender, about 15 minutes. Add the beans, season with salt and black pepper, and cook for 5 minutes longer.
3. Spoon the beans into an 8-inch square baking dish and spread the polenta over the top. Bake for 20 minutes.

Shepherd's Pie

RECIPE BY JUDY MICKLEWRIGHT

THE MOST POPULAR version of this dish is made with minced meat, as well as a large quantity of dairy. The Shepherdess's Pie (a vegetarian version) is commonly made with cheese, butter, milk, and/or cream. This plant-based version uses a wide variety of flavorful vegetables. The recipe makes a full six to eight servings—and it reheats well at the end of a busy weekday. Its flavors intensify overnight as the vegetables and mushrooms meld into the sauces. For best results, use a deep-dish pan rather than a shallow one, but avoid using any type of dish that will crack under broiling heat. I use a 3-quart clay baker (4 inches deep, with a 3-inch-tall lid), which is easy to clean—just soak it without any soap and the food comes off easily. Plus, food rarely gets stuck to it during cooking, even when cooking without oil.

SERVES 6 TO 8

FOR THE POTATO LAYER:

4 pounds Yukon Gold potatoes (about 9 large), quartered

3 cloves garlic, peeled and minced

4 cups Vegetable Stock (page 23), or low-sodium vegetable broth

2 cups unsweetened plain almond milk

2 tablespoons prepared mustard

3 tablespoons thyme

½ teaspoon white pepper

Salt to taste

FOR THE MUSHROOM AND GRAVY LAYER:

½ medium onion, peeled and diced (about ¼ cup)

½ pound cremini mushrooms, sliced

1½ teaspoons thyme

½ teaspoon minced tarragon

3 tablespoons red grape juice (no sugar added)

¼ cup brown rice flour

1 tablespoon prepared mustard

2 tablespoons low-sodium soy sauce

2 teaspoons 100% pure maple syrup

Pinch of ground white pepper or freshly ground black pepper

FOR THE TOMATO LAYER:

One 24-ounce can crushed or diced tomatoes (see tip, page 261)

½ medium onion, peeled and diced (about ¼ cup)

2 cloves garlic, peeled and minced

1 tablespoon oregano

2 tablespoons basil

1 cup peas

3 medium carrots, peeled and cut into ¼-inch slices

2 cups cauliflower florets (from about 1 medium head)

2 cups green beans

Salt to taste

TO MAKE THE POTATO LAYER:

1. Place the potatoes, garlic, and vegetable stock in a large saucepan and bring to a boil over high heat. Reduce the heat to medium and simmer for about 15 minutes, or until the potatoes are tender. Drain the potatoes, reserving the cooking water. Return the potatoes to the pot, cover, and keep over low heat, shaking periodically, for about 5 minutes or until dry.

2. Add the almond milk, mustard, thyme, and pepper. Mash until only a few small lumps of potato are left. Season with salt.

TO MAKE THE MUSHROOM AND GRAVY LAYER:

3. Add 1 cup of reserved potato liquid and the onion to a large saucepan and bring to a boil over high heat. Reduce the heat to medium and simmer for 5 minutes. Add the mushrooms, thyme, and tarragon and simmer for another 10 minutes, or until all the liquid is reduced. Add the grape juice to deglaze the pan and cook until mostly reduced, about 5 minutes.

4. Combine the brown rice flour, an additional 2 cups of reserved potato liquid, and the mustard in a medium bowl and whisk until smooth. Pour into the pan and cook, stirring constantly until it thickens. Remove from the heat. Stir in the soy sauce, maple syrup, and pepper.

TO MAKE THE TOMATO LAYER:

5. Add the tomatoes, onion, garlic, oregano, basil, peas, and carrots to a large saucepan and sauté for 10 minutes. Add the cauliflower and green beans and cook for another 5 minutes. Drain any excess water and season with salt.

TO ASSEMBLE THE CASSEROLE:

6. Preheat the oven to 350°F.

7. Spread the tomato later in the bottom of a 9 x 13-inch baking dish. Pour the mushroom and gravy layer over the tomato layer. Spread the potato layer over the mushroom layer.

8. Cover the dish with a lid or aluminum foil and bake for 30 minutes. Remove the cover and broil for 10 minutes, or until bits of the potato layer turn golden brown.

TIPS

▶ I've used different types of potatoes for this recipe and I've found that Yukon Gold potatoes yield the most flavor and the creamiest texture. If Yukon Golds are not available, use any medium- to high-starch potato. Be sure to not over-mash the potatoes, which will create a gummy consistency.

▶ If you can find the San Marzano crushed tomatoes that come in a glass jar, use them instead of canned. The tomato sauce layer has to be thick, or the potato layer will sink into the dish.

▶ If you want to vary the vegetables, try this dish with zucchini, parsnips, or eggplant.

▶ Save any extra sauce and gravy that will not fit into the dish and keep it on hand for serving reheated leftovers.

Lentil Shepherd's Pie with Rustic Parsnip Crust

MY FAMILY EATS mashed potatoes at every holiday meal, and as a kid I never liked them, except as a bowl for gravy, which I adored. Imagine my surprise when I learned that you could add other things to mashed potatoes to make them good—such as roasted garlic, leeks, and, as in this dish, parsnips.

SERVES 6 TO 8

1 large yellow onion, peeled and diced small

1 large carrot, peeled and diced small

2 stalks celery, diced small

2 cloves garlic, peeled and minced

1 sprig rosemary

1½ cup green lentils, rinsed

1 bay leaf

3 tablespoons tomato paste

Salt and freshly ground black pepper to taste

8 medium red-skin potatoes, peeled and chopped

4 parsnips, peeled and chopped

1. Place the onion, carrot, and celery in a large saucepan and sauté over medium heat for 10 minutes. Add water 1 to 2 tablespoons at a time to keep the vegetables from sticking to the pan. Add the garlic and cook for another minute. Stir in the rosemary, lentils, bay leaf, and enough water to cover the lentils by 3 inches. Bring the pot to a boil over high heat. Reduce the heat to medium and cook, covered, for 30 minutes.
2. Preheat the oven to 350°F.
3. Add the tomato paste to the saucepan and cook for another 15 minutes, or until the lentils are tender. Season with salt and pepper. Remove from the heat, discard the bay leaf and rosemary sprig, and pour the lentils into a 9 x 13-inch baking dish.
4. Meanwhile, add the potatoes and parsnips to a medium saucepan and add enough water to cover. Bring the pot to a boil over high heat. Reduce the heat to medium and cook, covered, until the vegetables are tender, about 15 minutes.
5. Remove the potatoes and parsnips from the heat and drain all but ½ cup of the water. Mash the vegetables until smooth and creamy, then season with additional salt and spread the mixture evenly over the lentils.
6. Bake the casserole for 25 minutes, or until bubbly. Let sit for 10 minutes before serving.

Moroccan-Style Shepherd's Pie

I'VE NEVER HAD traditional, meat-containing Shepherd's Pie—the first I ever tried was a vegetarian recipe made with textured vegetable protein. In this version, green lentils are cooked with Moroccan spices and spinach, then topped with a mashed-yam crust and baked. It's fantastic, whether or not you've tasted the original.

SERVES 6 TO 8

1 large onion, peeled and diced

2 medium carrots, peeled and diced

2 celery stalks, diced

6 cloves garlic, peeled and minced

2 tablespoons sweet paprika

1 tablespoon cumin seeds, toasted (see page 10) and ground

1 teaspoon turmeric

1 teaspoon crushed red pepper flakes

2 cups green lentils, rinsed

8 cups Vegetable Stock (page 23), or low-sodium vegetable broth

3 large yams, peeled and diced

2 cinnamon sticks

12 cups packed spinach (about 2 pounds)

1 cup chopped cilantro

Salt and freshly ground black pepper to taste

Zest and juice of 2 lemons

1. Place the onion, carrots, and celery in a large saucepan and sauté over medium heat for 10 minutes. Add water 1 to 2 tablespoons at a time to keep the vegetables from sticking to the pan. Add the garlic and cook for another minute. Add the paprika, cumin, turmeric, crushed red pepper flakes, lentils, and vegetable stock. Bring to a boil over high heat, reduce the heat to medium, and cook, covered, for 45 minutes, or until the lentils are tender.
2. Meanwhile, place the yams and the cinnamon sticks in a separate saucepan. Add enough water to cover, bring to a boil, and cook over medium heat until tender, about 15 minutes. Remove from the heat, drain the excess water from the pan, and discard the cinnamon sticks. Mash the yams until smooth and creamy and set aside.
3. Preheat the oven to 350°F.
4. Add the spinach and cilantro to the lentil mixture and cook until the spinach is wilted, about 5 minutes. Season with salt and pepper and add the lemon zest and juice. Pour the mixture into a 9 x 13-inch baking dish.
5. Spread the mashed yams evenly over the lentil mixture and bake the casserole for 20 minutes. Let sit for 10 minutes before serving.

Moussaka

TRADITIONAL MOUSSAKA IS made with lamb or beef—a version I've never had. The first time I had it, the dish was made with some kind of meat analog, and it had almost no flavor. So of course I had to make my own version, and here it is. The lentils are perfectly spiced with cinnamon and allspice, and the traditional béchamel sauce that goes on top has been replaced with a variation on our own no-fuss No-Cheese Sauce (page 29). This dish takes a little effort, but the flavor makes it well worth it for special occasions.

SERVES 6 TO 8

FOR THE LENTILS:

2 cups green lentils, rinsed

2 medium yellow onions, peeled and diced small

4 cloves garlic, peeled and minced

¼ cup tomato paste

1 teaspoon ground cinnamon

1 teaspoon ground allspice

Salt to taste

FOR THE EGGPLANT:

3 tablespoons low-sodium soy sauce

¼ cup Vegetable Stock (page 23), or low-sodium vegetable broth

2 large eggplants, stemmed and cut into ½-inch slices

FOR THE CUSTARD LAYER:

2 large yellow onions, peeled and coarsely chopped

1 large red bell pepper, seeded and coarsely chopped

¼ cup cashews, toasted (see page 10)

Salt or low-sodium soy sauce to taste

2 tablespoons tahini

1 teaspoon ground nutmeg

2 tablespoons arrowroot powder

1 cup nutritional yeast

TO MAKE THE LENTIL LAYER:

1. Add the lentils to a medium saucepan and add enough water to cover by 2 inches. Bring to a boil over high heat. Reduce the heat to medium and cook, covered, for 40 minutes, or until the lentils are tender. Drain any excess water and set the lentils aside.

2. Place the onions in a large saucepan and sauté over medium heat for 6 minutes. Add water 1 to 2 tablespoons at a time to keep the onions from sticking to the pan. Add the garlic and cook for 3 minutes. Add the tomato paste, cinnamon, and allspice and cook for 1 minute. Add the lentils to the onion mixture, season with salt, and mix well. Set aside.

TO MAKE THE EGGPLANT:

3. Preheat the oven to 350°F.

4. Combine the soy sauce and vegetable stock in a small bowl and set aside.

5. Line a baking sheet with parchment paper. Place the eggplant slices on the parchment paper—do not overlap—and brush each piece with some of the soy sauce mixture. Bake the eggplant until it is tender, about 15 minutes. (Do not overcook, it as it will continue cooking in the casserole.)

TO MAKE THE CUSTARD LAYER:

6. Combine the onions, red pepper, cashews, salt, tahini, nutmeg, and arrowroot powder in a blender and puree until smooth and creamy. Add the nutritional yeast and process until the yeast is well incorporated, scraping down the sides with a spatula as needed.

TO ASSEMBLE THE CASSEROLE:

7. Place half of the lentil mixture on the bottom of a 9 x 13-inch baking dish. Arrange half of the eggplant on top of the lentils. Top with the remaining lentils, followed by the rest of the eggplant. Top with the custard mixture.
8. Bake for 45 to 50 minutes, or until the casserole is hot and bubbly.

Scalloped Potatoes

TAKE THIS DISH to a potluck and don't tell anyone how healthy it is. They won't know the difference.

SERVES 6 TO 8 AS A SIDE

> **2 large yellow onions, peeled and thinly sliced into rings**
> **6 medium Yukon Gold or other waxy potatoes (about 2 pounds),**
>   **peeled and sliced into thin rounds**
> **Salt and freshly ground black pepper to taste**
> **2 batches No-Cheese Sauce (page 29)**
> **Spanish paprika to taste**
> **¼ cup chopped chives**

1. Place the onions in a large skillet and sauté over medium-high heat, stirring frequently, for 10 minutes, or until browned. Add water 1 to 2 tablespoons at a time to keep the onions from sticking to the pan.
2. Bring a large pot of salted water to boil. Add the potatoes and parboil for 3 minutes. Drain and set aside.
3. Preheat the oven to 350°F.
4. Layer half of the parboiled potatoes in the bottom of a 9 x 13-inch baking dish. Season with salt and pepper. Spread half of the No-Cheese Sauce over the potatoes, then sprinkle half of the onions over the sauce. Repeat with the remaining potatoes and sauce and top with the rest of the onions. Sprinkle with paprika and bake for 35 to 45 minutes, or until the casserole is bubbly. Remove the casserole from the oven and let rest for 10 minutes. Garnish with the chives and serve.

Spinach and Sweet Potato Lasagna

I HAVE NEVER been a fan of traditional Italian-American lasagna made with a red sauce. But I do like anything made with a cream sauce, so of course I like lasagna made that way. This unusual lasagna is very rich without all the fat, thanks to a tasty sauce made from cauliflower.

SERVES 6 TO 8

2 to 3 large sweet potatoes (about 2 pounds), peeled and cut into ½-inch rounds

2 large heads cauliflower, cut into florets

¼ cup pine nuts, toasted (see page 10)

Unsweetened plain almond milk, as needed

3 tablespoons nutritional yeast, optional

½ teaspoon ground nutmeg

1½ teaspoons salt

1 large yellow onion, peeled and diced small

4 cloves garlic, peeled and minced

1 tablespoon minced thyme

½ cup finely chopped basil

12 cups spinach (about 2 pounds)

Salt and freshly ground black pepper to taste

12 ounces whole-grain or Jerusalem artichoke–flour lasagna noodles, cooked according to package directions, drained, and rinsed until cool

1. Place the sweet potatoes in a double boiler or steamer basket and steam for 6 minutes, or until tender but not mushy. Rinse until cool, then drain and set aside.
2. Steam the cauliflower for 6 to 8 minutes until very tender. Combine the cauliflower and pine nuts in a blender, in batches if necessary, and puree until smooth and creamy, adding almond milk if needed. Add the puree to a large bowl and stir in the nutritional yeast (if using), nutmeg, and salt. Set aside.
3. Place the onion in a large skillet and sauté over medium heat for 10 minutes. Add water 1 to 2 tablespoons at a time to keep the onion from sticking to the pan. Add the garlic, thyme, basil, and spinach and cook for 4 to 5 minutes, or until the spinach wilts. Add to the cauliflower puree and mix well. Season with additional salt and pepper.
4. Preheat the oven to 350°F.
5. To assemble the lasagna, pour 1 cup of the cauliflower mixture into the bottom of a 9 x 13-inch baking dish. Add a layer of lasagna noodles. Place a layer of sweet potatoes on top of the noodles. Pour 1½ cups of the cauliflower mixture over the sweet potatoes. Top with another layer of noodles, followed by a layer of sweet potatoes. Add another layer of the cauliflower mixture. Top with a final layer of noodles and the remaining cauliflower sauce. Cover with aluminum foil and bake for 30 minutes. Uncover and bake for another 15 minutes, or until the casserole is hot and bubbly. Let sit for 15 minutes before serving.

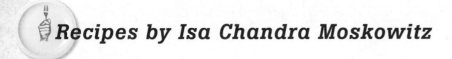

Recipes by Isa Chandra Moskowitz

Lunchbox Chocolate Chip Cookies

I CALL THESE "lunchbox" cookies because they hold up well to being knocked about a bit *and* because you're definitely going to want one of these for an afternoon treat. Even though they are soft-baked, they are not cake-like at all (as lower-fat cookies tend to be). Almond butter is the perfect secret ingredient! It gives the cookies great texture while providing a yummy flavor people won't quite be able to put their finger on.

MAKES 24 COOKIES

⅓ **cup unsweetened applesauce**

⅓ **cup almond butter**

½ **cup dry sweetener (see page 13)**

1 **tablespoon ground flaxseeds**

2 **teaspoons pure vanilla extract**

1⅓ **cups oat flour**

½ **teaspoon baking soda**

½ **teaspoon salt**

¼ **cup sorghum flour, or whole wheat pastry flour**

½ **cup grain-sweetened chocolate chips**

1. Preheat the oven to 350°F. Line two large baking sheets with parchment paper or Silpat baking mats.
2. In a large mixing bowl, use a strong fork to beat together the applesauce, almond butter, dry sweetener, and flaxseeds. Once relatively smooth, mix in the vanilla.
3. Add in the oat flour, baking soda, and salt and mix well. Add the sorghum flour and chocolate chips and mix well.
4. Drop spoonfuls of batter onto the prepared baking sheets in about 1½-tablespoon scoops, about 2 inches apart. Flatten the cookies a bit, so that they resemble thick discs (they won't spread much at all during baking). Bake for 8 to 10 minutes. The longer you bake them, the crispier they will be.
5. Remove the cookies from the oven and let them cool on the sheets for 5 minutes, then transfer to a cooling rack to cool completely.

'Nilla Cookies

THIS COOKIE IS so bursting with vanilla! Vanilla bean *and* extract to be exact. And a top-secret ingredient gives the cookie a hint of extra mysterious vanilla-ness—it's coconut flour! These cookies are cute and crackle-topped, just like a cookie should be. The recipe makes 36 cookies, but since the cookies don't spread while baking, you should be able to fit them all on two large baking sheets.

MAKES 36 COOKIES

⅔ cup unsweetened plant-based milk

¼ cup almond butter

¼ cup unsweetened applesauce

⅔ cup dry sweetener (see page 13)

1 teaspoon pure vanilla extract

1 vanilla bean, halved

1 cup oat flour

⅔ cup coconut flour

1 tablespoon cornstarch

2 teaspoons baking powder

½ teaspoon salt

1. Preheat the oven to 350°F. Line 2 large baking sheets with parchment paper or Silpat baking mats.
2. In a large mixing bowl, use a strong fork to beat together the plant-based milk, almond butter, applesauce, and dry sweetener. Once relatively smooth, mix in the vanilla. Scrape the seeds from the vanilla bean and add to the batter. Mix well.
3. Add in the oat flour, coconut flour, cornstarch, baking powder, and salt. Mix well. The dough will be stiff.
4. Roll the dough into walnut-size balls and place them on the prepared baking sheets, a little over an inch apart. Flatten the cookies a bit, so that they resemble thick discs (they don't spread much at all during baking). Bake for 8 to 10 minutes. The longer you bake them, the crispier they will be.
5. Remove the cookies from the oven and let them cool on the baking sheets for 5 minutes, and then transfer to a cooling rack to cool completely.

Nutty Raspberry Thumbprint Cookies 📷

THESE ARE FUN and festive cookies with a beautiful ruby-red center. The cookies are dense with nuts and oats, and they go great with a cup of tea. Of course, you don't have to limit yourself to raspberry. Apricot or strawberry jam are both strongly vying for the spotlight as well.

MAKES 18 COOKIES

⅓ cup unsweetened applesauce

¼ cup almond butter

½ cup dry sweetener (see page 13)

1 tablespoon ground flaxseeds

2 teaspoons pure vanilla extract

1¾ cups oat flour

½ teaspoon baking soda

½ teaspoon salt

½ cup rolled oats

½ cup finely chopped walnuts

⅓ cup raspberry jam, or to taste

1. Preheat the oven to 350°F. Line a large baking sheet with parchment paper or a Silpat baking mat.
2. In a large mixing bowl, use a strong fork to beat together the applesauce, almond butter, sweetener, and flaxseeds. Once relatively smooth, mix in the vanilla.
3. Add the oat flour, baking soda, and salt and mix well. Fold in the oats and walnuts.
4. Roll about 2 tablespoons of batter into a ball and place on the prepared baking sheet. Repeat with the remaining batter until you have 18 balls. They can all fit on one sheet because they don't spread much at all during baking. Moisten your thumb (or index finger) and make a deep indent in the center of each cookie. Place about ½ teaspoon of jam in each indentation.
5. Bake for 10 to 12 minutes, or until the bottoms of the cookies are golden brown.
6. Remove the cookies from the oven and let them cool on the sheets for 5 minutes, then transfer to a cooling rack to cool completely.

Oatmeal Raisin Cookies

THESE ARE GOOD, old-fashioned oatmeal raisin cookies, just like Grandma used to make them: with cinnamon, oats and—what in the world is sorghum flour?! Anyway, you will love these. They are gluten-free, but if you don't care one way or the other then whole wheat pastry flour can easily stand in for the sorghum.

MAKES 24 COOKIES

⅓ cup almond butter

¼ cup unsweetened applesauce

½ cup dry sweetener (see page 13)

1 teaspoon pure vanilla extract

⅔ cups oat flour

⅓ cup sorghum flour, or whole wheat pastry flour

½ teaspoon baking soda

¼ teaspoon salt

½ teaspoon ground cinnamon

1 cup rolled oats (not quick-cooking or instant)

½ cup raisins

1. Preheat the oven to 350°F. Line two large baking sheets with parchment paper or Silpat baking mats.
2. In a large mixing bowl, use a strong fork to beat together the almond butter, applesauce, and sweetener. Once relatively smooth, mix in the vanilla.
3. Add in the oat flour, sorghum flour, baking soda, salt, and cinnamon. Mix well. Stir in the oats and raisins and mix well. The dough will be stiff.
4. Roll the dough into walnut-size balls and place on the prepared baking sheets, 2 inches apart. Flatten the cookies a bit, so that they resemble thick discs (they don't spread much at all during baking). Bake for 8 to 10 minutes. The longer you bake them, the crispier they will be.
5. Remove the cookies from the oven and let cool on the baking sheets for 5 minutes, and then transfer to a cooling rack to cool completely.

Gingerbread Mamas

THESE ARE FUN little cookies that will make your mouth tingle with ginger and holiday cheer. They're soft and puffy and perhaps more reminiscent of gingerbread muffin tops than of cookies.

MAKES 12 COOKIES

> **1 cup plus 2 tablespoons whole wheat pastry flour**
> **½ teaspoon baking soda**
> **¼ teaspoon salt**
> **1¼ teaspoons ground ginger**
> **¼ teaspoon ground cinnamon**
> **⅛ teaspoon ground cloves**
> **¼ cup unsweetened applesauce**
> **⅓ cup 100% pure maple syrup**
> **2 tablespoons molasses**
> **1 teaspoon pure vanilla extract**
> **1 tablespoon dry sweetener, plus more as needed**

1. Preheat the oven to 350°F. Line a baking sheet with parchment paper or Silpat baking mats.
2. In a mixing bowl, sift together the flour, baking soda, salt, ginger, cinnamon, and cloves. Make a well in the center of the mixture and add the applesauce, maple syrup, molasses, and vanilla. Mix well.
3. Use a spoon or cookie scoop and drop 12 large tablespoonfuls of dough onto the prepared baking sheet, about 2 inches apart. Sprinkle pinches of dry sweetener on top of each cookie.
4. Bake for 8 to 10 minutes, or until the tops are slightly crackly and puffed up. Let cool on the baking sheet for 5 minutes, and then transfer to a cooling rack to cool completely.
5. Store the cookies in a tightly sealed container at room temperature.

Cranberry Orange Biscotti

THESE BISCOTTI JUST personify a crunchy holiday treat! Always have a plate of these citrus-scented cookies at the table for guests to nibble on.

MAKES 18 SLICES

⅓ cup fresh orange juice

2 tablespoons ground flaxseeds

¾ cup dry sweetener (see page 13)

¼ cup unsweetened applesauce

¼ cup almond butter

1 teaspoon pure vanilla extract

1⅔ cups whole wheat pastry flour

2 tablespoons cornstarch

2 teaspoons baking powder

½ teaspoon ground allspice

½ teaspoon salt

¾ cup fruit-sweetened dried cranberries

1. Line a baking sheet with parchment paper or a Silpat baking mat. Preheat the oven to 350°F.
2. In a large mixing bowl, use a fork to vigorously mix together orange juice and flaxseeds until frothy. Mix in the dry sweetener, applesauce, almond butter, and vanilla.
3. Sift in the flour, cornstarch, baking powder and allspice, then add the salt and mix until well combined. Knead in the cranberries using your hands because the dough will be stiff.
4. On the prepared baking sheet, form the dough into a rectangle about 12 inches long by 3 to 4 inches wide. Bake for 26 to 28 minutes, or until lightly puffed and browned. Remove the sheet from the oven and let cool for 30 minutes.
5. Turn the oven temperature up to 375°F. With a heavy, very sharp knife, slice the biscotti into ½-inch-thick slices. The best way to do this is in one motion, pushing down; don't "saw" the slices or they may crumble. Lay the slices down on the cookie sheet and bake for 10 to 12 minutes, flipping the slices halfway through. Allow to cool for a few minutes on the baking sheet before transferring the slices to cooling racks.

Almond Anise Biscotti 📷

YOUR KITCHEN WILL smell like an Italian bakery as this classic biscotti bakes. *Biscotti* means "twice-baked," and these are first baked in a loaf, then sliced and baked again. They are perfect alongside your coffee or any hot drink.

MAKES 18 SLICES

⅓ cup unsweetened plant-based milk

2 tablespoons ground flaxseeds

¾ cup dry sweetener (see page 13)

¼ cup unsweetened applesauce

¼ cup almond butter

½ teaspoon pure vanilla extract

½ teaspoon almond extract

1⅔ cups whole wheat pastry flour

2 tablespoons cornstarch

2 teaspoons baking powder

2 teaspoons anise seeds

½ teaspoon salt

1 cup slivered almonds

1. Preheat the oven to 350°F. Line a baking sheet with parchment paper or a Silpat baking mat.
2. In a large mixing bowl, use a fork to vigorously mix together the plant-based milk and flaxseeds until frothy. Mix in the dry sweetener, applesauce, almond butter, vanilla, and almond extract.
3. Sift in the flour, cornstarch, and baking powder. Add the anise seeds and salt and mix until well combined. Knead in the almonds using your hands because the dough will be stiff.
4. On the prepared baking sheet, form the dough into a rectangle about 12 inches long by 3 to 4 inches wide. Bake for 26 to 28 minutes, or until lightly puffed and browned. Remove the sheet from the oven and let cool for 30 minutes.
5. Turn the oven temperature up to 375°F. With a heavy, very sharp knife, slice the biscotti loaf into ½-inch-thick slices. The best way to do this is in one motion, pushing down; don't "saw" the slices or they may crumble. Lay the slices down on the baking sheet and bake for 10 to 12 minutes, flipping the slices halfway through. Allow to cool for a few minutes on the baking sheet before transferring the slices to cooling racks.

Tea Scones

THESE SCONES ARE perfect for any tea party! Spread with a little jam, or enjoy one of the variations.

MAKES 1 DOZEN SCONES

½ cup unsweetened plant-based milk

1 teaspoon apple cider vinegar

1 teaspoon pure vanilla extract

3 cups oat flour

2 tablespoons baking powder

½ cup dry sweetener (see page 13)

½ teaspoon salt

½ cup unsweetened applesauce

⅓ cup almond butter

1. Preheat oven to 350°F. Line a baking sheet with parchment paper or a Silpat baking mat.
2. In a glass measuring cup, whisk together the plant-based milk and apple cider vinegar. Set aside to curdle for a few minutes and then add the vanilla.
3. In a medium bowl, sift together the oat flour, baking powder, dry sweetener, and salt.
4. In a small bowl, mix together applesauce and almond butter with a fork. Use the fork to cut the applesauce mixture into the flour mixture, until crumbly. Add the milk mixture and stir until just moistened. Do not overmix.
5. Use a ¼-cup measuring cup (or ice-cream scoop) to scoop the scones out onto the baking sheet. Mist it with a little water first so that the batter comes out easier. Bake for 20 to 24 minutes, or until a knife inserted through the center comes out clean.
6. Allow the scones to cool on the baking sheet for a few minutes before transferring them to a cooling rack to cool completely.

VARIATIONS:

▶ **FOR BERRY SCONES:** Fold in 1 cup of fresh blueberries or raspberries just before scooping onto the baking sheet.

▶ **FOR CHOCOLATE CHIP SCONES:** Fold in ½ cup of grain-sweetened chocolate chips just before scooping onto the baking sheet.

▶ **FOR CINNAMON SCONES:** In a separate bowl, mix together 2 tablespoons of dry sweetener and 1 teaspoon of ground cinnamon. Sprinkle over the scones before baking.

▶ **FOR ALMOND SCONES:** Add ½ teaspoon of almond extract with the milk and fold in ½ cup of slivered almonds just before scooping onto the baking sheet.

Graham Crackers

THESE CRUNCHY GRAHAM crackers have a great cinnamon-sugar topping. For a s'mores-like treat, serve them smeared with Fudgy Chocolate Frosting (page 286) and Vanilla Bean Whip (page 302).

MAKES 12 CRACKERS

> 1½ cups spelt flour, plus additional for dusting
> ¼ cup plus 1 tablespoon dry sweetener (see page 13)
> ½ teaspoon baking soda
> 1 teaspoon ground cinnamon
> ½ teaspoon salt
> ¼ cup unsweetened applesauce
> 2 tablespoons molasses
> 1 teaspoon pure vanilla extract
> ¼ cup unsweetened plant-based milk
> 1 tablespoon ground flaxseeds

1. Preheat the oven to 350°F.
2. In a large bowl, mix together the flour, ¼ cup of the dry sweetener, the baking soda, ½ teaspoon of the cinnamon, and the salt. Make a well in the middle of the bowl and add the applesauce, molasses, and vanilla. Mix the ingredients together with a fork until well combined and crumbly.
3. In a large measuring cup, whisk together the plant-based milk and ground flaxseeds. Pour the mixture into the dough and stir to combine. Use your hands to knead the dough a few times until it holds together; add an extra tablespoon of milk or water if needed. You should be able to form a pliable ball of dough.
4. Line a work surface with parchment paper or a Silpat baking mat. Place the dough on the parchment and flatten it into a rectangle. Sprinkle the dough lightly with spelt flour. Use a rolling pin to roll the dough into a roughly 10 x 14-inch rectangle. The dough should be about ⅛-inch thick.
5. Using a sharp knife, trim the edges so that you have a relatively even 8 x 12-inch rectangle. Cut the dough into eight crackers. Transfer the parchment onto a large baking sheet. Gather up the remaining scraps of dough and form them into a ball. On a separate sheet of parchment paper, roll out the scraps into a 4 x 8-inch rectangle, or whatever size you can manage to make. Trim the edges and cut into four crackers. Transfer the parchment to a baking sheet.
6. Mix together the remaining tablespoon of dry sweetener and ½ teaspoon of cinnamon and sprinkle evenly over the crackers. Score each cracker with a fork four times in two columns. You don't need to poke all the way through. Bake for 10 to 12 minutes.
7. Remove the crackers from the oven and let cool on the baking sheet for 5 minutes, and then transfer to a cooling rack to cool completely.

Apple Cinnamon Granola Bars

THIS IS A classic combo—you can't go wrong with apple and cinnamon! These are the perfect on-the-go treat, but you can also smash up a bar in a cereal bowl and pour on some plant-based milk; it makes a great breakfast granola.

MAKES 8 BARS

½ cup cashew butter

¼ cup 100% pure maple syrup

¼ cup brown rice syrup

1 teaspoon pure vanilla extract

2 cups whole rolled oats (not quick-cooking or instant)

1 cup finely chopped dried apple

½ teaspoon salt

1 teaspoon ground cinnamon

1. Preheat the oven to 350°F. Line an 8 x 8-inch baking pan with a 10-inch square of parchment paper.
2. In a small saucepan or saucier, mix together the cashew butter, maple syrup, and brown rice syrup. Gently heat the mixture over low heat, whisking with a fork, just until it's warm enough for the ingredients to incorporate and become smooth.
3. Remove the mixture from the heat. Let the mixture cool a bit so that it's still warm but not hot. Mix in the vanilla, and then add the oats, apple, salt, and cinnamon. Mix very well.
4. Now wet your hands and press the mixture into the pan. If your hands aren't wet, things will get kind of sticky! Firmly press the oat mixture into the pan, pressing on the top and packing the bars as tightly as you can. Bake for 18 minutes, or until the sides of the bars are lightly browned.
5. Remove the pan from oven and let cool for about 10 minutes. Remove the bars from the pan by lifting up the corners of the parchment paper. Transfer to a cooling rack to cool completely (with the parchment underneath).
6. Use an 8-inch knife to slice the bars into eight rectangles. It's best to press down firmly in one motion to slice, rather than using a sawing motion, which may make the bars crumble a bit. Slice once down the middle, and then 4 times across the other way.
7. Store the bars in a tightly sealed container at room temperature.

Peanut Butter Granola Bars

OH, THESE ARE so good and so simple! They are full of crunchy, toasty, peanut-buttery deliciousness, with just a hint of cinnamon. These granola bars are a must for your lunchbox. This recipe calls for smooth peanut butter, but feel free to use chunky peanut butter if you want an extra peanut kick in your bars.

MAKES 8 BARS

½ cup smooth peanut butter
¼ cup 100% pure maple syrup
¼ cup brown rice syrup
1 teaspoon pure vanilla extract
2 cups whole rolled oats (not quick-cooking or instant)
½ teaspoon salt
½ teaspoon ground cinnamon

1. Preheat the oven to 350°F. Line an 8 x 8-inch baking pan with a 10-inch square of parchment paper.
2. In a small saucepan or saucier, mix together the peanut butter, maple syrup, and brown rice syrup. Gently heat the mixture over low heat, whisking with a fork, just until it's warm enough for the ingredients to incorporate and become smooth.
3. Remove from the heat. Let the mixture cool a bit so that it's still warm but not hot. Mix in the vanilla, then add the oats, salt, and cinnamon and mix very well.
4. Now wet your hands and press the oats into the pan. Firmly press the oat mixture into the pan, pressing on the top and packing the bars as tightly as you can. Bake for 18 minutes, or until the sides of the bars are lightly browned.
5. Remove the pan from oven and let cool for about 10 minutes. Remove the bars from the pan by lifting up by corners of the parchment paper. Transfer to a cooling rack to cool completely (with the parchment underneath).
6. Use an 8-inch knife to slice the bars into eight rectangles. It's best to press down firmly in one motion to slice, rather than using a sawing motion, which may make the bars crumble a bit. Slice once down the middle, and then 4 times across the other way.
7. Store the bars in a tightly sealed container at room temperature.

Apricot Fig Squares 📷

FIGS AND APRICOTS make for the most deliciously sultry filling, surrounded by a soft, cookie-like gluten-free dough. It's like the classic fig bar cookie, but all grown up.

MAKES 16 SQUARES

FOR THE FILLING:

8 ounces (about 1½ cups) dried unsulfured apricots, roughly chopped (see page 9 for more on sulfites and sulfur dioxide)

8 ounces (about 1½ cups) dried figs, roughly chopped

¼ cup 100% pure maple syrup

2 teaspoons finely grated orange zest

¼ teaspoon ground ginger

FOR THE DOUGH:

2 tablespoons ground flaxseeds

¼ cup unsweetened plant-based milk

¼ cup unsweetened applesauce

¼ cup almond butter

⅓ cup dry sweetener (see page 13)

2 teaspoons pure vanilla extract

1 cup oat flour

¾ cup sorghum flour

½ teaspoon baking powder

½ teaspoon baking soda

½ teaspoon salt

1. Preheat the oven to 350°F. Line an 8 x 8-inch pan with a 10-inch square of parchment paper or have ready an 8 x 8-inch nonstick or silicone baking pan (see page 17 for recommendations).

TO MAKE THE FILLING:

2. In a large saucepan, combine ⅔ cup of water with the apricots, figs, maple syrup, orange zest, and ginger. Bring to a boil over medium heat, reduce the heat to a simmer, and stir occasionally. Cook until very soft, about 15 minutes, and mash with a spatula as you go along. Remove from the heat and puree with an immersion blender, or transfer the mixture to a blender and puree, being careful not to let the steam in the blender build up. Set the filling aside.

TO MAKE THE DOUGH:

3. In a large bowl, stir together ground flaxseeds, plant-based milk, applesauce, almond butter, and sweetener. Mix well with a strong fork and stir in the vanilla.

4. Add the oat flour, sorghum flour, baking powder, baking soda, and salt. Stir well to combine. Use your hands to knead the dough a few times until it holds together; add

an extra tablespoon of milk if needed. You should be able to form a pliable ball of dough. Divide the dough into two balls.

TO ASSEMBLE THE BARS:

5. Put the first half of the dough into the bottom of the prepared baking pan and press firmly to create an even layer. Spread the filling over the top of the dough and smooth with a spatula.
6. Shape or roll the second half of the dough into a square the size of the pan and place on top of the filling.
7. Bake for 22 to 24 minutes. The top should be firm and lightly golden.
8. Remove the pan from oven and place on a cooling rack until cooled completely. Slice into 16 squares.

Raspberry Truffle Brownies

THESE DENSE, FUDGY brownies have loads and loads of melt-in-your-mouth raspberry yumminess. Frozen berries actually will work better here because the dough is very stiff, and frozen berries are easier to fold in.

The brownies are still very gooey after the baking time is complete, but don't worry—that's what you want with brownies! Gooey out of the oven means that they will be nice and fudgy when they cool. Allow them to cool completely and chill in the fridge for a few hours for best results.

MAKES 12 BROWNIES

> **4 ounces unsweetened chocolate, chopped**
> **½ cup raspberry jam**
> **½ cup dry sweetener (see page 13)**
> **½ cup unsweetened applesauce**
> **2 teaspoons pure vanilla extract**
> **½ teaspoon almond extract**
> **1½ cups whole wheat pastry flour**
> **¼ cup unsweetened cocoa powder**
> **¼ teaspoon baking powder**
> **½ teaspoon baking soda**
> **¼ teaspoon salt**
> **1 cup raspberries, frozen or fresh**

1. Preheat the oven to 350°F. Line an 8 x 8-inch pan with a 10-inch square of parchment paper or have ready an 8 x 8-inch nonstick or silicone baking pan (see page 17 for recommendations).
2. Melt the chocolate in either a double boiler or the microwave. Set aside.
3. In a large mixing bowl, vigorously mix together the jam, sweetener, and applesauce. Stir in the vanilla, almond extract, and the melted chocolate.
4. Sift in the flour, cocoa powder, baking powder, baking soda, and salt. Mix very well until a stiff dough forms. Fold in the raspberries.
5. Spread the mixture into the prepared pan. It will be very thick; you'll need to use your hands to even the batter out in the pan.
6. Bake the brownies for 16 to 18 minutes. Remove them from the oven and let cool completely. These taste especially good and fudgy after being refrigerated for a few hours.

Walnut Brownies

IF A LITTLE dose of chocolate is what you need to get through the day, then these brownies ought to do the trick! Bake for 17 minutes for a more fudgy brownie, or 20 minutes if you prefer a cakey treat. All of the liquid ingredients need to be very hot before adding them, so either heat them in a microwave or briefly boil them on the stovetop before using.

MAKES 12 BROWNIES

3 ounces extra-firm silken tofu, drained

⅓ cup pitted prunes, rough stems removed

½ cup unsweetened plant-based milk, heated until very hot but not boiling

¾ cup 100% pure maple syrup

½ cup plus 2 tablespoons unsweetened cocoa powder

¾ cup water, heated until very hot but not boiling

2 teaspoons pure vanilla extract

1 cup whole wheat pastry flour

½ teaspoon baking soda

½ teaspoon salt

½ cup walnuts, roughly chopped

1. Preheat the oven to 325°F. Line an 8 x 8-inch pan with a 10-inch square of parchment paper or have ready an 8 x 8-inch nonstick or silicone baking pan (see page 17 for recommendations).

2. Crumble the tofu into a blender. Add the prunes. Pour in the hot plant-based milk and puree for about 30 seconds. Add the maple syrup and puree until relatively smooth. Some flecks of prune are okay, but there should be no chunks of tofu left. Scrape down the sides of the blender with a rubber spatula to make sure all the ingredients are incorporated.

3. Sift the cocoa powder into a mixing bowl. Add the hot water and mix with a fork until well combined. It should look like a thick chocolate sauce.

4. Add the prune mixture to the chocolate in the mixing bowl and stir to combine. Mix in the vanilla.

5. Sift in half of the flour and add the baking soda and salt. Mix well. Mix in the remaining flour and fold in the walnuts.

6. Spread the batter into the prepared baking pan. It will be rather thick, but you don't need to push it into the corners, as it will spread as it bakes.

7. Bake for 17 to 20 minutes. The top should be set and firm to the touch.

8. Remove the pan from the oven and let cool for at least 20 minutes. Slice the brownies into 12 squares and serve!

Carrot Cake

THIS CAKE COMBINES the classic flavors of carrot, pineapple, and shredded coconut, studded with sweet bursts of raisins and lots of spice. This cake never goes out of style! It's moist and delicious on its own, but serve with sliced fresh pineapple rings on top and/or Vanilla Bean Whip (page 302) if you're feeling fancy.

SERVES 9

¾ cup 100% pure maple syrup

One 8-ounce can crushed pineapple, drained (about ¾ cup)

⅓ cup unsweetened applesauce

1 tablespoon ground flaxseeds

1⅔ cups spelt flour

2¼ teaspoons baking powder

¾ teaspoon baking soda

½ teaspoon salt

1½ teaspoons ground cinnamon

½ teaspoon ground nutmeg

½ teaspoon ground ginger

¼ teaspoon ground allspice

3 medium carrots, peeled and grated (about 1½ cups)

¾ cup golden raisins

½ cup unsweetened shredded coconut

1 batch Vanilla Bean Whip (page 302), optional

1. Preheat the oven to 350°F. Have ready an 8 x 8-inch nonstick or silicone baking pan (see page 17 for recommendations).
2. In a large bowl, vigorously whisk together the maple syrup, crushed pineapple, applesauce, and ground flaxseeds.
3. Sift in the spelt flour, baking powder, baking soda, salt, cinnamon, nutmeg, ginger, and allspice. Mix well. Fold in the grated carrots, raisins, and shredded coconut.
4. Pour the batter into the prepared pan. Bake for 28 to 32 minutes, or until a toothpick inserted into the center comes out clean.
5. Remove the cake from the oven and let cool in the pan for about 30 minutes. Invert the cake onto a cooling rack and cool completely before frosting with Vanilla Bean Whip (page 302) or serving alone.

Double Chocolate Cupcakes 📷

THESE ARE RICH and delicious chocolate cupcakes—what more do you need to know? The frosting is made with dates and gets surprisingly fudgy. You can top each cupcake with a berry to make them extra special.

MAKES 12 CUPCAKES

> **2 ounces unsweetened chocolate**
> **1 cup unsweetened plant-based milk**
> **1 teaspoon apple cider vinegar**
> **⅔ cup dry sweetener (see page 13)**
> **¼ cup unsweetened applesauce**
> **1 teaspoon pure vanilla extract**
> **1 cup whole wheat pastry flour, or spelt flour**
> **⅓ cup cocoa powder, either Dutch-processed or regular unsweetened**
> **¾ teaspoon baking soda**
> **½ teaspoon baking powder**
> **¼ teaspoon salt**
> **1 batch Fudgy Chocolate Frosting (page 286)**

1. Preheat the oven to 350°F. Line a 12-cup muffin pan with silicone liners or have ready a nonstick or silicone muffin pan (see page 17 for recommendations).
2. Melt the chocolate in a small bowl in the microwave. Set aside.
3. In a large bowl, whisk together the plant-based milk and vinegar. Let it sit for a few minutes, until curdled. Stir in the dry sweetener, applesauce, vanilla, and melted chocolate.
4. In a separate bowl, sift together the flour, cocoa powder, baking soda, baking powder, and salt. Add the mixture to the wet ingredients, one half at a time, and beat until no large lumps remain.
5. Scoop the batter into the prepared pan, filling each cup three-quarters full. Bake for 18 to 20 minutes, or until a toothpick inserted into the center comes out clean.
6. Remove the pan from the oven and let the cupcakes cool for at least 20 minutes, then carefully run a knife around the edges of each cupcake to remove. The cupcakes should be completely cool before frosting with the Fudgy Chocolate Frosting.

Fudgy Chocolate Frosting 📷

THIS FROSTING GOES great on Double Chocolate Cupcakes (page 285), but once you get a taste of how delicious it is, you'll find lots of places to use it.

MAKES 1 CUP

> **1 cup boiling water**
> **⅓ cup unsweetened cocoa powder**
> **1½ cups dried, pitted dates, tough ends removed**
> **1 tablespoon brown rice syrup**
> **Pinch salt**
> **½ teaspoon pure vanilla extract**

1. Put the boiling water and cocoa powder in a blender. Blend on high speed for about 30 seconds, or until the mixture is relatively smooth. Scrape down the sides of the blender. Be careful not to let steam build up.
2. Add the dates, brown rice syrup, and salt to the blender. Blend until smooth, stopping occasionally to scrape down the sides of the blender with a spatula to make sure all the ingredients are incorporated. Add the vanilla and blend until combined.
3. Transfer the mixture to an airtight container. Let chill completely, for at least 3 hours, until it becomes firm and spreadable.

TIP
▶ Spread the frosting onto cooled cupcakes with the back of a spoon or an offset spatula. You can also pipe the frosting with a pastry bag fitted with a wide metal tip.

Ginger Peach Muffins 📷

THERE'S SOMETHING PERFECT about the ginger-peach marriage and there's no better way to enjoy it than in a muffin. This batter is thick, so you can fill each muffin cup all the way up; that way, you'll get nice, big muffin domes.

MAKES 12 MUFFINS

- 1 cup unsweetened plant-based milk
- 1 tablespoon ground flaxseeds
- 1 teaspoon apple cider vinegar
- 2¼ cups spelt flour
- ¾ cup dry sweetener (see page 13)
- 1 tablespoon baking powder
- ½ teaspoon salt
- 2 teaspoons ground ginger
- 1 teaspoon ground cinnamon
- ¾ cup unsweetened applesauce
- 1 teaspoon pure vanilla extract
- 4 medium peaches, peeled, halved, pitted, and cut into ¼-inch slices (about 2 cups)

1. Preheat the oven to 350°F. Line a 12-cup muffin pan with silicone liners or have ready a nonstick or silicone muffin pan (see page 17 for recommendations).
2. In a large measuring cup, use a fork to vigorously mix together the plant-based milk, flaxseeds, and vinegar. Mix for about a minute, or until it appears foamy. Set aside.
3. In a medium mixing bowl, sift together the flour, dry sweetener, baking powder, salt, ginger, and cinnamon. Make a well in the center of the mixture and pour in the milk mixture. Add the applesauce and vanilla and stir together with the milk mixture in the well. Incorporate the dry ingredients into the wet ingredients in the well just until the dry ingredients are moistened (do not overmix). Fold in the peaches.
4. Fill each muffin cup all the way to the top. Bake for 24 to 27 minutes, or until a knife inserted through the center comes out clean.
5. Remove the pan from the oven. Let the muffins cool completely, about 20 minutes, then carefully run a knife around the edges of each muffin to remove.

Oatberry Yogurt Muffins

THIS IS ANOTHER great muffiny option! This recipe uses oat flour, so it's gluten-free if your oats are. Soy yogurt lends this muffin a wonderful pillowy texture.

MAKES 12 MUFFINS

2¼ cups oat flour

1 tablespoon baking powder

¾ teaspoon salt

½ cup dry sweetener (see page 13)

⅔ cup unsweetened plant-based milk

½ cup unsweetened applesauce

½ cup unsweetened plain soy yogurt

2 teaspoons pure vanilla extract

1¼ cup berries (such as blueberries, raspberries, or blackberries), halved

1. Preheat the oven to 350°F. Line a 12-cup muffin pan with silicone liners or have ready a nonstick or silicone muffin pan (see page 17 for recommendations).
2. In a medium mixing bowl, sift together the flour, baking powder, salt, and dry sweetener. Make a well in the center and pour in the plant-based milk, applesauce, yogurt, and vanilla. Stir together the wet ingredients in the well. Then mix the wet and dry ingredients together just until moistened (do not overmix). Fold in the berries.
3. Fill each muffin cup three quarters of the way and bake for 22 to 26 minutes. A knife inserted through the center should come out clean.
4. Let the muffins cool completely, about 20 minutes, then carefully run a knife around the edges of each muffin to remove.

Whole Wheat Berry Muffins 📷

THESE ARE A perfectly delicious breakfast muffin with loads of berry goodness and a tasty, wheaty backdrop. If you can find wild blueberries, use them—they are perfect for muffins because they're tiny and distribute beautifully without making the muffin soggy. If you use larger berries, like blackberries, slice them in half; otherwise they'll be too large. If you use frozen berries, bake the muffins for 26 minutes. If you use fresh, then 22 minutes should do it. Either way, check after 22 minutes to make sure you don't overbake.

MAKES 12 MUFFINS

> ⅔ cup unsweetened plant-based milk
> 1 tablespoon ground flaxseeds
> 1 teaspoon apple cider vinegar
> 2 cups whole wheat pastry flour
> 2 teaspoons baking powder
> ¼ teaspoon baking soda
> ¾ teaspoon salt
> ½ cup unsweetened applesauce
> ½ cup 100% pure maple syrup
> 1½ teaspoons pure vanilla extract
> 1 cup berries

1. Preheat the oven to 350°F. Line a 12-cup muffin pan with silicone liners or have ready a nonstick or silicone muffin pan (see page 17 for recommendations).
2. In a large measuring cup, use a fork to vigorously mix together the plant-based milk, flaxseeds, and vinegar. Mix for about a minute, until it appears foamy. Set aside.
3. In a medium mixing bowl, sift together the flour, baking powder, baking soda, and salt. Make a well in the center of the mixture and pour in the milk mixture. Add the applesauce, maple syrup, and vanilla, and stir together the wet ingredients in the well. Incorporate the dry ingredients into the wet ingredients until the dry ingredients are moistened (do not overmix). Fold in the berries.
4. Fill each muffin cup three-quarters of the way to the top and bake for 22 to 26 minutes, or until a knife inserted through the center of a muffin comes out clean.
5. Let the muffins cool completely, about 20 minutes, then carefully run a knife around the edges of each muffin to remove.

Quinana Muffins (Quinoa Banana Muffins)

QUINOA ADDS A fun texture to banana muffins, and it also adds lots of protein, making this the perfect wholesome breakfast muffin that will also satisfy your morning sweet tooth.

MAKES 12 MUFFINS

2 cups spelt flour

2 teaspoons baking powder

½ teaspoon baking soda

¾ teaspoon salt

½ teaspoon ground cinnamon

½ cup dry sweetener (see page 13)

1 cup mashed banana (from about 2 large bananas, peeled)

¼ cup unsweetened plant-based milk

⅓ cup unsweetened applesauce

2 teaspoons pure vanilla extract

1 cup cooked quinoa (see page 6), drained and rinsed until cool

1. Preheat the oven to 350°F. Line a 12-cup muffin pan with silicone liners or have ready a nonstick or silicone muffin pan (see page 17 for recommendations).
2. In a medium mixing bowl, sift together the spelt flour, baking powder, baking soda, salt, cinnamon, and dry sweetener. Make a well in the center of the mixture and add the mashed banana, plant-based milk, applesauce, and vanilla. Stir together the wet ingredients in the well. Then incorporate the dry ingredients into the wet ingredients just until the dry ingredients are moistened (do not overmix). Fold in the quinoa.
3. Fill each muffin cup all the way to the top. Bake for 22 to 24 minutes, or until a knife inserted through the center of a muffin comes out clean.
4. Let the muffins cool completely, about 20 minutes, then carefully run a knife around the edges of each muffin to remove.

Better-Than-Mom's Banana Bread

MAYBE YOUR MOM'S banana bread has 2 sticks of butter and 7 eggs. Well, give her this recipe and tell her there's a new banana bread in town! This is just pure, unadulterated banana goodness. Such simple ingredients but such satisfying bread! I know most recipes list a specific number of bananas to use, but instead measure them out to keep the results consistent. It will be about 2 to 3 bananas, depending on their size. You can add all the usual suspects to this bread if you're the type who likes banana bread with "stuff"; a cup of walnuts or pecans, half a cup of grain-sweetened chocolate chips, or a cup of berries would be mighty fine.

MAKES ONE 8 X 4-INCH LOAF

> **2 cups whole wheat pastry flour**
> **¾ teaspoon baking soda**
> **¾ teaspoon salt**
> **1 cup mashed banana**
> **½ cup 100% pure maple syrup**
> **⅓ cup unsweetened applesauce**
> **¼ cup unsweetened plant-based milk**
> **1½ teaspoons pure vanilla extract**

1. Preheat the oven to 350°F. Have ready an 8 x 4-inch nonstick or silicone baking pan (see page 17 for recommendations).
2. In a large mixing bowl, sift together the flour, baking soda, and salt.
3. In a separate mixing bowl, combine the mashed banana, maple syrup, applesauce, plant-based milk, and vanilla.
4. Make a well in the center of the dry ingredients and pour in the wet ingredients, mixing just until everything is evenly moistened.
5. Spoon the batter into the prepared loaf pan. Distribute the batter evenly along the length of the pan but don't spread the batter to the edges; the batter will spread as it bakes. Bake for 55 to 60 minutes. It's hard to test for doneness with a knife because the banana tends to stay moist, so judge by the edges of bread. They should be golden brown and pulling away from the sides of the pan.
6. Let the bread cool for at least 30 minutes, then run a knife around the edges and carefully invert the loaf onto a cooling rack. Be sure it is fully cooled before slicing.

Zecret Zucchini Bread

THERE'S A SECRET ingredient in this zucchini bread and no, it isn't the zucchini! Avocado is a wonderful complement to the green veggie and gives this loaf a great crumb. Hints of cinnamon and spice make it a warm and inviting afternoon snack. Use the large holes of a box grater to get perfectly grated zucchini.

MAKES ONE 8 X 4-INCH LOAF

⅓ cup unsweetened plant-based milk

1 avocado, halved, pitted, peeled, and mashed

1 tablespoon ground flaxseeds

½ cup dry sweetener (see page 13)

2 teaspoons pure vanilla extract

1 teaspoon lemon zest

1½ cups spelt flour

½ teaspoon baking soda

½ teaspoon baking powder

½ teaspoon salt

1½ teaspoons ground cinnamon

¼ teaspoon ground allspice

1 cup grated zucchini (from about 1 medium zucchini)

½ cup chopped walnuts, optional

½ cup raisins, optional

1. Preheat the oven to 350°F. Have ready an 8 x 4-inch nonstick or silicone baking pan (see page 17 for recommendations).
2. In a large mixing bowl, combine the plant-based milk, mashed avocado, flaxseeds, and sweetener and use a handheld electric mixer to beat until creamy and smooth. Mix in the vanilla and lemon zest.
3. Sift in the flour, baking soda, baking powder, salt, cinnamon, and allspice. Mix until all the ingredients are well incorporated.
4. Fold in the zucchini and mix in the walnuts and raisins (if using). Pour the batter into the prepared baking pan. Bake for 60 to 70 minutes, or until the top is very firm to the touch and the sides are pulling away from the pan.
5. Let the bread cool for at least 30 minutes, then run a knife around the edges and carefully invert the loaf onto a cooling rack. Be sure it is fully cooled before slicing.

Pumpkin Spice Bread

THIS IS PUMPKIN pie in bread form! I like my pumpkin bread pure and unadulterated, but if you like, raisins and walnuts make nice additions.

MAKES ONE 8 X 4-INCH LOAF

> **2 cups whole wheat pastry flour**
> **2 teaspoons baking powder**
> **1 teaspoon baking soda**
> **2 teaspoons ground cinnamon**
> **½ teaspoon ground ginger**
> **¼ teaspoon ground allspice**
> **⅛ teaspoon ground cloves**
> **One 15-ounce can pumpkin puree (about 2 cups)**
> **½ cup 100% pure maple syrup**
> **⅓ cup apple butter**
> **1 teaspoon pure vanilla extract**
> **½ cup golden raisins, optional**
> **½ cup chopped walnuts, optional**

1. Preheat the oven to 350°F. Have ready an 8 x 4-inch nonstick or silicone baking pan (see page 17 for recommendations).
2. In a large mixing bowl, sift together the flour, baking powder, baking soda, cinnamon, ginger, allspice, and cloves.
3. In a separate mixing bowl, vigorously mix together the pumpkin, maple syrup, apple butter, and vanilla.
4. Pour the wet mixture into the dry mixture and combine until everything is evenly moistened (the batter will be stiff). Fold in the raisins and walnuts (if using).
5. Spoon the batter into the prepared loaf pan. Distribute the batter evenly along the length of the pan but don't spread the batter to the edges; the batter will spread as it bakes. Bake for 50 to 60 minutes, or until a knife inserted through the center comes out clean.
6. Remove the pan from the oven and let the bread cool for at least 30 minutes, then run a knife around the edges and carefully invert the loaf onto a cooling rack. Be sure it is fully cooled before slicing.

Chocolate Pumpkin Loaf

THIS LOAF IS dense, chocolaty, and moist, with undertones of pumpkin and autumnal spices laced throughout. I throw in some chocolate chips, and you may like to add other yummy things too, like pecans or walnuts.

MAKES ONE 8 X 4-INCH LOAF

¼ cup unsweetened applesauce

⅓ cup unsweetened cocoa powder

1½ cups all-purpose flour

½ teaspoon ground cinnamon

¼ teaspoon ground nutmeg

¼ teaspoon ground ginger

⅛ teaspoon ground cloves

¾ teaspoon baking soda

¾ teaspoon salt

1 cup pumpkin puree (about ½ of a 15-ounce can)

1 cup dry sweetener (see page 13)

3 tablespoons almond butter, at room temperature

1 teaspoon pure vanilla extract

½ cup grain-sweetened chocolate chips

1. Preheat the oven to 350°F. Have ready an 8 x 4-inch nonstick or silicone baking pan (see page 17 for recommendations). Also, boil some water in a tea kettle (no need to measure yet).
2. Combine the applesauce and cocoa powder in a large mixing bowl. In a separate bowl, sift together the flour, cinnamon, nutmeg, ginger, cloves, baking soda, and salt.
3. Measure out ⅓ cup of the boiling water and pour it into the bowl with the chocolate mixture, mixing quickly to make a smooth chocolate sauce. Add the pumpkin, sweetener, almond butter, and vanilla and mix well.
4. Dump about half of the flour mixture into the chocolate mixture and gently stir just to incorporate, then measure out 1 tablespoon of the boiling water, add it to the mixture, and stir again. Add the rest of the flour mixture, and another tablespoon of boiling water, and stir just until smooth (do not overmix). Fold in the chocolate chips.
5. Spoon the batter into the prepared loaf pan. It will be good and thick. You can smooth out the top with a spatula.
6. Bake for 55 to 60 minutes. Stick a steak knife into the center of the loaf to check for doneness. A little bit of wetness is okay, since it could be from a chocolate chip, but the knife should come out mostly dry.
7. Remove the loaf from the oven. Let it cool for 10 minutes, then run a knife around the edges and carefully invert the loaf onto a cooling rack to cool most of the way. It's yummy a little bit warm or thoroughly cooled. Slice and serve!

NOTE ▶ There's a funny little method with boiling water in this recipe and you may wonder why I use it. The answer is simple: I don't exactly know. Well, I know why *I* use it, but I'm not positive why it works. What you do is add boiling water alternately as you add the dry ingredients to the wet. I was introduced to this method in Nigella Lawson's monumental book *How to Be a Domestic Goddess,* with her recipe for a chocolate loaf cake, and I've used it ever since. I've tried to disobey it, thinking it was frivolous and unneeded, only to be greeted by a loaf whose crumb was not as fine and rise was not as perfectly formed. And so I've stopped fighting it. Maybe it has to do with the baking soda, I don't know. Just use it and be rewarded with perfect loaves every time.

Pumpkin Bread Pudding

CHEWY BREAD IN a decadent, creamy pumpkin custard, this is the perfect dessert to put front and center on the Thanksgiving table. Serve with Vanilla Bean Whip (page 302).

SERVES 8

1¼ cups pumpkin puree (a little over ½ of a 15-ounce can)

1 cup unsweetened plant-based milk

½ cup 100% maple syrup

2 teaspoons pure vanilla extract

2 tablespoons cornstarch

½ teaspoon salt

½ teaspoon ground cinnamon

¾ teaspoon ground ginger

¼ teaspoon ground nutmeg

¼ teaspoon ground allspice

⅛ teaspoon ground cloves

8 slices stale whole wheat bread, cut into 1-inch cubes (about 6 cups)

½ cup golden raisins

1. Preheat the oven to 350°F. Have ready an 8 x 8-inch nonstick or silicone baking pan (see page 17 for recommendations).

2. In a large bowl, whisk together the pumpkin puree, plant-based milk, maple syrup, and vanilla. Add the cornstarch, salt, cinnamon, ginger, nutmeg, allspice, and cloves and whisk well. Stir in the bread cubes and raisins, and toss to coat completely.

3. Transfer the mixture to the prepared pan. Bake for 25 minutes, or until the top is golden brown and firm to the touch. Serve warm.

Apple Crisp

THIS IS A comforting, cinnamony, juicy apple dessert with a crisp oaty topping, perfect for a blustery winter evening. Make sure that your cashew butter is a spreadable consistency at room temperature so that it coats the oats evenly and they get nicely crisped.

SERVES 6 TO 8

FOR THE FILLING:

   3 pounds Granny Smith apples (about 8 apples), peeled, cored, and cut into ¼-inch slices

   2 tablespoons cornstarch

   1 teaspoon ground cinnamon

   ½ teaspoon ground ginger

   ⅛ teaspoon ground cloves

   ½ cup 100% pure maple syrup

FOR THE TOPPING:

   ¼ cup 100% pure maple syrup

   3 tablespoons cashew butter

   2 tablespoons unsweetened applesauce

   1 teaspoon pure vanilla extract

   1½ cup rolled oats

   ½ teaspoon ground cinnamon

   ¼ teaspoon salt

1. Preheat the oven to 400°F. Line an 8 x 8-inch pan with parchment paper, making sure that the parchment goes all the way up the sides of the pan, or have ready an 8 x 8-inch nonstick or silicone baking pan (see page 17 for recommendations).

TO MAKE THE FILLING:

2. Place the apples in a large mixing bowl.
3. Sprinkle the cornstarch, cinnamon, ginger, and cloves over the apple slices and toss well to coat. Pour the maple syrup over the mixture and stir to combine. Place the apple mixture into the prepared baking pan.

TO MAKE THE TOPPING:

4. In a small bowl, use a fork to stir together the maple syrup, cashew butter, applesauce, and vanilla, until relatively smooth. Add the oats, cinnamon, and salt, and toss to coat.

TO ASSEMBLE THE CRISP:

5. Spread the topping over the apple mixture. Place the pan in the preheated oven and bake for 20 minutes. Reduce the oven temperature to 350°F and bake for an additional 30 minutes, or until the topping is golden and filling is bubbly.
6. Remove the pan from the oven and transfer it to a cooling rack. Serve the crisp warm.

Bursting with Berries Cobbler 📷

THE TITLE SAYS it all—fruity berries bubble up under a biscuity dough. It's beautiful and delicious! For the topping, treat it like a pastry: The applesauce and almond butter mixture acts as the fat. Cut it into the flour instead of vigorously mixing it. This way the topping will stay tender and biscuity.

SERVES 8

FOR THE FILLING:

5 cups mixed berries (such as blueberries, raspberries, and strawberries)

2 tablespoons fresh lemon juice

⅓ cup dry sweetener (see page 13)

3 tablespoons cornstarch

Pinch salt

FOR THE BISCUIT TOPPING:

½ cup unsweetened plant-based milk

1 teaspoon apple cider vinegar

1 teaspoon pure vanilla extract

1½ cups oat flour

1 tablespoon baking powder

¼ cup dry sweetener

¼ teaspoon salt

3 tablespoons unsweetened applesauce

2 tablespoons almond butter

FOR SPRINKLING:

1 tablespoon dry sweetener

¼ teaspoon ground cinnamon

1. Preheat the oven to 425°F. Line an 8 x 8-inch pan with parchment paper, making sure that the parchment goes all the way up the sides of the pan, or have ready an 8 x 8-inch nonstick or silicone baking pan (see page 17 for recommendations).

TO MAKE THE FILLING:

2. In a large bowl, mix together the berries, lemon juice, sweetener, cornstarch, and salt until well combined. Place the mixture in the prepared pan. Cover the pan with aluminum foil and bake for 25 minutes.

TO MAKE THE BISCUIT TOPPING:

3. In a large measuring cup, whisk together the plant-based milk and apple cider vinegar. Set aside to let curdle for a few minutes and then add the vanilla.
4. In a large bowl, sift together the oat flour, baking powder, sweetener, and salt.
5. In a small bowl, mix together the applesauce and almond butter.
6. Cut the applesauce mixture into the flour mixture with a fork, until crumbly. Add the milk mixture and stir until just moistened. Do not overmix.

TO ASSEMBLE THE COBBLER:

7. Reduce the oven temperature to 350°F. Remove the foil from the pan and plop spoonfuls of the batter over the berry filling. Combine the sweetener and cinnamon and sprinkle evenly over the top of the biscuit dough. Return the pan to the oven, uncovered, and bake for 20 more minutes.

8. Remove the pan from the oven and transfer it to a cooling rack. Serve the cobbler warm.

Ginger Peach Parfaits

THESE PARFAITS ARE the perfect ending to a summer meal, with layers of gingery peach, crumbled scone, and crunchy pecans.

SERVES 6

FOR THE PEACHES:

8 medium peaches, peeled, halved, pitted, and cut into ¼-inch slices (about 4 cups)

⅓ cup 100% pure maple syrup

2 tablespoons fresh lemon juice

1 tablespoon grated ginger

Pinch salt

6 Tea Scones (page 276)

1 cup chopped pecans

1 batch Vanilla Bean Whip (page 302)

TO PREPARE THE PEACHES:

1. Stir together the peaches, maple syrup, lemon juice, ginger, and salt in a large bowl and let sit for at least 30 minutes.

TO ASSEMBLE THE PARFAITS:

2. Chop the scones into roughly ½-inch pieces. Have ready 6 parfait glasses or wineglasses. Layer some peaches in the bottom of a glass. Add a layer of scone pieces and a sprinkle of chopped pecans. Add more peaches and a layer of Vanilla Bean Whip. Top with additional scone pieces, another dollop of Vanilla Bean Whip, and another sprinkle of pecans. Repeat with the remaining glasses. Serve immediately.

Strawberry Shortcakes

NOTHING BEATS FRESH, tart, and sweet strawberries in syrup, oozing over a flaky scone and topped with creamy vanilla. Make these fancy by serving in wine or parfait glasses, so that you can devour the beautiful layers with your eyes first.

SERVES 6

FOR THE STRAWBERRIES:

1 pound strawberries, trimmed and cut into ¼-inch slices

¼ cup 100% pure maple syrup

2 tablespoons fresh lemon juice

Pinch salt

6 Tea Scones (page 276)

1 batch Vanilla Bean Whip (page 302)

TO PREPARE THE STRAWBERRIES:

1. Stir together the strawberries, maple syrup, lemon juice, and salt in a large bowl and let sit for at least 30 minutes.

TO ASSEMBLE THE SHORTCAKES:

2. Split the scones in half, as if you were going to make a sandwich. Place the bottom half of a scone on an individual serving plate. Top with some of the strawberries, and add a dollop of Vanilla Bean Whip. Top with the second scone half, spoon on another layer of strawberries, and top with a dollop of Vanilla Bean Whip. Repeat with the remaining scones. Serve immediately.

TIP

▶ To assemble the shortcakes as parfaits, have ready 6 wine- or parfait glasses. Add some strawberries to the bottom of a wineglass. Add the bottom half of one of the scones, breaking it into pieces to make it fit if necessary. Add more strawberries, and add a layer of Vanilla Bean Whip. Top with the remaining scone half, another dollop of Vanilla Bean Whip, and finally more strawberries. Repeat for the remaining glasses.

Vanilla Bean Whip

THIS IS A light and fluffy cream with lots of vanilla flavor, and you'll want to top everything with this whip. Cobblers, cakes, your cat—everything! If you don't have a vanilla bean handy, then use 2 teaspoons of pure vanilla extract instead. But definitely seek out some vanilla beans—you don't want to miss out on their pure vanilla flavor. This whip isn't quite as firm as traditional nondairy whipped topping, but you should definitely be able to scoop it out.

MAKES 2 CUPS

> One 12-ounce package extra firm silken tofu, drained
> ½ cup cashews, soaked overnight and drained
> ½ cup 100% pure maple syrup
> 2 tablespoons fresh lemon juice
> Pinch salt
> 1 vanilla bean

1. Combine the tofu, cashews, maple syrup, lemon juice, and salt in a blender. Puree until smooth. Scrape down the sides of the blender to incorporate all the ingredients.
2. Slice the vanilla bean in half lengthwise with a sharp knife and scrape the seeds into the blender. Blend the mixture until very smooth.
3. Transfer the mixture to a bowl and cover with plastic wrap. Chill for several hours in the refrigerator, or until firm.

NOTE: All ingredient weights are averages based on information from product manufacturers; gram amounts may vary based on brand.

NUTS AND SEEDS

¼ cup slivered almonds	27 grams
¼ cup cashews	30 grams
¼ cup chopped pecans	28 grams
½ cup chopped walnuts	64 grams
¼ cup peanuts	37 grams
½ cup pecan halves	61 grams
¼ cup pine nuts	32 grams
¼ cup sunflower seeds	30 grams
½ cup walnuts	60 grams

GRAINS

1 cup uncooked pearled barley	200 grams
1 cup uncooked brown rice	187 grams
1 cup cooked brown rice	195 grams
1 cup uncooked brown basmati rice	182 grams
½ cup uncooked brown basmati rice	91 grams
1 cup uncooked bulgur	140 grams
1 cup uncooked millet	200 grams
1 cup dry rolled oats	81 grams
1 cup steel-cut oats	181 grams
1 cup uncooked quinoa	170 grams
½ cup uncooked quinoa	85 grams
1 cup whole spelt berries	180 grams
1 cup whole wheat berries	159 grams
1 cup uncooked wild rice	160 grams

DRIED FRUITS AND JAMS

1 cup chopped dried apple	83 grams
1 cup dried, unsulfured apricots	170 grams
¼ cup dried, unsulfured apricots	43 grams
1 cup fruit-sweetened dried cherries	114 grams
¾ cup fruit-sweetened dried cranberries	113 grams
½ cup pitted dates	76 grams
½ cup raisins	78 grams
¼ cup raisins	39 grams
½ cup raspberry jam	152 grams
⅓ cup raspberry jam	101 grams

SYRUPS, BUTTERS, SAUCES, ETC.

⅓ cup almond butter	83 grams
¼ cup almond butter	63 grams
⅓ cup apple butter	94 grams
¼ cup brown rice syrup	80 grams
½ cup cashew butter	128 grams
¼ cup date molasses	156 grams
½ cup ketchup, optional	120 grams
⅓ cup 100% pure maple syrup	105 grams
¼ cup 100% pure maple syrup	80 grams
½ cup smooth peanut butter	129 grams
1¼ cups pumpkin puree	287 grams
¼ cup tomato puree	62 grams
¼ cup tomato sauce	63 grams
⅓ cup unsweetened applesauce	79 grams
¼ cup unsweetened applesauce	59 grams
½ cup unsweetened plain soy yogurt	113 grams

DRY INGREDIENTS

1½ cups all-purpose flour	188 grams
¼ cup brown rice flour	35 grams
⅓ cup cocoa powder	29 grams
¼ cup cocoa powder	22 grams
¼ cup unsweetened dried coconut	15 grams
⅔ cup coconut flour	75 grams
½ cup cornmeal	69 grams
¼ cup nutritional yeast	12 grams
1 cup oat flour	120 grams
1½ cups spelt flour	182 grams
1 cup spelt flour	121 grams
⅓ cup spelt flour	40 grams
¼ cup spelt flour	31 grams
⅓ cup sorghum flour	43 grams
¼ cup sorghum flour	32 grams
½ cup Sucanat (dry sweetener)	96 grams
⅓ cup Sucanat (dry sweetener)	64 grams
1 cup sugar (dry sweetener)	200 grams
½ cup sugar (dry sweetener)	100 grams
⅓ cup sugar (dry sweetener)	66 grams
¾ cup whole-grain breadcrumbs	101 grams
1⅔ cups whole-wheat pastry flour	200 grams
1 cup whole-wheat pastry flour	120 grams

LENGTHS

18 inches	46 cm
13 inches	33 cm
12 inches	30 cm
9 inches	23 cm
8 inches	20 cm
6 inches	15 cm
5 inches	13 cm
4 inches	10 cm
3 inches	8 cm
2 inches	5 cm
1 inch	2.5 cm
¾ inch	2 cm
½ inch	1.25 cm
¼ inch	5 mm

TEMPERATURES

450°F	230°C
425°F	220°C
400°F	200°C
375°F	190°C
365°F	185°C
350°F	175°C
325°F	163°C
275°F	135°C

WEIGHTS

2 pounds	32 dry ounces	907 grams
1¾ pounds	28 dry ounces	794 grams
1½ pound	24 dry ounces	680 grams
1 pound	16 dry ounces	454 grams
–	15 dry ounces	425 grams
½ pound	8 dry ounces	227 grams
¼ pound	4 dry ounces	113 grams
–	1 dry ounces	28 grams
–	½ dry ounces	14 grams

VOLUMES

1 quart	4 cups	950 ml
1 pint	2 cups	475 ml
	1 cup	237 m
	¾ cup	178 ml
	½ cup	125 ml
	⅓ cup	80 ml
	¼ cup	60 ml
	2 tablespoons	30 ml

RESOURCES

TO LEARN MORE

For more information, or to become actively involved in the field of plant-based nutrition, check out these websites:

- ▶ Forks Over Knives: www.forksoverknives.com
- ▶ Farms 2 Forks (Forks Over Knives and Engine 2 Diet educational retreats): www.farms2forks.com
- ▶ The Engine 2 Diet: www.engine2diet.com
- ▶ Farm Sanctuary: www.farmsanctuary.org
- ▶ FoodnSport: www.foodnsport.com
- ▶ Happy Cow, the Healthy Eating Guide: www.happycow.net
- ▶ Dr. McDougall's Health and Medical Center: www.drmcdougall.com
- ▶ Physicians Committee for Responsible Medicine: www.pcrm.org
- ▶ Prevent and Reverse Heart Disease: www.heartattackproof.com
- ▶ The T. Colin Campbell Foundation: www.tcolincampbell.org
- ▶ TrueNorth Health Center: www.healthpromoting.com
- ▶ Wellness Forum: www.wellnessforum.com

BOOKSHELF

Some essential books for the plant-based bibliophile:

- ▶ *Forks Over Knives: The Plant-Based Way to Health* by Gene Stone (ed.), The Experiment, 2011.
- ▶ *21-Day Weight-Loss Kickstart* by Neal D. Barnard, MD, Grand Central, 2011.
- ▶ *Bravo!: Health-Promoting Meals from the TrueNorth Kitchen* by Ramses Bravo, Book Publishing Company, 2012.
- ▶ *Breaking the Food Seduction* by Neal D. Barnard, MD, St. Martin's Press, 2003.
- ▶ *The China Study* by T. Colin Campbell, PhD, and Thomas M. Campbell II, BenBella Books, 2006.
- ▶ *Dr. Neal Barnard's Program for Reversing Diabetes* by Neal D. Barnard, MD, Rodale, 2007.
- ▶ *The Engine 2 Diet* by Rip Esselstyn, Grand Central Books, 2009.
- ▶ *Farm Sanctuary* by Gene Baur, Touchstone, 2008.
- ▶ *The Happy Herbivore Cookbook* and *Everyday Happy Herbivore* by Lindsay S. Nixon, BenBella Books, 2011.

- *Keep It Simple, Keep It Whole* by Alona Pulde, MD, and Matthew Lederman, MD, Exsalus Health & Wellness Center, 2009.
- *The McDougall Program: 12 Days to Dynamic Health* by John A. McDougall, MD, Plume, 1991.
- *The McDougall Quick & Easy Cookbook* by John A. McDougall, MD, and Mary McDougall, Plume, 1999.
- *The Pleasure Trap* by Douglas J. Lisle, PhD, and Alan Goldhamer, DC, Book Publishing Company, 2006.
- *Prevent and Reverse Heart Disease* by Caldwell B. Esselstyn Jr., MD, Avery Books, 2007.
- *The Starch Solution* by John A. McDougall, MD, and Mary McDougall, Rodale Books, 2012.

ACKNOWLEDGMENTS

FROM CHEF DEL:

Many, many thanks go out to those who, in one way or another, have encouraged, prodded, pushed, and waited patiently for me while I wrote this cookbook. Thanks, Dad, for letting me into the kitchen at such an early age, and for giving me that first box of Bisquick, with which I made many bad batches of pancakes before I got it right. Thanks, Mom, for being one of the best cooks I've ever known and for sharing your secrets for making food taste good. Thanks, Jean and Paul, for many wonderful late-night vegetarian meals.

Thanks to everyone who has eaten my food in one venue or another.

A special thank-you to Brian Wendel for liking my food and giving me this opportunity, and to all of the talented people at The Experiment for their amazing eyes for detail and seemingly endless patience. Thanks to Pam Popper for putting up with my moods as I finished the manuscript for this book and for being my biggest fan. Thanks, Jane Belt, for your gentle encouragement. And a big thank-you to Robert Metzger, Libby Gregory, and a whole bunch of other people from King Avenue Coffeehouse for being part of what would become the best job I ever had.

FROM BRIAN WENDEL, EXECUTIVE PRODUCER OF *FORKS OVER KNIVES*:

First and foremost, thank you to Chef Del for his amazing skill and for logging long, hard hours putting together so many delectable recipes in a relatively short time. Thanks also to Julieanna Hever, Judy Micklewright, Isa Chandra Moskowitz, and Darshana Thacker for their love of plant-based food, and for sharing their delicious recipes with us.

I'm grateful to everyone at The Experiment, especially Matthew Lore, for believing in our work and making so many good things happen. And a special thank-you to Robby Barbaro and Kathie Pomposo, who bring a lot of talent and enthusiasm to the office every day and make sure all the important work gets done. Finally, thank you to my family and friends for their support, without which *Forks Over Knives* and this book would not be possible.

INDEX

About the Author and Contributors

DEL SROUFE has worked for six years as chef and co-owner of Wellness Forum Foods, a plant-based meal delivery and catering service that emphasizes healthy, minimally processed foods; produces a line of "in-the-bag mixes"; and offers cooking classes to the public. He has worked in vegan and vegetarian kitchens for 22 years, including spending time as a vegan personal chef. He lives, works, and cooks in Columbus, Ohio.

JULIEANNA HEVER, MS, RD, CPT, is known as the Plant-Based Dietitian. She is the author of *The Complete Idiot's Guide to Plant-Based Nutrition*, co-author of *The Complete Idiot's Guide to Gluten-Free Vegan Cooking*, nutrition columnist for *VegNews*, and co-producer and star of the infotainment documentary *To Your Health*. Visit her at www.PlantBasedDietitian.com.

JUDY MICKLEWRIGHT always had an affinity for plants but never realized their full potential, or how one day they would change her life. After battling numerous ailments unsuccessfully, it occurred to her to give a plant-based diet a try, and the results were profound. She has since set out on a path of discovery into plant-based living, personalizing the diet, and enjoying newfound vigor in her mind, body, and soul. Now a mother, Judy continues to dedicate herself to unearthing tasty, plant-based good-for-you goodness.

ISA CHANDRA MOSKOWITZ is an American cookbook author, magazine columnist, and former host of the community access cooking show *Post Punk Kitchen*. Her bestselling cookbooks include *Vegan with a Vengeance*, *Vegan Cupcakes Take Over the World*, *Veganomicon*, *Vegan Brunch*, *Vegan Cookies Invade Your Cookie Jar*, and *Appetite for Reduction*. She maintains the popular vegan website Post Punk Kitchen and lives in Omaha, Nebraska.

DARSHANA THACKER teaches contemporary vegan interpretations of traditional Ayurvedic food preparation at Vapika Spirit in Los Angeles (www.vapikaspirit.com). Her intimate, kitchen-based classes illustrate the simple preparation of well-balanced meals planned according to the body constitution, lifestyle, and seasons of the year.

MORE FROM FORKS OVER KNIVES

THE FILM THAT LAUNCHED THE MOVEMENT

The hit documentary *Forks Over Knives* examines the profound claim that most, if not all, of the degenerative diseases that afflict us can be controlled, or even reversed, by rejecting animal-based and processed foods. The film also uncovers the history that led to the modern "Western diet"—high in meat, dairy, and processed foods—and presents the challenges and triumphs of several patients with chronic diseases who benefited by switching to a plant-based diet.

DVD or Blu-ray | Includes English closed captioning, and English and Spanish subtitles
NTSC all regions | 96 minutes | Rated PG | $24.99 U.S.

THE EXTENDED INTERVIEWS

Forks Over Knives—The Extended Interviews includes never-before-seen footage from the original film's interviews with experts including Dr T. Colin Campbell, Dr. Caldwell B. Esselstyn, Jr., Dr. Neal Barnard, and Dr. John McDougall.

DVD or Blu-ray | Includes English closed captioning and Spanish subtitles
NTSC all regions | 110 minutes | $19.99 U.S.

THE #1 *NEW YORK TIMES* BESTSELLING COMPANION BOOK

Forks Over Knives: The Plant-Based Way to Health is an indispensable guide to adopting and maintaining a whole-foods, plant-based diet, complete with:

▶ Insights from the luminaries behind the film—Dr. T. Colin Campbell, Dr. Caldwell B. Esselstyn, Jr., Dr. Neal Barnard, Dr. John McDougall, Rip Esselstyn, and many others
▶ Success stories from real-life converts to plant-based eating
▶ The many benefits of a whole-foods, plant-based diet—for you, for animals and the environment, and for our future
▶ And 125 recipes from twenty-five champions of plant-based eating.

Trade paperback | 6¼ x 8½ inches | 224 pages | With 22 black-and-white photos
ISBN 978-1-61519-045-4 | Ebook ISBN 978-1-61519-146-8 | $14.95 U.S.

THE FOUR-WEEK PLAN TO TRANSFORM YOUR DIET

The Forks Over Knives Plan shows you how to put this life-saving (and delicious) diet into practice in your own life. This easy-to-follow meal-by-meal makeover from Drs. Alona Pulde and Matthew Lederman (featured in *Forks Over Knives*) provides a clear, simple plan that focuses on hearty comfort foods and does not involve portion control or worrying about obtaining single nutrients like protein and calcium.

Published by Touchstone in September 2014 | Hardcover | 336 pages
ISBN 978-1-47675-329-4 | $24.99 | Also available as an ebook